ORDNANCE SURVEY

C000130041

Cycle

TOURS

24 one-day routes in

Cumbria &
the Lakes

Compiled by
Nick Cotton

HAMLYN

Contents

On-road routes

Acknowledgements
AA Photo Library 25, 85 top, 91, 109, 111
• E A Bowness 115, 123 • Reed International Books
(John Freeman) 107 • B & S Thomlinson 19, 31, 37, 55,
61, 139 • Judy Todd back cover, 43, 49, 79
• Douglas Wood 85 bottom, 119

Off-road routes

Back cover photograph: A view from Skiddaw

First published 1995 by

Ordnance Survey and Hamlyn, an imprint of
Romsey Road   Reed Consumer Books Ltd
Maybush   Michelin House
Southampton   81 Fulham Road
SO16 4GU   London SW3 6RB

Text and compilation
Copyright © Reed International Books Ltd 1995
Maps Copyright © Crown Copyright 1995
First edition 1995
Second impression 1995

A catalogue record for this atlas is available from the British Library

ISBN 0 600 58126 8
(Ordnance Survey ISBN 0 319 00484 8)

Made, printed and published in Great Britain

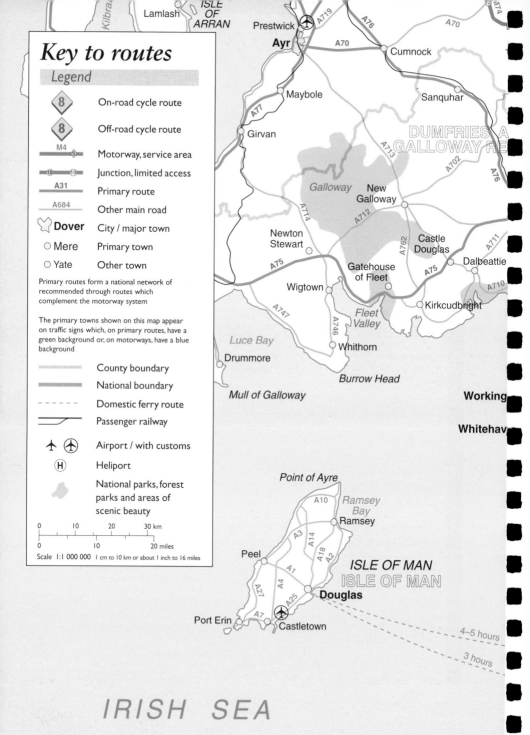

Key to routes

Legend

8 (in diamond)	On-road cycle route
8 (in diamond)	Off-road cycle route
M4 —S—	Motorway, service area
18 — 19	Junction, limited access
A31	Primary route
A684	Other main road
Dover	City / major town
○ Mere	Primary town
○ Yate	Other town

Primary routes form a national network of recommended through routes which complement the motorway system

The primary towns shown on this map appear on traffic signs which, on primary routes, have a green background or, on motorways, have a blue background

⋯⋯⋯	County boundary
▬▬▬	National boundary
– – –	Domestic ferry route
───	Passenger railway
✈ ✈ (in circle)	Airport / with customs
(H)	Heliport
(shape)	National parks, forest parks and areas of scenic beauty

Scale 0 10 20 30 km
0 10 20 miles

Scale 1:1 000 000 1 cm to 10 km or about 1 inch to 16 miles

Kilbra…
Lamlash
ISLE OF ARRAN
Prestwick
A719
A70
A76
A70
Ayr
Cumnock
A70
Maybole
Sanquhar
A77
Girvan
A713
DUMFRIES A
GALLOWAY RE
A702
A76
Galloway
New Galloway
A714
A712
A762
Castle Douglas
A711
Newton Stewart
A75
Gatehouse of Fleet
A75
Dalbeattie
A710
Wigtown
A747
Fleet Valley
Kirkcudbright
A746
Whithorn
Luce Bay
Drummore
Burrow Head
Mull of Galloway
Working
Whitehav

Point of Ayre
A10
Ramsey Bay
Ramsey
A3
A14
A18
A2
Peel
A1
ISLE OF MAN
ISLE OF MAN
A27
A4
A25
Douglas
Port Erin
A7
Castletown
4–5 hours
3 hours

IRISH SEA

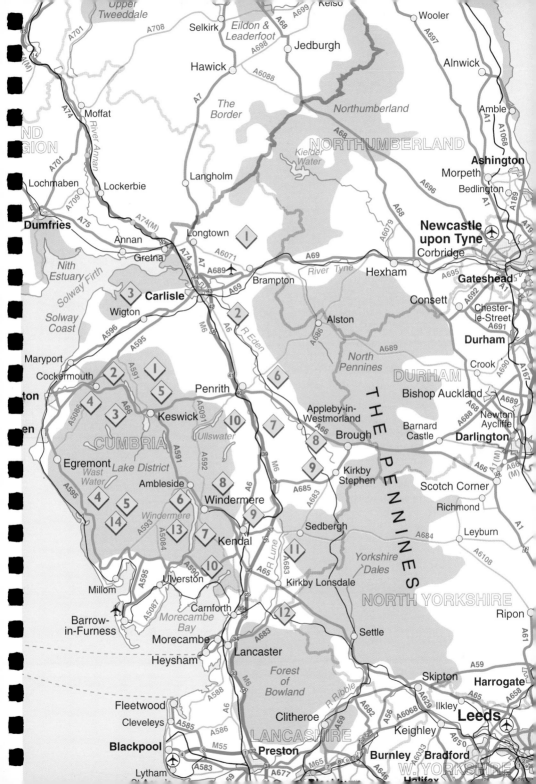

Quick reference chart

[1]Links with other routes Use this information to create a more strenuous ride or if you are planning to do more than one ride in a day or on a weekend or over a few days. The rides do not necessarily join: there may be a distance of up to three miles between the closest points. Several rides are in pairs, sharing the same starting point, which may be a good place to base yourself for a weekend.

[2]Tourist Information Centres You can contact them for details about accommodation. If they cannot help, there are many books that recommend places to stay. If nothing is listed for the place where you want to stay, try phoning the post office or the pub in the village to see if they can suggest somewhere.

Cumbria and the Lakes

Although the Lake District is largely concentrated into an area formed by a circle 15 miles around a central point of Thirlmere, for many people Cumbria and the Lake District are synonymous. This is far from the case – Cumbria stretches 60 miles from the coast at St Bees Head in the west to the Pennines beyond Brough in the east and more than 80 miles from Barrow-in-Furness to the border with Scotland, north of Carlisle. Indeed much of the central area of the Lake District, unless one is highly selective about the time and the season, is unsuitable for cycling – the roads, even the small lanes, are clogged with cars and caravans and off-road many of the bridleways in the heart of the fells are either too steep, too rocky, too boggy, too vague, too full of people or a combination of all of these to be of much value for a book of this nature.

This is a blessing in disguise as much of the best cycling in the Cumbria lies in the fringes around the Lake District: the Eden Valley provides some of the very finest cycling territory. Appleby-in-Westmorland is the base of three rides and the two rides from the attractive town of Kirkby Lonsdale explore stretches of the valley formed by the River Lune. Closer to Carlisle the rides starting in Brampton and Wigton show different aspects of Cumbria – the benignly neglected countryside of rolling green hills towards the Scottish Borders and the flatlands that stretch towards the Solway Firth

Other road rides come closer to the lakes and hills of the Lake District itself – Skiddaw is circumnavigated in a loop from Keswick; the route from Cockermouth provides some excellent views of the western fells; Broughton-in-Furness is the base for the toughest challenge in the book; Coniston Water and Lake Windermere are touched upon on the ride from Hawkshead and finally Kendal is the start of two easily-linked rides.

While a compass is always useful if riding off-road, these rides do not require advanced mountaineering skills and should be within the scope of anyone with a reasonable degree of fitness. In some cases they have a high proportion of road for an off-road ride but these sections are almost always on tiny lanes which are very beautiful and may well have an 'Unsuitable for motors' sign at either end of them. Mention should be made of the Forestry Commission's waymarked mountain bike trails in Grizedale and Whinlatter Forests, the lakeside trail alongside Ennerdale Water and the dismantled railway from Whitehaven, all of which offer all-year off-road riding.

Abbreviations and instructions

Instructions are given as concisely as possible to make them easy to follow while you are cycling. Remember to read one or two instructions ahead so that you do not miss a turning. This is most likely to occur when you have to turn off a road on which you have been riding for a fairly long distance and these junctions are marked **Easy to miss** to warn you.

If there appears to be a contradiction between the instructions and what you actually see, always refer to the map. There are many reasons why over the course of a few years instructions will need updating as new roads are built and priorities and signposts change.

If giving instructions for road routes is at times difficult, doing so for off-road routes can often be almost impossible, particularly when the route passes through woodland. With few signposts and buildings by which to orientate yourself, more attention is paid to other features, such as gradient and surface. Most of these routes have been explored between late spring and early autumn and the countryside changes its appearance very dramatically in winter. If in doubt, consult

your map and check your compass to see that you are heading in the right direction.

Where I have encountered mud I have mentioned it, but this may change not only from summer to winter but also from dry to wet weather at any time during the year. At times you may have to retrace your steps and find a road alternative.

Some routes have small sections that follow footpaths. The instructions will highlight these sections where you must get off and push your bike. You may only ride on bridleways and by-ways so be careful if you stray from the given routes.

Directions

L	left
LH	left-hand
RH	right-hand
SA	straight ahead or straight across
bear L or R	make less than a 90-degree (right-angle) turn at a fork in the road or track or at a sharp bend so that your course appears to be straight ahead; this is often written as *in effect SA*
sharp L or R turn	is more acute than 90 degrees
sharp R/L back on yourself	an almost U-turn
sharp LH/RH bend	a 90-degree bend
R then L or R	the second turning is visible then immediately L from the first
R then 1st L	the second turning may be some distance from the first; the distance may also be indicated: *R, then after 1 mile L*

Junctions

T-j	T-junction, a junction where you have to give way
X-roads	crossroads, a junction where you may or may not have to give way
offset X-roads	the four roads are not in the form of a perfect cross and you will have to turn left then right, or vice versa, to continue the route

Signs

'Placename 2'	words in quotation marks are those that appear on signposts; the numbers indicate distance in miles unless stated otherwise
NS	not signposted
trig point	a trigonometrical station

Instructions

An example of an easy instruction is:

4 At the T-j at the end of Smith Road by the White Swan PH R on Brown Street 'Greentown 2, Redville 3'.

There is more information in this instruction than you would normally need, but things do change: pubs may close down and signs may be replaced, removed or vandalized.

An example of a difficult instruction is:

8 Shortly after the brow of the hill, soon after passing a telephone box on the right next L (NS).

As you can see, there is no T-junction to halt you in your tracks, no signpost indicating where the left turn will take you, so you need to have your wits about you in order not to miss the turning.

Fact boxes

The introduction to each route includes a fact box giving useful information:

Start

This is the suggested start point coinciding with instruction 1 on the map. There is no reason why you should not start at another point if you prefer.

Distance and grade

The distance is, of course, that from the beginning to the end of the route. If you wish to shorten the ride, however, the maps enable you to do so.

The number of drinks bottles indicates the grade:

🍶 Easy
🍶🍶🍶 Moderate
🍶🍶🍶🍶🍶 Strenuous

Page diagrams

The on-road routes occupy four pages of mapping each. The page diagrams on the introductory pages show how the map pages have been laid out, how they overlap and if any inset maps have been used.

This section of the route is shown on pages 92 and 93

This overlap area appears at the foot of pages 92 and 93 and at the top of pages 94 and 95

This area is shown as an inset on page 94

This section of the route is shown on pages 94 and 95

92   93
94   95

The grade is based on the amount of climbing involved and, for off-road rides, the roughness of the surface rather than the distance covered.

Remember that conditions may vary dramatically with the weather and seasons, especially along off-road routes

Terrain

This brief description of the terrain may be read in conjunction with the cross-profile diagram at the foot of the page to help you to plan your journey.

Nearest railway

This is the distance to the nearest station from the closest point on the route, not necessarily from the start. Before starting out you should check with British Rail for local restrictions regarding the carrying of bicycles.
(See page 15)

Refreshments

Pubs and teashops on or near the route are listed. The tankard symbols indicate pubs particularly liked by the author.

Before you go

Preparing yourself

Fitness

Cycling uses muscles in a different way from walking or running, so if you are beginning or returning to it after a long absence you will need time to train your muscles and become accustomed to sitting on a saddle for a few hours. Build up your fitness and stamina gradually and make sure you are using a bicycle that is the right size for you and suits your needs.

Equipment

Attach the following items to the bike: bell, pump, light-brackets and lights, lock-holder and lock, rack and panniers or elastic straps for securing things to the rack, map holder. Unless it is the middle of summer and the weather is guaranteed to be fine, you will need to carry extra clothes, particularly a waterproof, with you, and it is well worth investing in a rack for this purpose.

Wearing a small pouch around your waist is the easiest and safest way of carrying small tools and personal equipment. The basics are: Allen keys to fit the various Allen bolts on your bike, chainlink extractor, puncture repair kit, reversible screwdriver (slot and crosshead), small adjustable spanner, spare inner tube, tyre levers (not always necessary with mountain bike tyres), coins and a phonecard for food and telephone calls, compass.

Additional tools for extended touring: bottom bracket extractor, cone spanners, freewheel extractor, headset spanners, lubricant, socket spanner for pedals, spare cables, spoke-key.

Clothing

What you wear when you are cycling should be comfortable, allowing you, and most especially your legs, to move freely. It should also be practical, so that it will keep you warm and dry if and when the weather changes.

Feet You can cycle in just about any sort of footwear, but bear in mind that the chain has oil on it, so do not use your very best shoes. Leather tennis shoes or something similar, with a smooth sole to slip into the pedal and toe clip are probably adequate until you buy specialist cycling shoes, which have stiffer soles and are sometimes designed for use with specialist pedals.

Legs Cycling shorts or padded cycling underwear worn under everyday clothing make long rides much more comfortable. Avoid tight, non-stretch trousers, which are very uncomfortable for cycling and will sap your energy, as they restrict the movement of your legs; baggy tracksuit bottoms, which can get caught in the chain and will sag around your ankles if they get wet. Almost anything else will do, though a pair of stretch leggings is probably best.

Upper body What you wear should be long enough to cover your lower back when you are leaning forward and, ideally, should have zips or buttons that you can adjust to regulate your temperature. Several thin layers are better than one thick layer.

Head A helmet may protect your head in a fall.

Wet weather If you get soaked to your skin and you are tired, your body core temperature can drop very quickly when you are cycling. A waterproof, windproof top is essential if it looks like rain. A dustbin bag would be better than nothing but obviously a breathable waterproof material is best.

Cold weather Your extremities suffer far more when you are cycling than when you are walking in similar conditions. A hat that covers your ears, a scarf around your neck, a pair of warm gloves and a thermal top and bottom combined with what you would normally wear cycling should cover almost all conditions.

Night and poor light Wearing light-coloured clothes or reflective strips is almost as important as having lights on your bike. Reflective bands worn around the ankles are particularly effective in making you visible to motorists.

Preparing your bicycle

You may not be a bicycle maintenance expert, but you should make sure that your bike is roadworthy before you begin a ride.

If you are planning to ride in soft, off-road conditions, fit fat, knobbly tyres. If you are using the bike around town or on a road route, fit narrower, smoother tyres.

Check the tyres for punctures or damage and repair or replace if necessary or if you are in any doubt. Keep tyres inflated hard (recommended pressures are on the side wall of the tyre) for mainly on-road riding. You do not need to inflate tyres as hard for off-road use; slightly softer tyres give some cushioning and get better traction in muddy conditions.

Ensure that the brakes work efficiently. Replace worn cables and brake blocks.

The bike should glide along silently. Tighten and adjust any part that is loose or rubbing against a moving part. Using a good-quality bike oil lubricate the hubs, bottom bracket, pedals where they join the cranks, chain and gear-changing mechanism from both sides. If the bike still makes grating noises, replace the bearings.

Adjust the saddle properly. You can raise or lower it, move it forwards or backwards or tilt it up or down. The saddle height should ensure that your legs are working efficiently: too low and your knees will ache; too high and your hips will be rocking in order for your feet to reach the pedals.

Some women find the average bike saddle uncomfortable because the female pelvis is a different shape from the male pelvis and needs a broader saddle for support. Some manufacturers make saddles especially for women.

Cross-profiles

The introduction to each route includes a cross-profile diagram. The vertical scale is the same on each diagram but the horizontal scale varies according to the length of the route

On-road route

Off-road route

Corfe Castle

Start / finish

Blashenwell Farm

Kingston

Swyre Head

Kimmeridge

Tips for touring

England and Wales have 120 000 miles of rights of way, but under the Wildlife and Countryside Act of 1968 you are allowed to cycle on only about 10 percent of them, namely on bridleways, by-ways open to all traffic (BOATs) and roads used as public paths (RUPPs).

The other 90 percent of rights of way are footpaths, where you may walk and usually push your bike, but not ride it. Local bylaws sometimes prohibit the pushing of bicycles along footpaths and although all the paths in this book have been checked, bylaws do sometimes change.

- You are not allowed to ride where there is no right of way. If you lose the route and find yourself in conflict with a landowner, stay calm and courteous, make a note of exactly where you are and then contact the Rights of Way Department of the local authority. It has copies of definitive maps and will take up the matter on your behalf if you are in the right.

- For further information on cycling and the law contact the Cyclists Touring Club (CTC) whose address can be found on the inside back cover.

If you are not used to cycling more than a few miles at a stretch, you may find initially that touring is tiring. There are ways of conserving your energy, however:

- Do not struggle in a difficult gear if you have an easier one. Let the gears help you up the hills. No matter how many gears a bike has, however, ultimately it is leg power that you need to get you up a hill. You may decide to get off and walk uphill with your bike to rest your muscles.

- You can save a lot of energy on the road by following close behind a stronger rider in his or her slipstream, but do not try this offroad. All the routes are circular, so you can start at any point and follow the instructions until you return to it. This is useful when there is a strong wind, as you can alter the route to go into the wind at the start of the ride, when you are fresh, and have the wind behind you on the return, when you are more tired.

- The main difference in technique between on-road and off-road cycling lies in getting your weight balanced correctly. When going down steep off-road sections, lower the saddle, keep the pedals level, stand up out of the saddle to let your legs absorb the bumps and keep your weight over the rear wheel. Control is paramount: keep your eyes on what lies ahead.

Steeple Hill

Grange Arch

Ridgeway Hill

Knowle Hill

Start / finish

Traffic

The rides in this book are designed to minimize time spent on busy roads, but you will inevitably encounter some traffic. The most effective way to avoid an accident with a motor vehicle is to be highly aware of what is going on around you and to ensure that other road users are aware of you.

- Ride confidently.
- Indicate clearly to other road users what you intend to do, particularly when turning right. Look behind you, wait for a gap in the traffic, indicate, then turn. If you have to turn right off a busy road or on a difficult bend, pull in and wait for a gap in the traffic or go past the turning to a point where you have a clear view of the traffic in both directions, then cross and return to the turning.
- Use your lights and wear reflective clothing at night and in poor light.
- Do not ride two-abreast if there is a vehicle behind you. Let it pass. If it cannot easily overtake you because the road is narrow, look for a passing place or a gate entrance and pull in to let it pass.

Maintenance

Mountain bikes are generally stronger than road bikes, but any bike can suffer. To prevent damage as far as possible:

- Watch out for holes and obstacles.
- Clean off mud and lubricate moving parts regularly.
- Replace worn parts, particularly brake blocks.

Riders also need maintenance:

- Eat before you get hungry, drink before you get thirsty. Dried fruit, nuts and chocolate take up little space and provide lots of energy.

- Carry a water bottle and keep it filled, especially on hot days. Tea, water and well-diluted soft drinks are the best thirst-quenchers.

Breakdowns

The most likely breakdown to occur is a puncture.

- Always carry a pump.
- Take a spare inner tube so that you can leave the puncture repair until later.
- Make sure you know how to remove a wheel. This may require an adjustable spanner or, in many cases, no tool at all, as many bikes now have wheels with quick-release skewers that can be loosened by hand.

Security

Where you park your bike, what you lock it with and what you lock it to are important in protecting it from being stolen.

- Buy the best lock you can afford.
- Lock your bike to something immovable in a well-lit public place.
- Locking two bikes together is better than locking them individually.
- Use a chain with a lock to secure the wheels and saddle to the frame. Keep a note of the frame number and other details, and insure, photograph and code the bike.

Lost and Found

The detailed instructions and the Ordnance Survey mapping in this book minimize the chances of getting lost. However, if you do lose your way:

- Ask someone for directions.
- Retrace the route back to the last point where you knew where you were.
- Use the map to rejoin the route at a point further ahead.

Code of Conduct

- Enjoy the countryside and respect its life and work
- Only ride where you know you have a legal right
- Always yield to horses and pedestrians
- Take all litter with you
- Don't get annoyed with anyone; it never solves any problems
- Guard against all risk of fire
- Fasten all gates

- Keep your dogs under close control
- Keep to public paths across farmland
- Use gates and stiles to cross fences, hedges and walls
- Avoid livestock, crops and machinery or, if not possible, keep contact to a minimum
- Help keep all water clean
- Protect wildlife, plants and trees
- Take special care on country roads
- Make no unnecessary noise

Transporting your bike

There are three ways of getting you and your bike to the start of a ride:

Cycle to the start or to a point along a route near your home.

Take the train. Always check in advance that you can take the bike on the train. Some trains allow only up to two bikes and you may need to make a reservation and pay a flat fee however long the journey. Always label your bike showing your name and destination station.

Travel by motor vehicle. You can carry the bikes:

- Inside the vehicle. With the advent of quick release mechanisms on both wheels and the seatpost, which allow a quick dismantling of the bike, it is possible to fit a bike in even quite small cars. It is unwise to stack one bike on top of another unless you have a thick blanket separating them to prevent scratching or worse damage. If you are standing them up in a van, make sure they are secured so they cannot slide around.

- On top of the vehicle. The advantages of this method are that the bikes are completely out of the way and are not resting against each other, you can get at the boot or hatch easily and the bikes do not obscure the number plate or rear lights and indicators. The disadvantages are that you use up more fuel, the car can feel uncomfortable in a crosswind and you have to be reasonably tall and strong to get the bikes on and off the roof.

- On a rack that attaches to the rear of the vehicle. The advantages are that the rack is easily and quickly assembled and disassembled, fuel consumption is better and anyone can lift the bikes on and off. The disadvantages are that you will need to invest in a separate board carrying the number plate and rear lights if they are obstructed by the bikes, you cannot easily get to the boot or hatch once the bikes have been loaded and secured, and the bikes are resting against each other so you must take care that they don't scrape off paint or damage delicate parts.

- Whichever way you carry the bikes on the outside of the vehicle, ensure that you regularly check that they are secure and that straps and fixings that hold them in place have not come loose. If you are leaving the bikes for any length of time, be sure they are secure against theft; if nothing else lock them to each other.

Legend to 1:50 000 maps

Roads and paths

Motorway

Service area — M 5 — Elevated
Junction number 20

Motorway under construction

Trunk road
Unfenced — Footbridge
A 46 (T)

Main road
Dual carriageway
A 420

Main road under construction

Secondary road
B 4348

Narrow road with passing places
A 855 — B 885

Road generally more than 4 m wide
Bridge

Road generally less than 4 m wide

Other road, drive or track

Path

Gradient: 1 in 5 and steeper, 1 in 7 to 1 in 5

Gates — Road tunnel

Passenger ferry — Vehicle ferry
Ferry P — Ferry V

Public rights of way (Not applicable to Scotland)

············· Footpath
- - - - - - - Bridleway
-·-·-·-·-·- Road used as a public footpath
-+-+-+-+-+- Byway open to all traffic

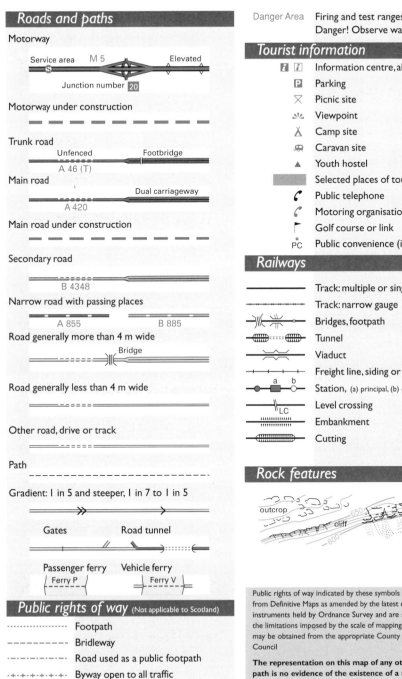

Danger Area — Firing and test ranges in the area. Danger! Observe warning notices

Tourist information

🄸 ⓘ Information centre, all year / seasonal
🅿 Parking
✕ Picnic site
᾿ᾳ᾿ Viewpoint
⋏ Camp site
🚐 Caravan site
▲ Youth hostel
▨▨▨ Selected places of tourist interest
𝐶 Public telephone
𝐶 Motoring organisation telephone
🏌 Golf course or link
PC Public convenience (in rural areas)

Railways

——————— Track: multiple or single
-+-+-+-+- Track: narrow gauge
)‖(⊥⊤ Bridges, footpath
◧┅┅┅◨ Tunnel
⌒⌒ Viaduct
—┼——┼— Freight line, siding or tramway
a b Station, (a) principal, (b) closed to passengers
‖ LC Level crossing
▨▨▨ Embankment
◧▨▨▨◨ Cutting

Rock features

outcrop cliff 650 scree 600

Public rights of way indicated by these symbols have been derived from Definitive Maps as amended by the latest enactments or instruments held by Ordnance Survey and are shown subject to the limitations imposed by the scale of mapping. Further information may be obtained from the appropriate County or London Borough Council

The representation on this map of any other road, track or path is no evidence of the existence of a right of way

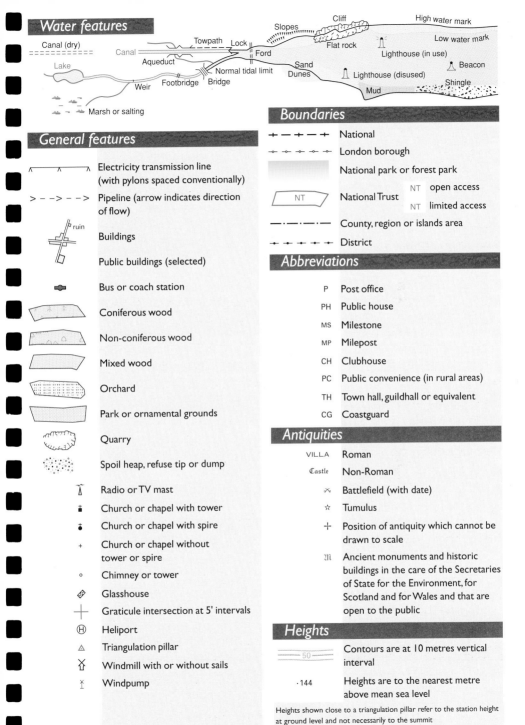

Water features

Canal (dry)
Canal
Aqueduct
Towpath
Lock
Ford
Lake
Weir
Footbridge
Bridge
Normal tidal limit
Marsh or salting

Cliff
Slopes
Flat rock
Sand
Dunes
Mud
High water mark
Low water mark
Lighthouse (in use)
Lighthouse (disused)
Beacon
Shingle

General features

Electricity transmission line (with pylons spaced conventionally)

Pipeline (arrow indicates direction of flow)

Buildings

Public buildings (selected)

Bus or coach station

Coniferous wood

Non-coniferous wood

Mixed wood

Orchard

Park or ornamental grounds

Quarry

Spoil heap, refuse tip or dump

Radio or TV mast

Church or chapel with tower

Church or chapel with spire

Church or chapel without tower or spire

Chimney or tower

Glasshouse

Graticule intersection at 5' intervals

Heliport

Triangulation pillar

Windmill with or without sails

Windpump

Boundaries

National

London borough

National park or forest park

National Trust
NT open access
NT limited access

County, region or islands area

District

Abbreviations

P   Post office
PH   Public house
MS   Milestone
MP   Milepost
CH   Clubhouse
PC   Public convenience (in rural areas)
TH   Town hall, guildhall or equivalent
CG   Coastguard

Antiquities

VILLA   Roman

Castle   Non-Roman

Battlefield (with date)

Tumulus

Position of antiquity which cannot be drawn to scale

Ancient monuments and historic buildings in the care of the Secretaries of State for the Environment, for Scotland and for Wales and that are open to the public

Heights

50   Contours are at 10 metres vertical interval

·144   Heights are to the nearest metre above mean sea level

Heights shown close to a triangulation pillar refer to the station height at ground level and not necessarily to the summit

North from Brampton to Bewcastle and the valleys of the Black and White Lyne

Start

Tourist Information Centre, Brampton

P Just off Front Street (on which the Tourist Information Centre is located) up Gelt Street then 1st left

Distance and grade

30 miles

///// Moderate

Terrain

Generally open, undulating country with large tracts of forestry land in the distance. Four climbs of between 230 and 300 feet on the outward section.

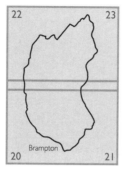

In years gone by this would have been lawless country close to the border between England and Scotland and subject to frequent raids from marauding cattle-rustlers. The ride stays on open country with fine views, avoiding the dense forestry plantations lying to the east and north. There is a feeling of gentle neglect to the tumble-down stone walls and green pastures beneath the rounded grassy slopes of The Beacon and Grey Hill. Unusual buildings along the route include the Priory at Lanercost, Askerton Castle (which is really just a farm), the castle and church at Bewcastle, and not least the unlikely situated Lime Kiln Inn. Several tributaries of the River Lyne, which empties its waters into the Solway Firth north of Carlisle, are crossed at the northern end of the route before the ride turns south. Any signpost with a collection of such curious names as Kinkry Hill, Cumcrook and Dodgsonford invites exploration and the ford crossing of the Black Lyne is one of the memorable moments of the ride. After a few quiet miles on roads through Boltonfellend and Hethersgill, the main A6071 is joined for three miles to return to the start.

Brampton   Lanercost   Banks   Askerton Castle   Tower Brae   Bewcastle

3 climbs of between 150 and 200 feet on the return. Highest point – 750 feet (225 mts) just north of Bewcastle. Lowest point –100 feet (30 mts) at the crossing of the River Irthing west of Brampton

Nearest railway

Brampton Station lies 2 miles southeast of Brampton

Refreshments

Plenty of choice in **Brampton** Appleby Bridge Inn PH, **Lanercost** Lime Kiln Inn PH, **Bewcastle** Pointers Dog Inn PH, **Bolton Fell End**

Places of interest

Brampton 1
Market town with cobbled streets and slate-roofed brick buildings where the octagonal Moot Hall, built in 1817, has clock tower cum belfry, external staircases and iron stocks. One of the shops in High Cross Street was Bonnie Prince Charlie's headquarters in 1745

Lanercost 3
The Priory was founded in 1166, damaged by Scottish raiders in the 13th and 14th centuries, and abandoned in 1536 during the Dissolution of the Monasteries. The aisle has windows by Victorian artists William Morris and Edward Burne-Jones

Naworth Castle (just off the route) 3
A border stronghold built in 1335, turned into a mansion in the 17th century and now the home of the Earl of Carlisle

Bewcastle 5
Village near to the 6-acre site of a Roman fort, an outpost of Hadrian's Wall. The shaft of a 1300 year old cross in the church yard, one of the finest Anglo-Saxon crosses in Europe, has runic inscriptions and carvings of figures

◄ Lanercost Bridge

Kinkry Hill   Black Lyne   Boltonfellend   Hethersgill   Newtown   River Irthing

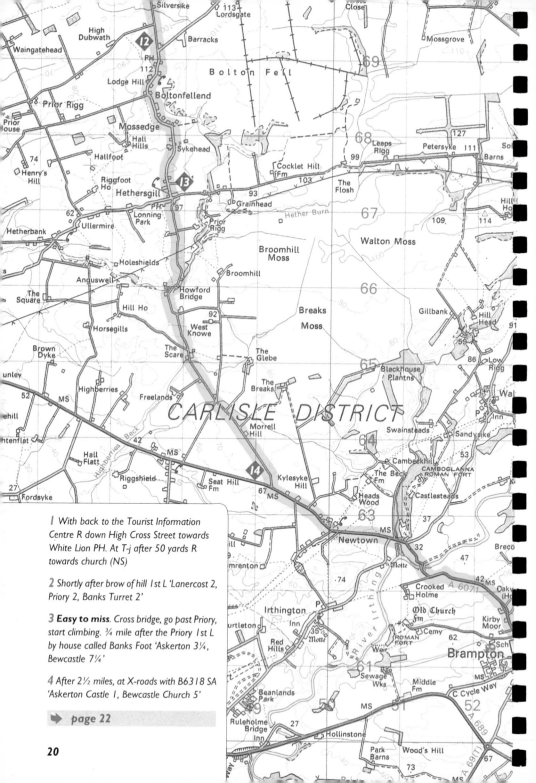

1 With back to the Tourist Information Centre R down High Cross Street towards White Lion PH. At T-j after 50 yards R towards church (NS)

2 Shortly after brow of hill 1st L 'Lanercost 2, Priory 2, Banks Turret 2'

3 *Easy to miss.* Cross bridge, go past Priory, start climbing. ¾ mile after the Priory 1st L by house called Banks Foot 'Askerton 3¼, Bewcastle 7¼'

4 After 2½ miles, at X-roads with B6318 SA 'Askerton Castle 1, Bewcastle Church 5'

➡ **page 22**

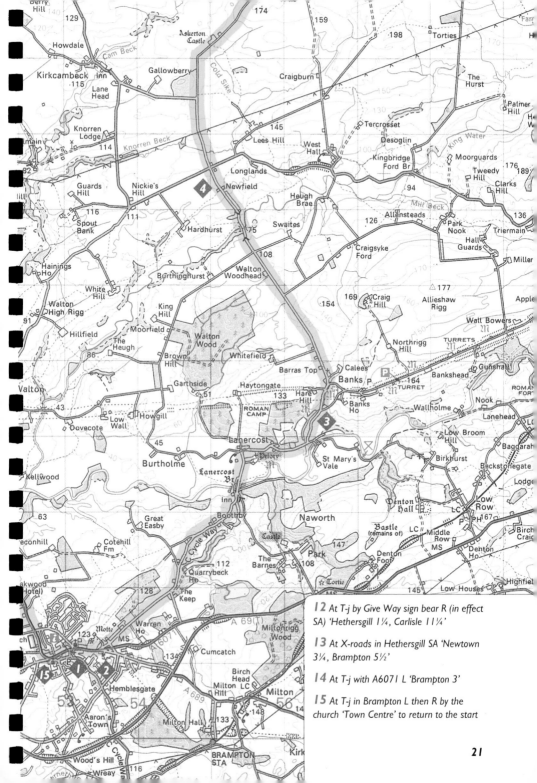

12 At T-j by Give Way sign bear R (in effect SA) 'Hethersgill 1¼, Carlisle 11¼'

13 At X-roads in Hethersgill SA 'Newtown 3¼, Brampton 5½'

14 At T-j with A6071 L 'Brampton 3'

15 At T-j in Brampton L then R by the church 'Town Centre' to return to the start

5 After 4 miles, shortly after passing the Lime Kiln Inn on your left, ignore 1st right to the church, take the 2nd R on a sharp LH bend

6 Climb, descend and climb again. At T-j after 2¼ miles L (NS)

7 Ignore left and right turns for 2 miles. At T-j L 'Roadhead 1½, Carlisle 18'

8 At T-j with B6318 bear L (in effect SA) 'Brampton 12, Gilsland 12'

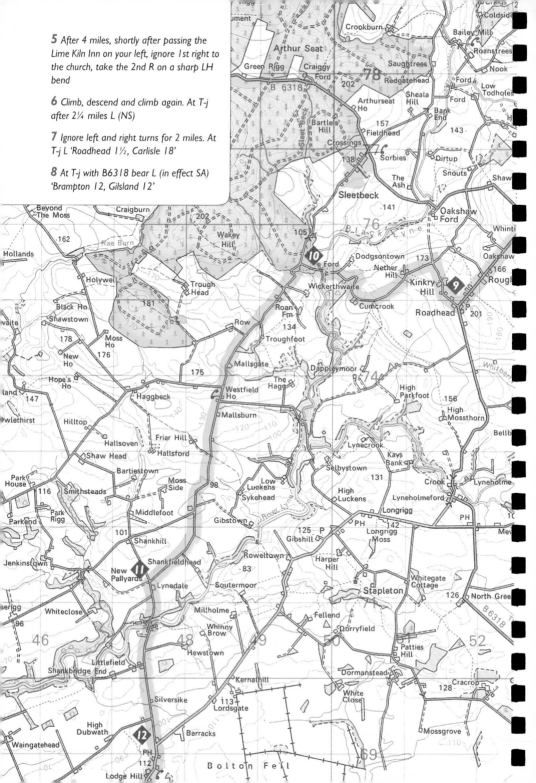

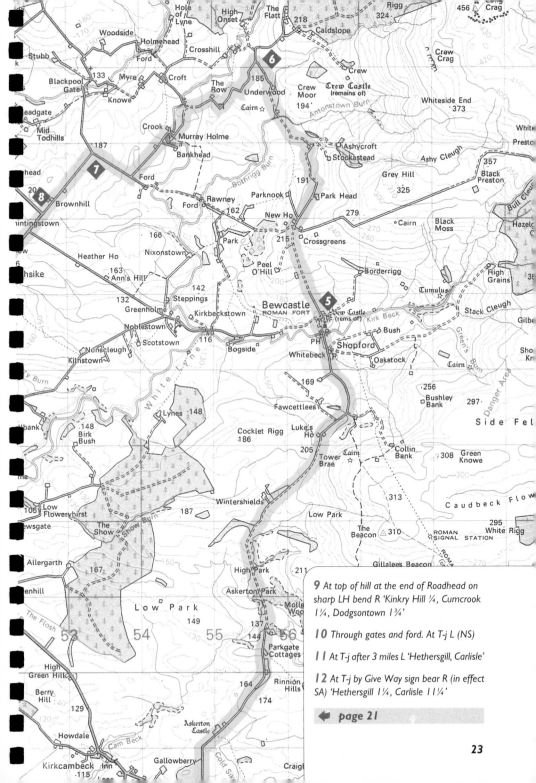

9 At top of hill at the end of Roadhead on sharp LH bend R 'Kinkry Hill ¼, Cumcrook 1¼, Dodgsontown 1¾'

10 Through gates and ford. At T-j L (NS)

11 At T-j after 3 miles L 'Hethersgill, Carlisle'

12 At T-j by Give Way sign bear R (in effect SA) 'Hethersgill 1¼, Carlisle 11¼'

← page 21

South from Wetheral along the Eden Valley

Start

The Post Office, Wetheral

P No specific car park. Some space near to the Post Office

2

Distance and grade

28 miles (or 16 miles if the River Eden is crossed at Armathwaite)
Easy / Moderate

Terrain

The valley of the River Eden is followed on its eastern side on the outward leg and on the western side on the return. However, the ride does not run along the banks of the river

The Eden Valley offers some of the finest cycling in Cumbria – it is relatively little-visited compared with the Lake District, there are fine views of both the Pennines and the Lakeland Fells, the hills are never too long or too steep and the River Eden itself is a constant delight. There are three rides based from Appleby-in-Westmorland plus this one, which explore the valley, all of which could be linked for longer rides, or, as most of the rides are cigar-shaped, could easily be shortened. An option to shorten this ride to sixteen miles is suggested. The route makes use of the railway bridge over the Eden in Wetheral to cross to the eastern side of the river. There are alternating views of the Pennines and the river as you climb beyond Cumwhitton then descend to the river near Holmwrangle. The steepest climb of the day is followed by a descent to the Nunnery House Hotel, a fine location for a coffee or tea stop. The river is crossed at Lazonby and is followed north through Armathwaite back to the start.

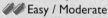

Wetheral Cumwhitton Holmwrangle Armathwaite Kirkoswald

and there are three climbs: 380 feet from Wetheral to Hornsby Gate, a steeper 350 feet south from Armathwaite above Coombs Wood, and 280 feet north from Lazonby back towards Armathwaite. Highest point – 530 feet (155 mts) betwen Lazonby and Armathwaite. Lowest point – 130 feet (40 mts) at the start

▲ *The Eden Valley*

Nearest railway

Wetheral, Armathwaite or Lazonby

Places of interest

Wetheral 1
Large stone houses stand around the triangular green, dominated by the 19th-century chateau-style Eden Bank

Corby Castle 2
The bulky 13th-century keep has 17th- and 19th-century additions. Terraced gardens overlook the River Eden with its medieval wood and stone salmon traps

Armathwaite 6
The village clusters around the bridge over the River Eden. The tower of the riverside castle was built into a Georgian mansion

Kirkoswald 7
Red-sandstone village with a 15th-century church and a ruined castle surrounded by a 13th-century moat. The college, the seat of the Featherstone family since 1613, was converted from a peel tower built in 1450

Refreshments

Wheatsheaf PH, Crown Hotel, **Wetheral**
Corby Bridge Inn PH, **Great Corby**
Pheasant Inn PH, **Cumwhitton**
Coffee and teas at Nunnery House Hotel, **Staffield**
Fetherston Arms PH, Crown Inn PH, **Kirkoswald**
Joiners Arms PH, Midland Hotel PH, **Lazonby**
Dukes Head PH 🍷, Fox and Pheasant PH,
Armathwaite

Lazonby

Baronwood Park

Armathwaite

Knott Hill

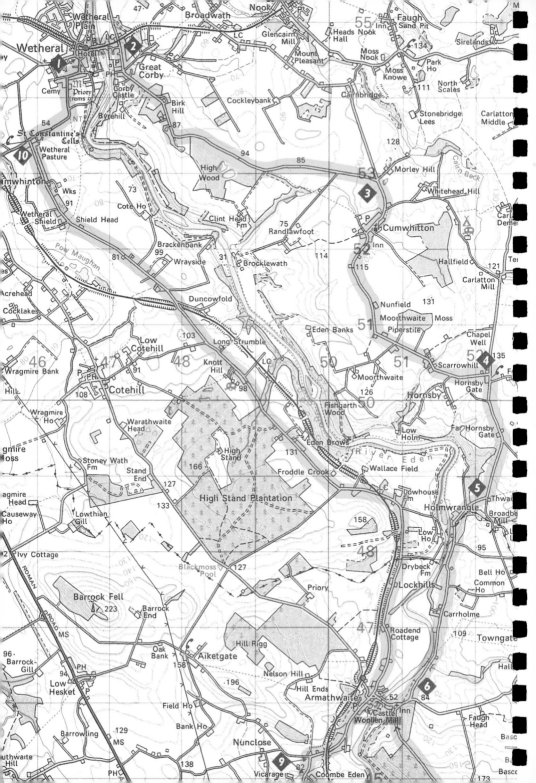

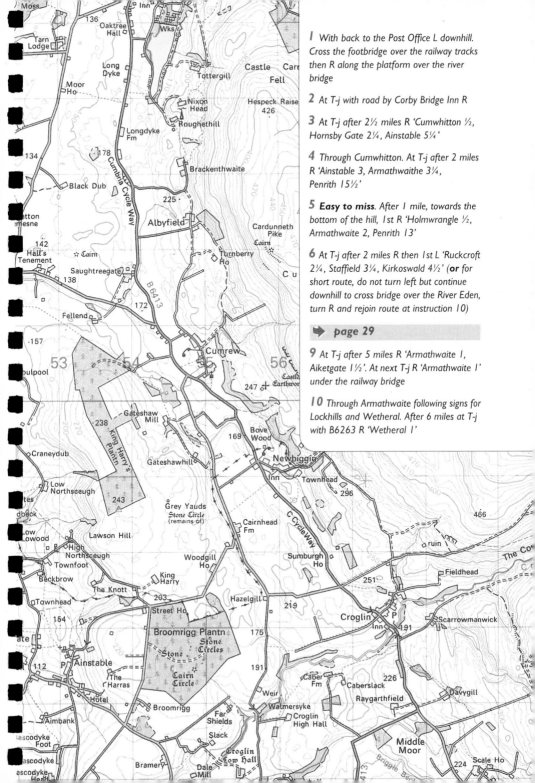

1 With back to the Post Office L downhill. Cross the footbridge over the railway tracks then R along the platform over the river bridge

2 At T-j with road by Corby Bridge Inn R

3 At T-j after 2½ miles R 'Cumwhitton ½, Hornsby Gate 2¼, Ainstable 5¼'

4 Through Cumwhitton. At T-j after 2 miles R 'Ainstable 3, Armathwaithe 3¼, Penrith 15½'

5 **Easy to miss**. After 1 mile, towards the bottom of the hill, 1st R 'Holmwrangle ½, Armathwaite 2, Penrith 13'

6 At T-j after 2 miles R then 1st L 'Ruckcroft 2¼, Staffield 3¼, Kirkoswald 4½' (**or** for short route, do not turn left but continue downhill to cross bridge over the River Eden, turn R and rejoin route at instruction 10)

➡ **page 29**

9 At T-j after 5 miles R 'Armathwaite 1, Aiketgate 1½'. At next T-j R 'Armathwaite 1' under the railway bridge

10 Through Armathwaite following signs for Lockhills and Wetheral. After 6 miles at T-j with B6263 R 'Wetheral 1'

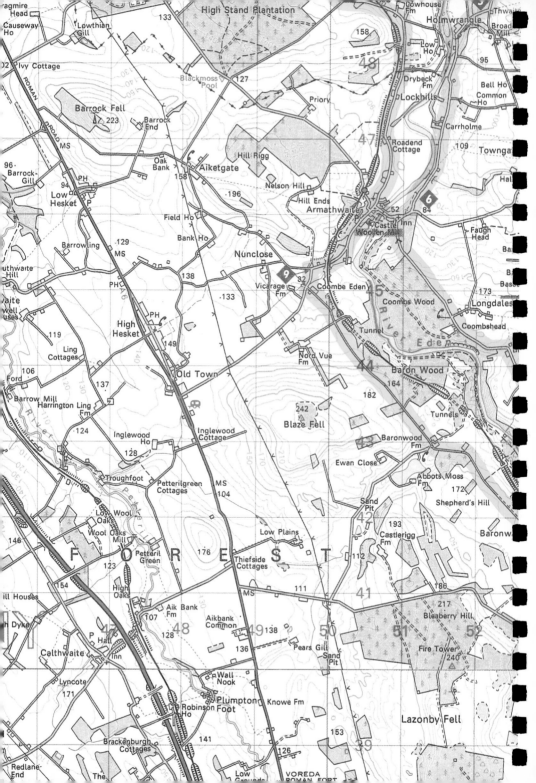

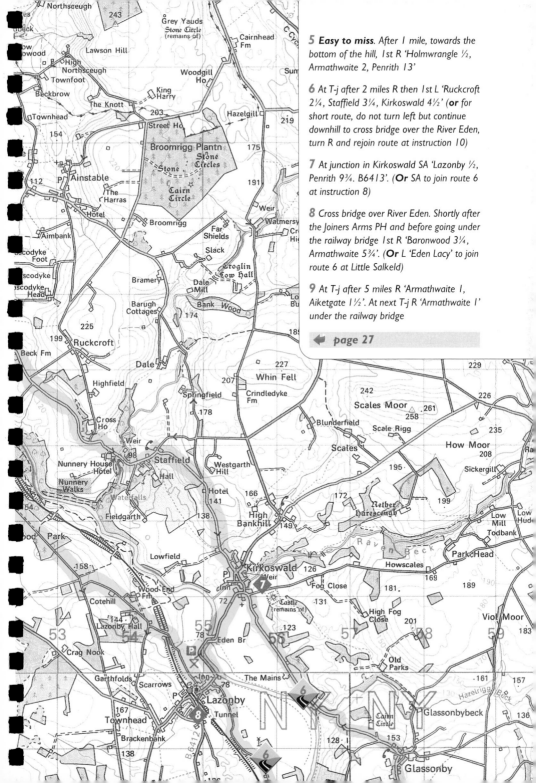

5 Easy to miss. *After 1 mile, towards the bottom of the hill, 1st R 'Holmwrangle ½, Armathwaite 2, Penrith 13'*

6 *At T-j after 2 miles R then 1st L 'Ruckcroft 2¼, Staffield 3¾, Kirkoswald 4½' (**or** for short route, do not turn left but continue downhill to cross bridge over the River Eden, turn R and rejoin route at instruction 10)*

7 *At junction in Kirkoswald SA 'Lazonby ½, Penrith 9¾. B6413'. (**Or** SA to join route 6 at instruction 8)*

8 *Cross bridge over River Eden. Shortly after the Joiners Arms PH and before going under the railway bridge 1st R 'Baronwood 3¼, Armathwaite 5¾'. (**Or** L 'Eden Lacy' to join route 6 at Little Salkeld)*

9 *At T-j after 5 miles R 'Armathwaite 1, Aiketgate 1½'. At next T-j R 'Armathwaite 1' under the railway bridge*

◄ **page 27**

North from Wigton to the coastline of the Solway Firth

3

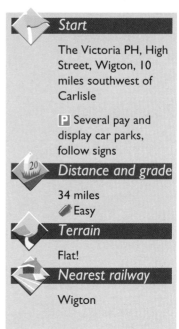

Start

The Victoria PH, High Street, Wigton, 10 miles southwest of Carlisle

P Several pay and display car parks, follow signs

Distance and grade

34 miles

Easy

Terrain

Flat!

Nearest railway

Wigton

It may come as a surprise to visitors to Cumbria that within the county boundaries there is an area that rivals East Anglia or the Somerset Levels for flatness! North of the A596 between Maryport on the coast

and Carlisle, is a large expanse of countryside that rarely rises to above 100 feet. Although Wigton itself is not a place to linger, dominated as it is by its cellophane factory, you soon escape into the maze of quiet lanes across the levels of Wedholme Flow. This is one of those good conversational rides where it would be possible for long stretches to cycle side by side and put the world to right with little fear of being mown down by vehicles. The masts between Anthorn and Cadurnock act as a beacon for the first half of the ride. Expect to see many birds on the salt marshes near to Newton Arlosh. From the coast you will be faced with clear views of Scotland across the Solway Firth, the fells to the south of Dumfries providing a pleasant contrast to the cooling towers of the power station at Annan. Soon after Port Carlisle the coast is left behind as the ride cuts inland through a series of unusual sounding hamlets such as Whitrigglees, Wampool, Biglands and Drumleaning to return to Wigton.

Wigton   Waverbridge   Raby   Newton Arlosh   Whitrigg   Anthorn

Abbeytown (just off the route) 5
Monks founded Holme Cultram Abbey in 1150, grew grain, raised sheep and cattle and traded in salt from the estuary. At the Dissolution of the Monasteries in the 16th century, its stones were hauled away to build houses

Refreshments

Hare and Hounds PH ●, plenty of choice in **Wigton**
Bush Inn PH, **Angerton**
Kings Arms PH, **Bowness-on-Solway**
Hope and Anchor PH, **Port Carlisle**
Highland Laddie Inn PH, **Glasson**

Bowness-on-Solway 9
Roman soldiers guarded the western end of Hadrian's Wall here and a defensive ditch (vallum) can be seen near Glasson. The wall was built between AD122 and 139 to discourage the independent Scottish tribes from marauding into the largely pacified territory to the south. It stretched 73 miles from Bowness to Wallsend-on-Tyne. It was built of the materials most readily to hand – stone in the east and turf in the west

◀ The Solway Firth in February

Bowness-on-Solway   Port Carlisle   Wampool   Biglands   Moorhouse

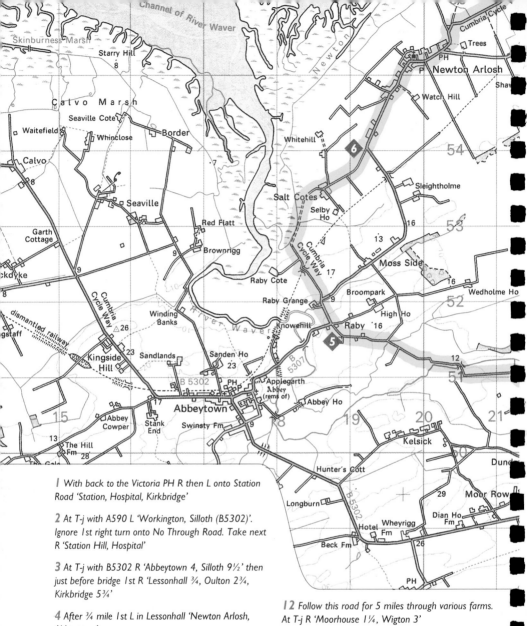

1 With back to the Victoria PH R then L onto Station Road 'Station, Hospital, Kirkbridge'

2 At T-j with A590 L 'Workington, Silloth (B5302)'. Ignore 1st right turn onto No Through Road. Take next R 'Station Hill, Hospital'

3 At T-j with B5302 R 'Abbeytown 4, Silloth 9½' then just before bridge 1st R 'Lessonhall ¾, Oulton 2¾, Kirkbridge 5¾'

4 After ¾ mile 1st L in Lessonhall 'Newton Arlosh, Abbeytown'

5 At T-j with B5307 R 'Newton Arlosh 2½, Kirkbride 5'. (Join the Cumbria Cycleway at this point). 1st L on sharp RH bend 'Cumbria Cycleway'

6 At T-j with B5307 L 'Kirkbride 3, Carlisle 14'

➡ **page 34**

12 Follow this road for 5 miles through various farms. At T-j R 'Moorhouse 1¼, Wigton 3'

13 **Easy to miss**. Ignore 1st left after ½ mile. Shortly after passing red sandstone terraced cottages to your right next L 'Wigton'

14 At T-j L 'Wigton 1'

15 At T-j with A596 R then L 'Wigton' to return to the start

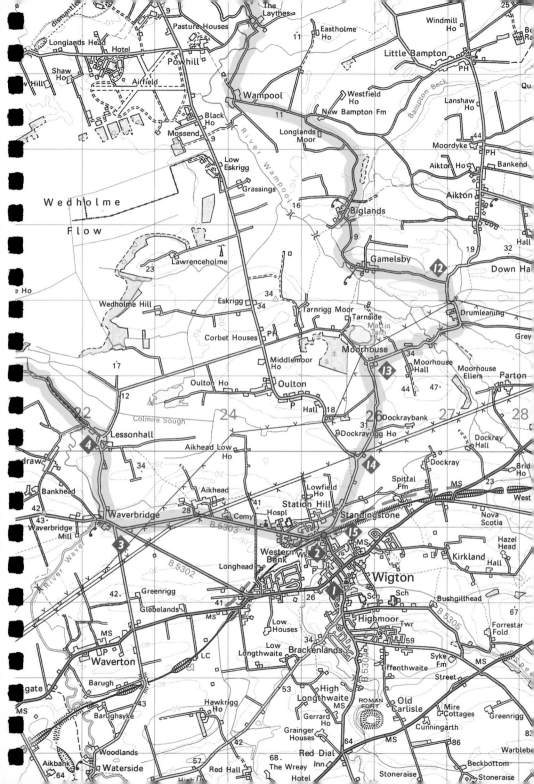

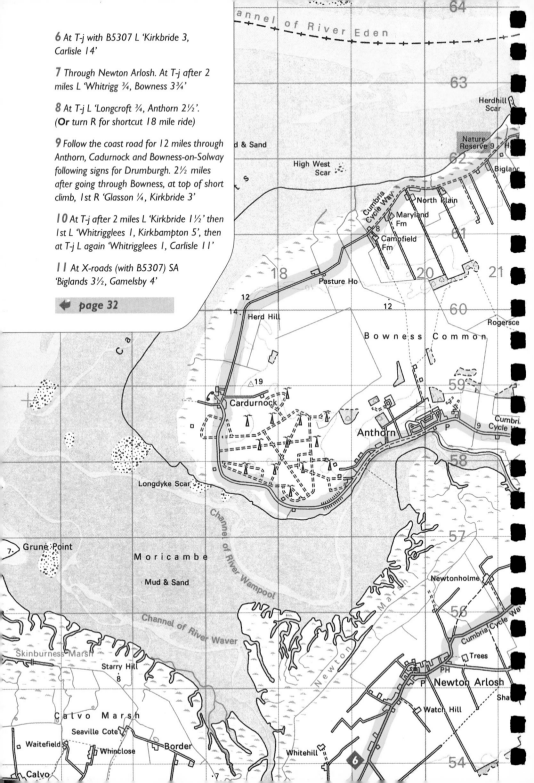

6 At T-j with B5307 L 'Kirkbride 3, Carlisle 14'

7 Through Newton Arlosh. At T-j after 2 miles L 'Whitrigg ¾, Bowness 3¾'

8 At T-j L 'Longcroft ¾, Anthorn 2½'. (**Or** turn R for shortcut 18 mile ride)

9 Follow the coast road for 12 miles through Anthorn, Cadurnock and Bowness-on-Solway following signs for Drumburgh. 2½ miles after going through Bowness, at top of short climb, 1st R 'Glasson ¼, Kirkbride 3'

10 At T-j after 2 miles L 'Kirkbride 1½' then 1st L 'Whitrigglees 1, Kirkbampton 5', then at T-j L again 'Whitrigglees 1, Carlisle 11'

11 At X-roads (with B5307) SA 'Biglands 3½, Gamelsby 4'

◀ **page 32**

annel of River Eden

64

63

Herdhill Scar

Nature Reserve 9

62

Biglan

High West Scar

d & Sand

Cumbria Cycle Way

North Plain

Maryland Fm

Campfield Fm

s

18

20

21

Pasture Ho

12

60

Rogersce

14

Herd Hill

12

Bowness Common

Ca

19

59

Cardurnock

Cumbri Cycle W

Anthorn

P

9

58

Longdyke Scar

Grune Point

7

57

Moricambe

Newtonholme

Mud & Sand

Channel of River Wampool

Newton Marsh

56

Channel of River Waver

Cumbria Cycle Way

Skinburness Marsh

Trees

Starry Hill

8

PH

P

Newton Arlosh

Calvo Marsh

Watch Hill

Sha

Seaville Cote

Waitefield

Whinclose

Border

Whitehill

6

54

Calvo

South from Cockermouth along the edge of the Lake District's Western Fells

This is a real gem of a ride with some of the best views of the fells in the whole book. On the first half of the ride you are slightly set back from the hills enabling you to appreciate them from afar. After Kirkland the route

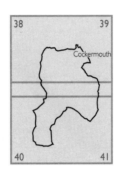

takes you into the heart of the hills. It is worth making a short detour from the T-junction beneath Murton Fell for some very fine views of Ennerdale Water with the backdrop of Ennerdale Fell. From Waterend the views are dominated by the mass of Melbreak and the charms of Loweswater but if you are lucky and the visibility is good you should be able to look right down the valley of Crummock Water and Buttermere to the very core of the central fells. There is an excellent pub in Loweswater should you need a break before the quiet lane through Lorton Vale alongside the River Cocker takes you back into Cockermouth.

Distance and grade

28 miles

Easy / Moderate

Terrain

For a ride with such stupendous views there are few climbs to worry about. Between the crossing of the River Marron in Ullock up to the road beneath Murton Fell there is 600 feet of climbing – 230 feet fairly steeply up to Dean Cross then 370 feet more gently from Asby to beyond Kirkland. Highest point – 850 feet (254 mts) beneath Murton Fell. Lowest point – 150 feet (45 mts) at the start

Nearest railway

Workington, 5 miles west of the route at Greysouthen

Cockermouth Brigham Greysouthen Ullock Asby Kirkland

Places of interest

Cockermouth 1

William Wordsworth was born in a Georgian house at the end of the main street. There are the remains of a largely 14th-century castle at the junction of the Cocker and Derwent rivers

Refreshments

Brown Cow PH ●, plenty of choice in **Cockermouth**
Royal Yew PH ●, **Dean**
Coffees and teas at the Grange Country House Hotel **at the northern end of Loweswater**
Kirkstile Inn PH ●●, **Loweswater**

The Lortons 16

Lorton Hall is partly a 15th-century peel tower, built as a refuge for the villagers against raiding Scots during the Border wars. The Jennings brewery in Cockermouth started off in what is now the village hall in High Lorton. At the rear stands a yew tree under which the founder of the Quaker movement, George Fox, preached pacifism to a large crowd that included Cromwellian soldiers. William Wordsworth in his poem Yew Trees wrote:

'There is a yew tree, pride of Lorton Vale
Which to this day stands single, in the midst
Of its own darkness, as it stood of yore'

▼ Crummock Water

Felldyke Lamplugh Waterend Loweswater Thackthwaite Low Lorton

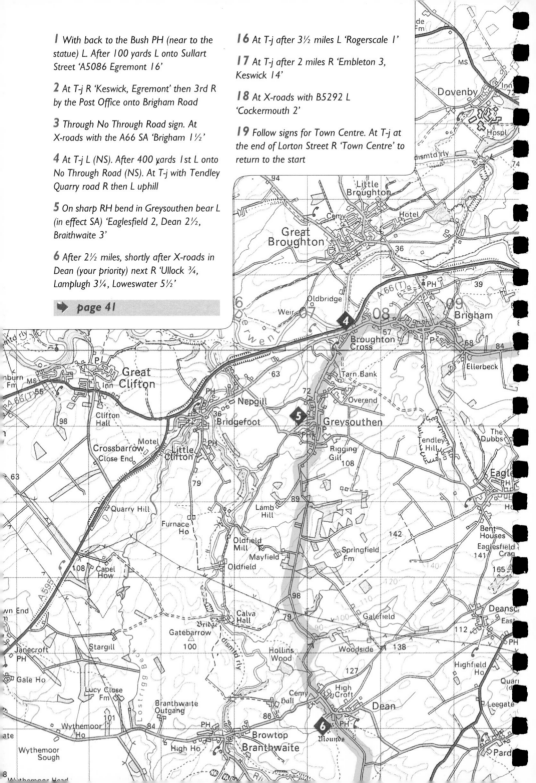

1 With back to the Bush PH (near to the statue) L. After 100 yards L onto Sullart Street 'A5086 Egremont 16'

2 At T-j R 'Keswick, Egremont' then 3rd R by the Post Office onto Brigham Road

3 Through No Through Road sign. At X-roads with the A66 SA 'Brigham 1½'

4 At T-j L (NS). After 400 yards 1st L onto No Through Road (NS). At T-j with Tendley Quarry road R then L uphill

5 On sharp RH bend in Greysouthen bear L (in effect SA) 'Eaglesfield 2, Dean 2½, Braithwaite 3'

6 After 2½ miles, shortly after X-roads in Dean (your priority) next R 'Ullock ¾, Lamplugh 3¼, Loweswater 5½'

16 At T-j after 3½ miles L 'Rogerscale 1'

17 At T-j after 2 miles R 'Embleton 3, Keswick 14'

18 At X-roads with B5292 L 'Cockermouth 2'

19 Follow signs for Town Centre. At T-j at the end of Lorton Street R 'Town Centre' to return to the start

➡ **page 41**

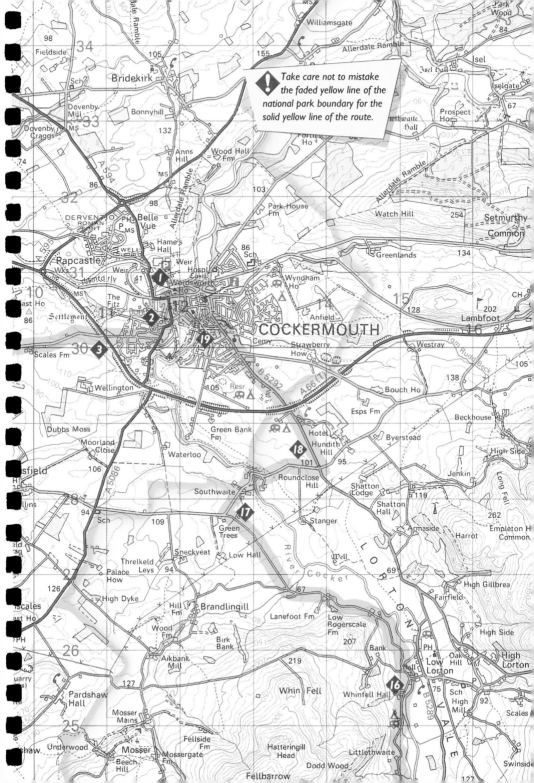

Take care not to mistake the faded yellow line of the national park boundary for the solid yellow line of the route.

Take care not to mistake the faded yellow line of the national park boundary for the solid yellow line of the route.

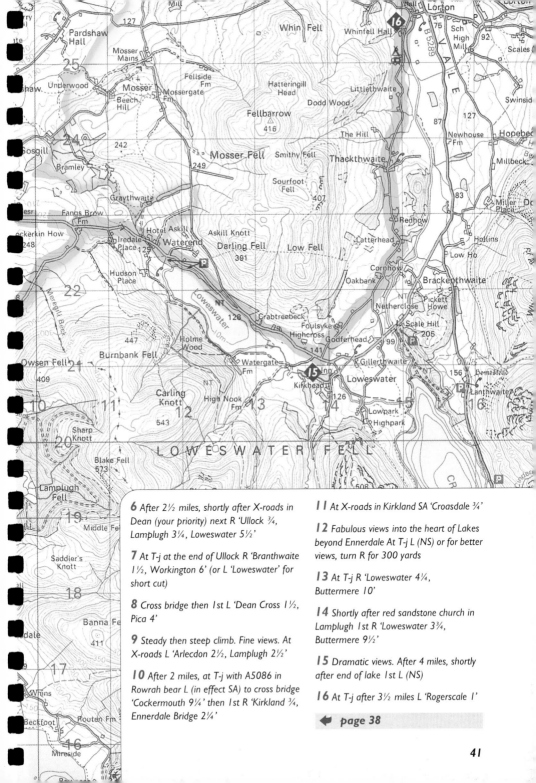

6 After 2½ miles, shortly after X-roads in Dean (your priority) next R 'Ullock ¾, Lamplugh 3¼, Loweswater 5½'

7 At T-j at the end of Ullock R 'Branthwaite 1½, Workington 6' (or L 'Loweswater' for short cut)

8 Cross bridge then 1st L 'Dean Cross 1½, Pica 4'

9 Steady then steep climb. Fine views. At X-roads L 'Arlecdon 2½, Lamplugh 2½'

10 After 2 miles, at T-j with A5086 in Rowrah bear L (in effect SA) to cross bridge 'Cockermouth 9¼' then 1st R 'Kirkland ¾, Ennerdale Bridge 2¼'

11 At X-roads in Kirkland SA 'Croasdale ¾'

12 Fabulous views into the heart of Lakes beyond Ennerdale At T-j L (NS) or for better views, turn R for 300 yards

13 At T-j R 'Loweswater 4¼, Buttermere 10'

14 Shortly after red sandstone church in Lamplugh 1st R 'Loweswater 3¾, Buttermere 9½'

15 Dramatic views. After 4 miles, shortly after end of lake 1st L (NS)

16 At T-j after 3½ miles L 'Rogerscale 1'

← **page 38**

5 A tour around Skiddaw and Blencathra, north from Keswick

Start

The Leisure Pool, Keswick (follow signs)

P As above, or alternatively a large pay and display car park near to the lake

Distance and grade

32 miles

Moderate

Terrain

6 climbs of between 200 and 300 feet spaced out evenly through the ride. The least welcome is that at the end from the main road up to

Skiddaw and Blencathra are completely circumnavigated on this ride, almost entirely on quiet lanes. The contrast between the described exit from Keswick, along the railway path, and the parallel A66 could not

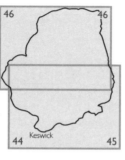

be greater. One is a delightful woodland trail crossing the River Greta some seven times on a gently graded trail popular with walkers and cyclists alike. By contrast the A66 is a fast, noisy, busy trunk road that holds no appeal whatsoever to cyclists. By using a section of old road at the end of Threlkeld it is possible to minimise to a couple of hundred yards the time spent on the A66. The views of Blencathra from the tiny lanes in the valley by Guardhouse are truly wonderful. The fell road from the White Horse Inn at Scales climbs then contours around the flanks of Souther Fell. There is a choice of refreshments at the inn at Mungrisdale or the coffee shop at Mosedale, or perhaps you will wish to cross the corner of the Caldbeck Fells before dropping down to Hesket Newmarket which is at the halfway stage of the ride. The views towards Skiddaw improve as you climb to a high point on Aughertree Fell. The short section on the A591 after Bassenthwaite and Scarness comes as something of a shock after so long on quiet roads but the first available exit is taken up to Applethwaite. All along this stretch the views across to Grisedale Pike and the fells above Bassenthwaite Lake are magnificent.

Keswick   Threlkeld   Scales   Mungrisdale   Mosedale

Applethwaite, but if the visibility is good then the views of the fells on the other side of the valley are more than adequate compensation. Highest point – 1030 feet (317 mts) at Calebreck, south of Hesket Newmarket. Lowest point – 280 feet (82 mts) at the start

Nearest railway

Penrith

Refreshments

Plenty of choice in **Keswick**
Horse and Farrier PH, Salutation Inn PH ❦, **Threlkeld** *White Horse Inn PH,* **Scales** *Mill Inn PH* ❦, **Mungrisdale** *Quakers coffee and tea shop at* **Mosedale** *Old Crown PH* ❦❦, **Hesket Newmarket** *Sun Inn PH* ❦❦, **Bassenthwaite**

Places of interest

Keswick 1
Several museums with a variety of displays including lead pencils made here since the 16th century, originally with local graphite, a relief model of the Lake District, works by Lakeland poets and cars used in films and TV series. Coleridge and Southey lived here

Castlerigg Stone Circle 1
A Bronze Age ring of stones up to 6 feet tall set in an amphitheatre of hills. Probably 3500 years old

Threlkeld 2
Famous for fox-hunting and sheepdog trials. Stagecoach travellers used to stay at the 17th-century Horse and Farrier Inn

Bassenthwaite 14
There are traces of Roman and Norse settlements around the village

▼ *Lake Derwentwater from Skiddaw*

Aughertree Fell · Longlands · Orthwaite · Bassenthwaite · Millbeck

1 From the leisure pool follow the broad track (the old railway track) past the old station through several gates and over many bridges to its end

2 Follow signs for Threlkeld village. At the A66 L and L again 'Threlkeld ¼'

3 Through Threlkeld past the Horse and Farrier PH and the Salutation Inn. 100 yards before rejoining the A66 L onto No Through Road just past the telephone box on the left

4 Through gates to the end of the tarmac. Descend on path to the A66. Turn L then 1st R 'Guardhouse'

5 At T-j after 1 mile, with No Through Road to the right, turn L

6 At T-j by triangle of grass and Give Way sign L. At T-j with A66 L then R 'White Horse Inn'. Just before Inn sharp R back on yourself 'Gates'

7 After 3 miles at T-j just past Mill Inn L (NS)

➡ **page 47**

17 At T-j with A591 R 'Keswick'

18 After 2½ miles 1st L 'Millbeck, Applethwaite, Skiddaw'

19 At T-j after 2½ miles L. At roundabout SA onto A5771 'Keswick'

20 1st L after the Pheasant Inn onto Brundholme Road 'Railway Station, Leisure Pool'

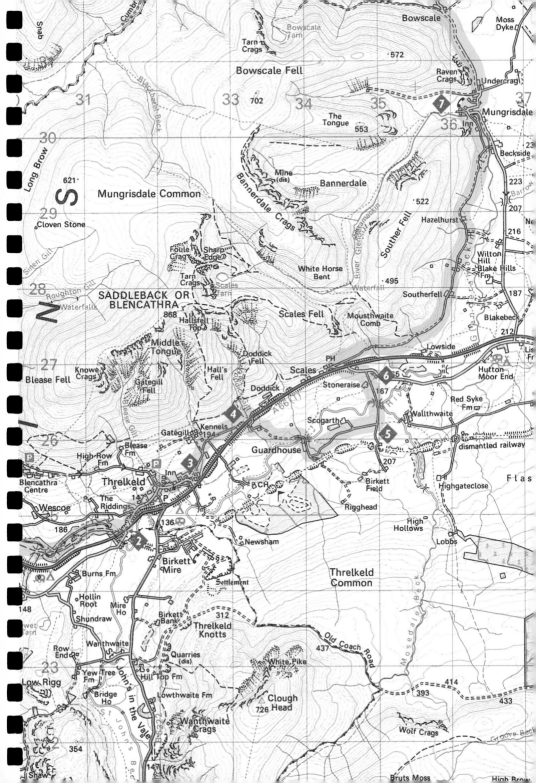

Take care not to mistake the faded yellow line of the national park boundary for the solid yellow line of the route.

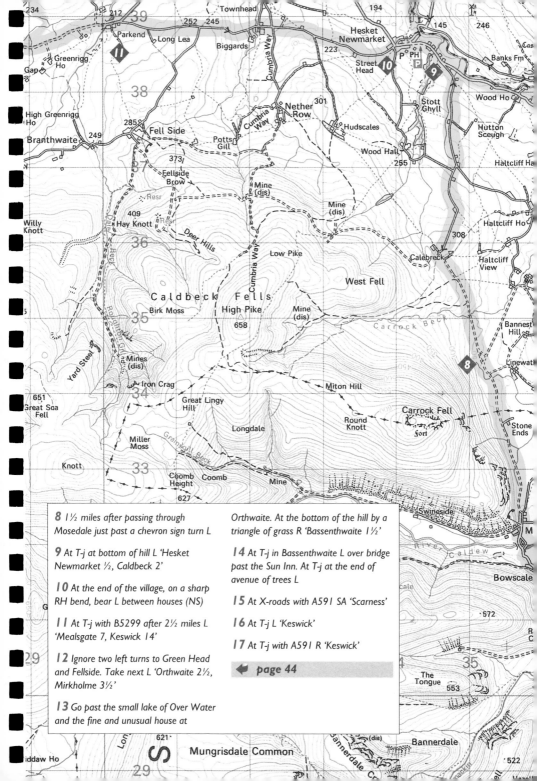

8 1½ miles after passing through Mosedale just past a chevron sign turn L

9 At T-j at bottom of hill L 'Hesket Newmarket ½, Caldbeck 2'

10 At the end of the village, on a sharp RH bend, bear L between houses (NS)

11 At T-j with B5299 after 2½ miles L 'Mealsgate 7, Keswick 14'

12 Ignore two left turns to Green Head and Fellside. Take next L 'Orthwaite 2½, Mirkholme 3½'

13 Go past the small lake of Over Water and the fine and unusual house at Orthwaite. At the bottom of the hill by a triangle of grass R 'Bassenthwaite 1½'

14 At T-j in Bassenthwaite L over bridge past the Sun Inn. At T-j at the end of avenue of trees L

15 At X-roads with A591 SA 'Scarness'

16 At T-j L 'Keswick'

17 At T-j with A591 R 'Keswick'

◀ page 44

6 Along the Eden Valley northwest from Appleby

The Eden Valley is a real delight for cyclists: to the east lie the Pennines, away to the west loom the fells of the Lake District, between the two runs the River Eden with long stretches of

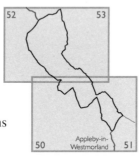

relatively easy cycling with fabulous views of both mountain ranges. This ride runs in a cigar-shaped loop northwest from Appleby through countryside which is more fertile and thus more cultivated than the surrounding fells. There are signs of red sandstone in the houses and the dry-stone walls enclosing rolling green pastures as you pass through solid, handsome villages and hamlets at the base of the western edge of the Pennines. The ride could easily be linked with route 8 near to Dufton forming a sixty mile loop.

Start

Tourist Information Centre, Appleby-in-Westmorland

P Long stay car park near the swimming pool at the end of Chapel Street. From the Tourist Information Centre turn R uphill then 1st R onto High Wiend and R again along Chapel Street

Distance and grade

37 miles

 Easy / moderate

Terrain

Undulating. Several climbs of between 100 and 200 feet. 30 feet climb west from Little Salkeld. Highest point – 710 feet (215 mts) at Knock, north of Dufton. Lowest point – 300 feet (90 mts) at Little Salkeld

Nearest railway

Appleby-in-Westmorland

Appleby-in-Westmorland — Long Marton — Kirkby Thore — Newbiggin — Culgaith — Langwathby — Little Salkeld

Appleby-in-Westmorland 1

▼ Long Meg, near Little Salked

The former capital of Westmorland consisting of two towns either side of the River Eden. The old town was a

10th-century Danish village on a bluff overlooking the 'new' town which grew around the 12th-century castle. The latter was restored in the 1650's and has the original keep and a rare breeds farm. The town contains many splendid buildings from Jacobean to Victorian times. The town is famous for its lively and colourful horse fair, held every June, when gypsy horse-dealers from all over the country come to the town for horse racing and trading

Milburn 3

Attractive village lying in the shadows of 2930-feet Cross Fell which rises up behind the sandstone cottages huddled around the spacious green. All face inwards, a reminder of the days when bands of bloodthirsty outlaws roamed the wild borderland between England and Scotland, killing, burning and rustling sheep and cattle. The narrow entrances at each corner were easily sealed against border raiders. A lofty maypole, topped by a weathercock, stands on the base of a long-gone preaching cross

 Refreshments

Royal Oak PH❦❦, plenty of choice in **Appleby-in-Westmorland**
Masons Arms PH, **Long Marton**
Shepherds Inn PH❦, **Langwathby**
Post Haste Cafe, Shepherds Inn PH❦❦, **Melmerby** *Fox Inn PH,* **Ousby**
Sun Inn PH, **Skirwith**
Stag Inn PH, **Milburn**
Stag Inn PH, **Dufton**

Great Salkeld *(just off the route)* 7

Red sandstone cottages and farmhouses cluster around the part-Norman church of St Cuthbert which has a Norman dog-tooth carving on the south doorway. The ivy-clad tower was built in 1380 as a refuge for villagers against border raiders

Gamblesby   Melmerby   Ousby   Blencarn   Milburn   Knock   Dufton

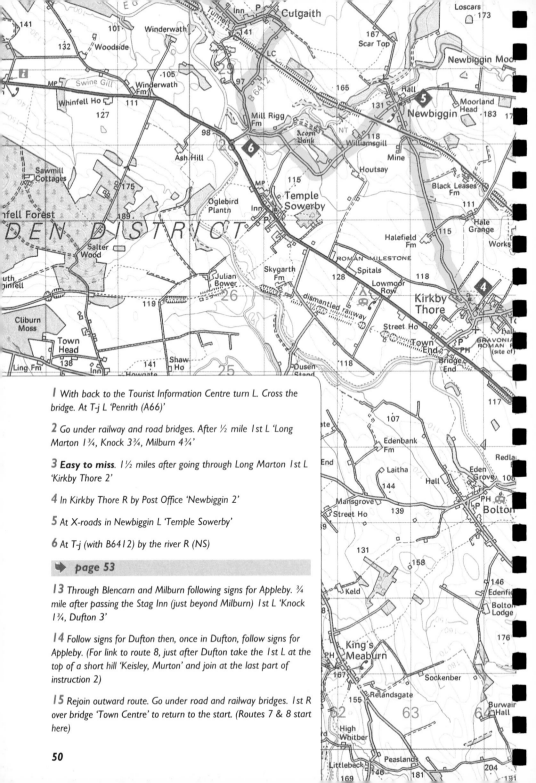

1 With back to the Tourist Information Centre turn L. Cross the bridge. At T-j L 'Penrith (A66)'

2 Go under railway and road bridges. After ½ mile 1st L 'Long Marton 1¾, Knock 3¾, Milburn 4¾'

3 Easy to miss. 1½ miles after going through Long Marton 1st L 'Kirkby Thore 2'

4 In Kirkby Thore R by Post Office 'Newbiggin 2'

5 At X-roads in Newbiggin L 'Temple Sowerby'

6 At T-j (with B6412) by the river R (NS)

➡ **page 53**

13 Through Blencarn and Milburn following signs for Appleby. ¾ mile after passing the Stag Inn (just beyond Milburn) 1st L 'Knock 1¾, Dufton 3'

14 Follow signs for Dufton then, once in Dufton, follow signs for Appleby. (For link to route 8, just after Dufton take the 1st L at the top of a short hill 'Keisley, Murton' and join at the last part of instruction 2)

15 Rejoin outward route. Go under road and railway bridges. 1st R over bridge 'Town Centre' to return to the start. (Routes 7 & 8 start here)

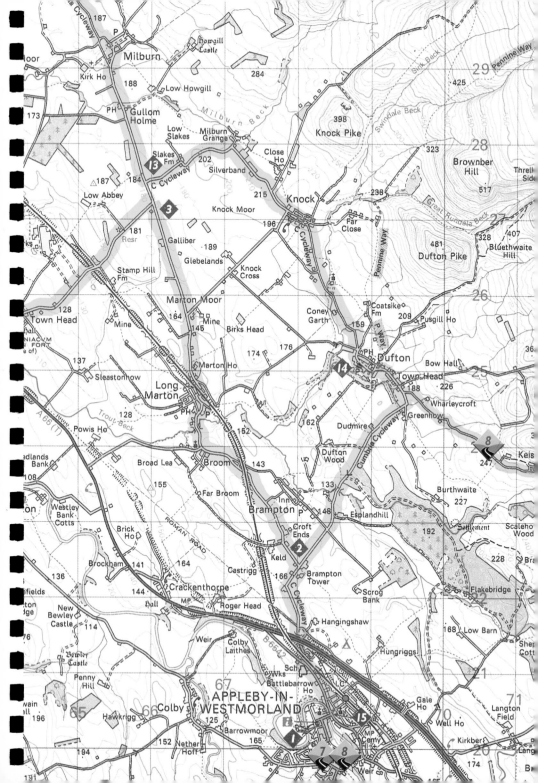

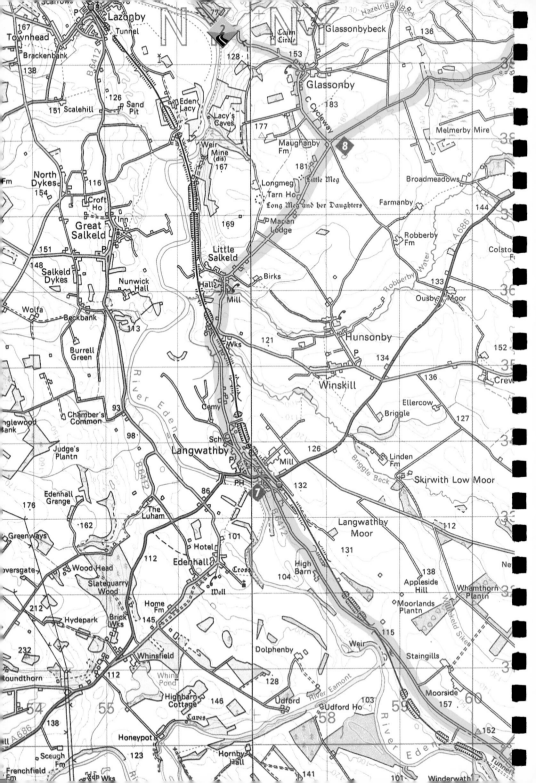

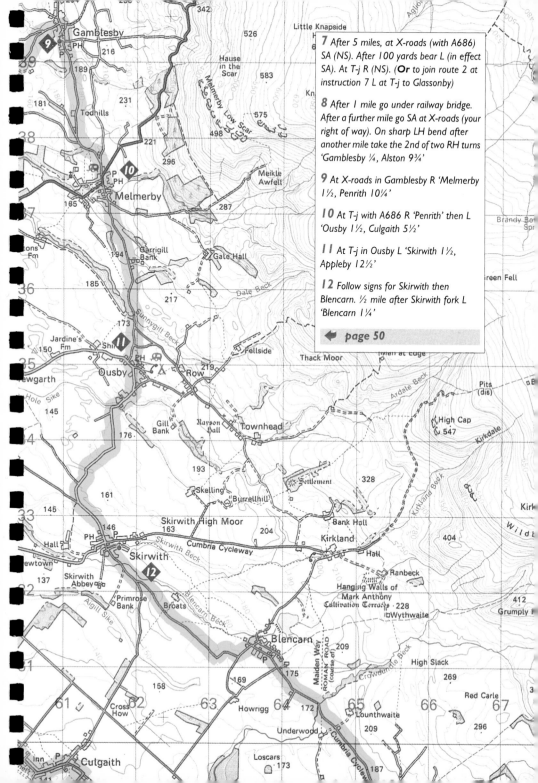

7 After 5 miles, at X-roads (with A686) SA (NS). After 100 yards bear L (in effect SA). At T-j R (NS). (**Or** to join route 2 at instruction 7 L at T-j to Glassonby)

8 After 1 mile go under railway bridge. After a further mile go SA at X-roads (your right of way). On sharp LH bend after another mile take the 2nd of two RH turns 'Gamblesby ¼, Alston 9¾'

9 At X-roads in Gamblesby R 'Melmerby 1½, Penrith 10¼'

10 At T-j with A686 R 'Penrith' then L 'Ousby 1½, Culgaith 5½'

11 At T-j in Ousby L 'Skirwith 1½, Appleby 12½'

12 Follow signs for Skirwith then Blencarn. ½ mile after Skirwith fork L 'Blencarn 1¼'

◀ page 50

7 West from Appleby to Shap and Askham, beneath the Lakeland Fells

The first half of this ride is characterised by climbs in and out of river valleys: the River Eden is 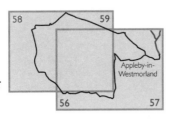 left behind at Appleby before a swift up and down to one of its tributaries, Hoff Beck at Colby. This in turn is crossed as the route heads east up over the hills and down into the valley of the River Lyvennet. There is a respite from the climbing as the valley is followed to Crosby Ravensworh with its lovely church and ring of pre-historic settlements. The steepest challenge of the day takes you up to over 1000 feet with fabulous views across to the Lakeland fells. After Shap you descend to the last important river valley – that formed by the River Lowther which drains the Haweswater Reservoir and borders Lowther Park with its dramatic castle facade. The last section of the ride seems to encourage you to stretch your legs and aim straight as an arrow for the gastronomic delights of Appleby.

Start

Tourist Information Centre, Appleby-in-Westmorland

P Long stay car park near the swimming pool at the end of Chapel Street. From the Tourist Information Centre turn R uphill then 1st R onto High Wiend and R again along Chapel Street

Distance and grade

34 miles

Moderate

Terrain

Three climbs: 250 feet west from Colby, 470 feet west from Crosby Ravensworth, with the first section very steep, 230 feet inside Lowther Park. Highest point – 1080 feet (325 mts) above Crosby Ravensworth. Lowest point – 380 feet (114 mts) at the end of the ride just before Appleby

Nearest railway

Appleby-in-Westmorland

Appleby-in-Westmorland

Colby

King's Meaburn

Maulds Meaburn

Crosby Ravensworth

Shap

Places of interest

Crosby Ravensworth 6

▼ *Near Shap*

The pre-historic settlements comprise many ruined huts, one measuring 50 feet across. St Lawrence's Church is a cathedral in miniature, much rebuilt since the 13th century and located in a picturesque setting

Askham 11

An immaculate village on the steep wooded bank of the River Lowther. The upper green has fine views to Lowther Castle and the Pennines. There is an ancient stone circle and burial sites on Askham Fell

Lowther 12

The fairy-tale facade of towers, turrets and battlements is the only remnant of the 19th-century castle which was demolished in 1957. Lowther Park was created in 1283 for the estate's deer and is now a country park with nature trails, children's entertainments, rare breeds and red deer whose ancestors roamed the original deer park

Refreshments

Royal Oak PH 🍺🍴, *plenty of choice in*
Appleby-in-Westmorland
Butchers Arms PH 🍴, **Crosby Ravensworth**
Cafe, Bulls Head PH 🍴, **Shap**
Crown and Mitre PH, St Patricks Well PH 🍴,
Bampton (just off the route)
Punchbowl PH 🍺🍴, Queens Head PH 🍴,
Askham

Whale   Askham   Cliburn   Bolton   Colby

Take care not to mistake the faded yellow line of the national park boundary for the solid yellow line of the route.

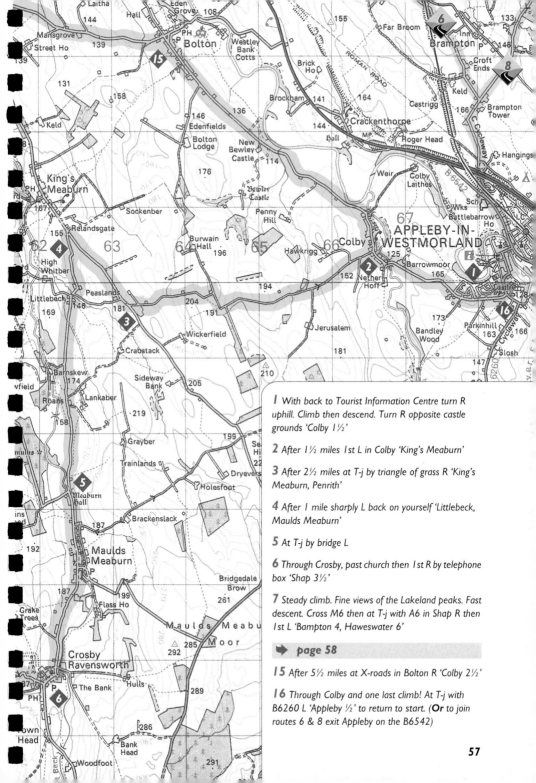

1 With back to Tourist Information Centre turn R uphill. Climb then descend. Turn R opposite castle grounds 'Colby 1½'

2 After 1½ miles 1st L in Colby 'King's Meaburn'

3 After 2½ miles at T-j by triangle of grass R 'King's Meaburn, Penrith'

4 After 1 mile sharply L back on yourself 'Littlebeck, Maulds Meaburn'

5 At T-j by bridge L

6 Through Crosby, past church then 1st R by telephone box 'Shap 3½'

7 Steady climb. Fine views of the Lakeland peaks. Fast descent. Cross M6 then at T-j with A6 in Shap R then 1st L 'Bampton 4, Haweswater 6'

➡ page 58

15 After 5½ miles at X-roads in Bolton R 'Colby 2½'

16 Through Colby and one last climb! At T-j with B6260 L 'Appleby ½' to return to start. (**Or** to join routes 6 & 8 exit Appleby on the B6542)

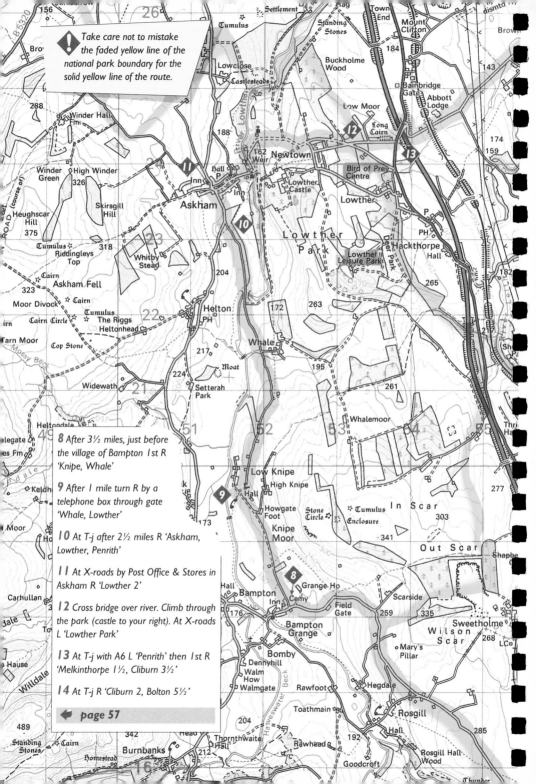

! Take care not to mistake the faded yellow line of the national park boundary for the solid yellow line of the route.

8 After 3½ miles, just before the village of Bampton 1st R 'Knipe, Whale'

9 After 1 mile turn R by a telephone box through gate 'Whale, Lowther'

10 At T-j after 2½ miles R 'Askham, Lowther, Penrith'

11 At X-roads by Post Office & Stores in Askham R 'Lowther 2'

12 Cross bridge over river. Climb through the park (castle to your right). At X-roads L 'Lowther Park'

13 At T-j with A6 L 'Penrith' then 1st R 'Melkinthorpe 1½, Cliburn 3½'

14 At T-j R 'Cliburn 2, Bolton 5½'

← **page 57**

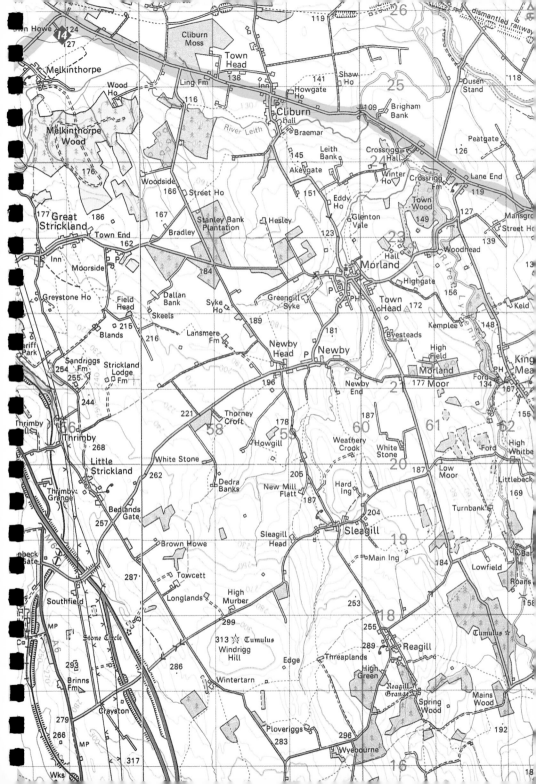

Southeast from Appleby-in-Westmorland to Brough and Kirkby Stephen

*T*his ride climbs out of the Eden valley, leaving behind the river, the railway and the main road (the A66) as it heads for quiet lanes running right along the base of the Pennines. The latter rise to over

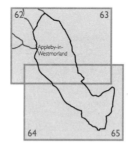

2000 feet within a couple of miles of the route. The ride passes through military firing ranges during the first section of the route before crossing to the south of the A66 and into Brough. There used to be seventeen inns here in its heyday as a staging post. The number has declined but you should find enough choice of cafés or pubs before turning south on a 2½ mile section of main road. You are soon back onto quiet lanes through Winton and the charms of Kirkby Stephen. The nine mile final stretch back to Appleby is truly wonderful cycling – a gently undulating road with fine views to both sides and little traffic.

 Start

Tourist Information Centre, Appleby-in-Westmorland

P Long stay car park near the swimming pool at the end of Chapel Street. From the Tourist Information Centre turn R uphill then 1st R onto High Wiend and R again along Chapel Street

 Distance and grade

30 miles

Easy / moderate

 Terrain

450 feet climb near the start from the crossing of Trout Beck north of Appleby towards Murton. Several climbs of between 100 and 200 feet. Highest point – 890 feet (268 mts) north of Murton. Lowest point – Appleby 410 feet (125 mts)

Nearest railway

Appleby-in-Westmorland

Appleby-in-Westmorland   Dufton   Murton   Hilton   Warcop   Great Musgrave

Brough 8

The castle was built by the Normans on the site of a Roman fort then rebuilt in medieval style but was gutted by fire in 1666. Castle Hotel has original stables and outbuildings and a

▼ Brough Castle

cobbled courtyard. Stone from the Roman fort was used in building the 11th-century St Michael's Church. Great prosperity came in the 18th and 19th centuries, with up to 60 stage coaches a day halting at the village, on their way from London to Carlisle and on to Glasgow, or from York to Lancaster. Seventeen inns attended to their needs, but decline set in when the railway was built and routed to the west, through Kirkby Stephen

Kirkby Stephen 12

Brightly painted shops and old coaching inns huddle among attractive cobbled squares above the Eden valley. Inside the 13th-century St Stephen's church is the shaft of the unique 10th-century cemetery cross of Loki, the Danish Devil

Refreshments

Royal Oak PH ✿ ✿, plenty of choice in **Appleby-in-Westmorland**
Chamley Arms PH, **Warcop**
Plenty of choice in **Brough**
Bay Horse Inn PH, **Winton**
Kings Arms PH ✿, White Lion PH ✿, **Kirkby Stephen**

Winton   Kirkby Stephen   Soulby

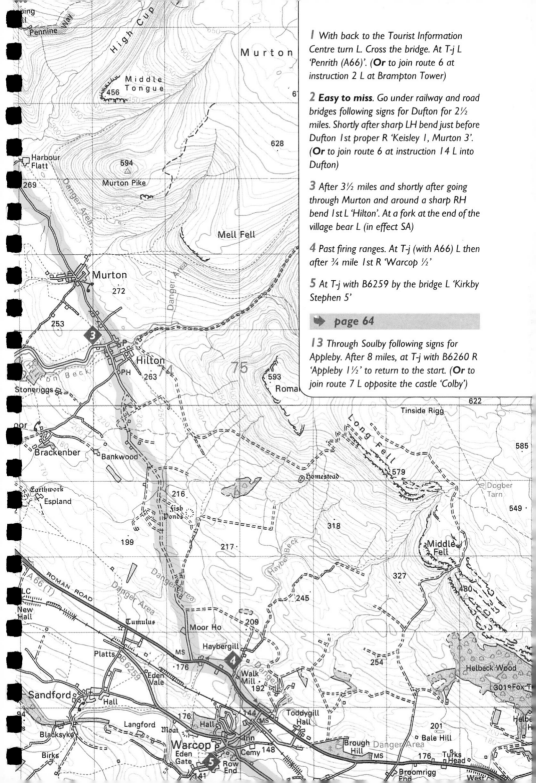

1 With back to the Tourist Information Centre turn L. Cross the bridge. At T-j L 'Penrith (A66)'. (**Or** to join route 6 at instruction 2 L at Brampton Tower)

2 Easy to miss. Go under railway and road bridges following signs for Dufton for 2½ miles. Shortly after sharp LH bend just before Dufton 1st proper R 'Keisley 1, Murton 3'. (**Or** to join route 6 at instruction 14 L into Dufton)

3 After 3½ miles and shortly after going through Murton and around a sharp RH bend 1st L 'Hilton'. At a fork at the end of the village bear L (in effect SA)

4 Past firing ranges. At T-j (with A66) L then after ¾ mile 1st R 'Warcop ½'

5 At T-j with B6259 by the bridge L 'Kirkby Stephen 5'

➡ **page 64**

13 Through Soulby following signs for Appleby. After 8 miles, at T-j with B6260 R 'Appleby 1½' to return to the start. (**Or** to join route 7 L opposite the castle 'Colby')

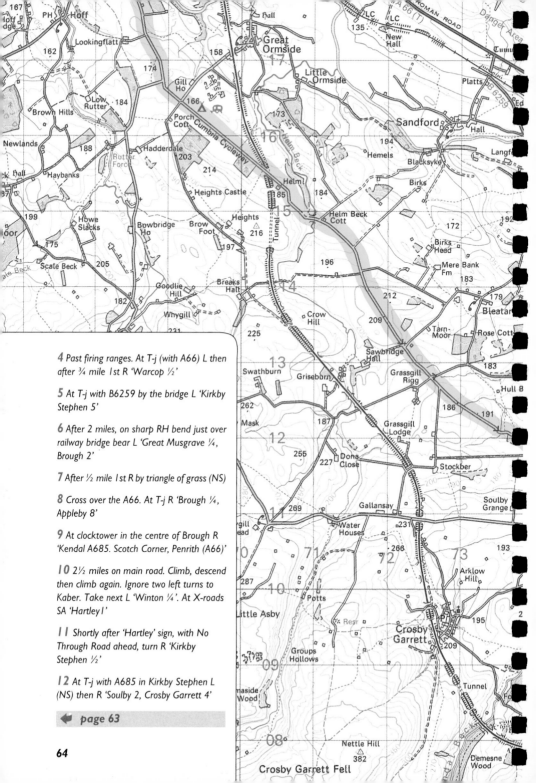

4 Past firing ranges. At T-j (with A66) L then after ¾ mile 1st R 'Warcop ½'

5 At T-j with B6259 by the bridge L 'Kirkby Stephen 5'

6 After 2 miles, on sharp RH bend just over railway bridge bear L 'Great Musgrave ¼, Brough 2'

7 After ½ mile 1st R by triangle of grass (NS)

8 Cross over the A66. At T-j R 'Brough ¼, Appleby 8'

9 At clocktower in the centre of Brough R 'Kendal A685. Scotch Corner, Penrith (A66)'

10 2½ miles on main road. Climb, descend then climb again. Ignore two left turns to Kaber. Take next L 'Winton ¼'. At X-roads SA 'Hartley1'

11 Shortly after 'Hartley' sign, with No Through Road ahead, turn R 'Kirkby Stephen ½'

12 At T-j with A685 in Kirkby Stephen L (NS) then R 'Soulby 2, Crosby Garrett 4'

← page 63

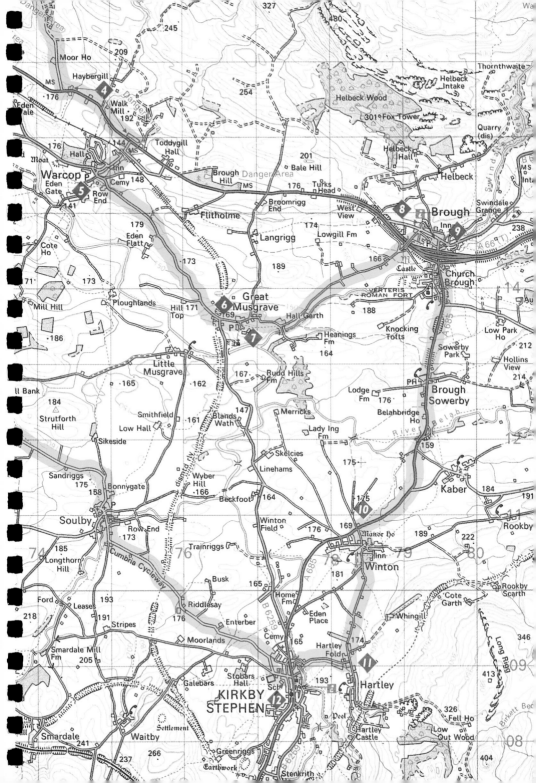

9 North from Kendal along quiet lanes into the valleys of the Mint, Sprint and Kent

Start

The Tourist Information Centre, Kendal

P Follow signs for long stay car parks

Distance and grade

33½ miles

Moderate / strenuous

Terrain

610 feet climb from the start to the edge of Hay Fell. 430 feet climb south from Staveley. 480 feet near the start of Underbarrow up

Although Kendal itself is dominated by motor traffic, within a mile or so of the town centre it is possible to escape onto quiet lanes with some of the most rewarding cycling in the Lake District. The price to be paid for this is a steep climb of over 600 feet on the old Sedbergh road to the edge of Hay Fell. From here on the route is truly delightful with

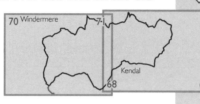

tiny hamlets, fine views, streams and sections of broadleaf woodland. Staveley is the only village of any size in the first half of the ride. From Staveley tiny, gated roads lead west then south through Borwick Fold. The route continues on to Winster and towards Bowland Bridge where there are two excellent pubs just off the route. At this point you may wish to opt for a longer route by linking this ride with route 10 and going down to the coast at Grange-over-Sands. If not, you are faced with a last climb over the southern end of Scout Scar to return to Kendal, the road dropping you right at the doorstep of the Tourist Information Centre. (The obvious direct route over Scout Scar is a steeper climb on a busier road, hence the southern route).

Kendal   Woodside   Beck Houses Grayrigg   Patton Bridge   Garnett Bridge   Staveley

Kendal I
Isolated above the 'auld grey town' of fine limestone buildings and narrow twisting streets is the ruined 12th-century castle, the birthplace in 1512 of Catherine Parr, Henry VIII's last wife. The elegant 18th-century Abbott Hall preserves local traditions in the Museum of Lakeland Life and Industry

over Scout Scar. Many of the black arrows in the middle section of the ride are for very short sections and should cause no worries. Highest point – 760 feet (230 mts) near the start, to the east of Kendal. Lowest point – 30 feet (10 mts) at Underbarrow

Nearest railway

Kendal

Refreshments

Plenty of choice in **Kendal**
Tea and coffee at farm at **Watchgate** *(east of the A6 north of Kendal)*
Eagle and Child PH, *Station Inn PH,*
Staveley
Brown Horse Inn PH, **Winster**
Hare and Hounds PH, **Bowland Bridge**
(just off the route)
Masons Arms PH, **Strawberry Bank**
(just off the route)
Punchbowl PH, **Crosthwaite**
Wheatsheaf PH, **Brigsteer**

Bowness-on-Windermere

Winster

Crosthwaite

Underbarrow

Brigsteer

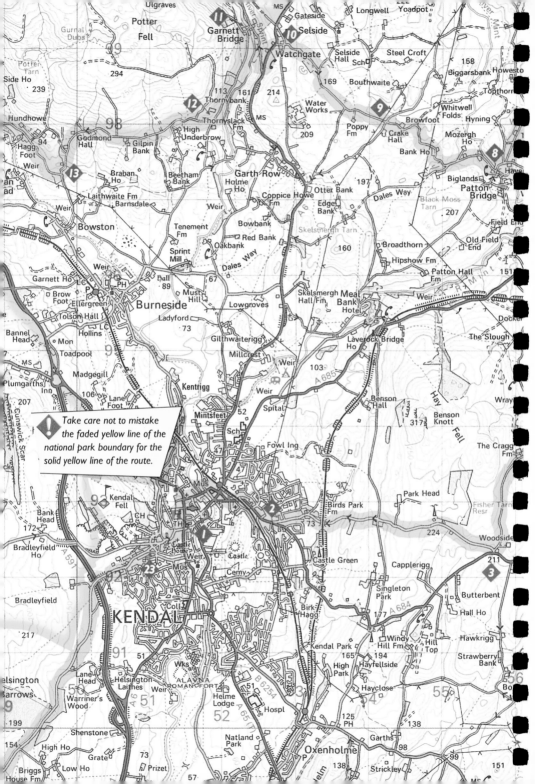

Take care not to mistake the faded yellow line of the national park boundary for the solid yellow line of the route.

1 With back to the Tourist Information Centre R following the one way system and signs for Sedbergh (A684). At T-j at the end of Castle Street bear R (in effect SA) 'A684 Sedbergh 9½' (the sign is on the wall to your right)

2 Ignore Sandylands Lane to your left. Shortly after passing allotments to your left, take the next proper L by a telephone box onto Sedbergh Road

3 Climb steeply. After 2 miles, and just before rejoining the main road turn L by a white cottage (NS)

4 At T-j L (NS). Continue downhill bearing R by Croft Foot Farm

5 At T-j just after Kiln Head Cottage L (NS) then R 'Moorfold, Thatchmoor Head'

6 At T-j / X-roads turn L towards cottage

7 At T-j with main road (A685) L then R by church 'Whinfell 3'

8 After 2 miles, immediately after crossing bridge turn R 'Selside, Watchgate 2'

9 At X-roads SA 'Watchgate 1'

10 At T-j with A6 L 'Kendal' then R 'Longsleddale 4½'

11 At bottom L over bridge 'Burnside 2½'

12 After 1 mile at top of short hill 1st R to continue uphill

13 At T-j after 1½ miles R 'Staveley'. Lovely wooded section

➡ **page 70**

23 Through Brigsteer, climb steeply, descend to cross bridge over Kendal bypass. 3 miles after Brigsteer, at X-roads on the edge of Kendal at the end of Brigsteer Road, SA. Shortly, at T-j R to return to the Tourist Information Centre

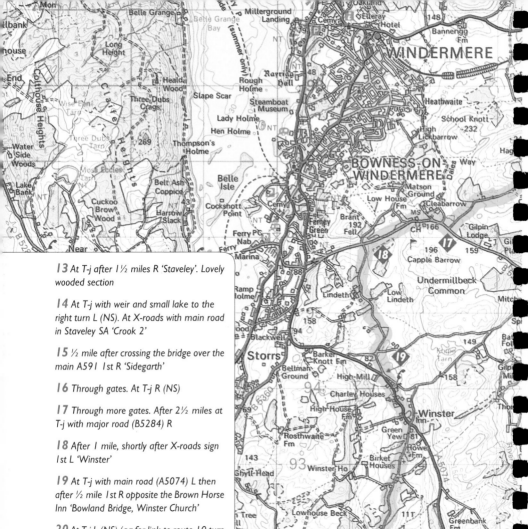

13 At T-j after 1½ miles R 'Staveley'. Lovely wooded section

14 At T-j with weir and small lake to the right turn L (NS). At X-roads with main road in Staveley SA 'Crook 2'

15 ½ mile after crossing the bridge over the main A591 1st R 'Sidegarth'

16 Through gates. At T-j R (NS)

17 Through more gates. After 2½ miles at T-j with major road (B5284) R

18 After 1 mile, shortly after X-roads sign 1st L 'Winster'

19 At T-j with main road (A5074) L then after ½ mile 1st R opposite the Brown Horse Inn 'Bowland Bridge, Winster Church'

20 At T-j L (NS) (**or** for link to route 10 turn R then 1st L by the Hare and Hounds PH at Bowland Bridge to join at last part of instruction 4 'Cartmel Fell')

21 At T-j (with A5074) R 'Kendal, Lancaster' then on sharp RH bend 1st L 'Crosthwaite, Kendal'

22 Follow this road for 2 miles, passing through Crosthwaite. At the start of the village of Underbarrow turn R 'Milnthorpe, Levens. 6 ft 6 ins width limit'. After ½ mile, at T-j R 'Brigsteer, Levens'

← page 69

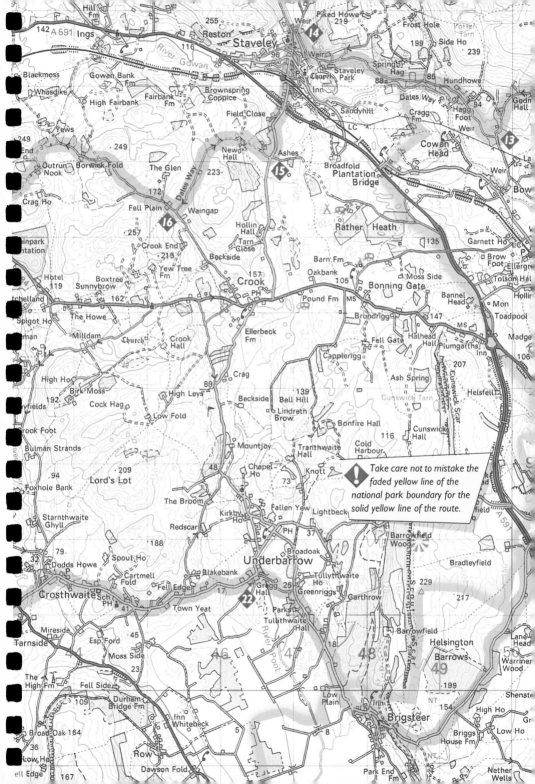

Take care not to mistake the faded yellow line of the national park boundary for the solid yellow line of the route.

10 South from Kendal to Cartmel and Grange-over-Sands

Start

The Tourist Information Centre, Kendal

P Follow signs for long stay car parks

Distance and grade

33½ miles
Moderate

Terrain

Steep 350 feet climb from Kendal onto Scout Scar above Brigsteer. Steep then more gentle 570 feet climb from Bowland Bridge south to Newton Fell. 310 feet climb from Gilpin Bridge to above

The fells to the east of Lake Windermere are little visited with the result that the roads are only lightly used – this more than anything else improves the enjoyment of the cycling. A steep climb that starts from right outside the Tourist Information Centre takes you around the southern end of Scout Scar to Underbarrow. From the crossing of the River Winster south of Crosthwaite the route climbs steeply at first then more gently onto Newton Fell with panoramic views opening up ahead and to the southeast. Cartmel is a real jewel of a

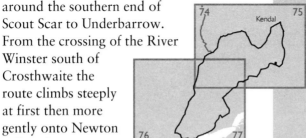

village with several fine refreshment stops. Grange-over-Sands has the feel of a large town after so many miles of little-used lanes. The section that follows, although easy cycling and passing through attractive scenery, is nevertheless affected by the noise of the busy A590, which is crossed via a small underpass near Town End then joined very briefly near to Gilpin Bridge. Beyond Levens you may be tempted to visit the Elizabethan Hall of Sizergh Castle with its lovely gardens. Two curiosities soon follow – the bridge carrying the A591 over the route near to Sizergh which forms a wonderful echo chamber and then the small wooden bridge over the River Kent just before Sedgwick. An easy lane through Sedgwick and Natland drops you near the start of the Kendal one-way system which you follow back to the start.

Kendal   Brigsteer   Underbarrow   Crosthwaite   Cartmel Fell   High Newton

Levens. Highest point – 570 feet (167 mts) on Newton Fell near to High Newton. Lowest point – sea level at the crossing of the River Gilpin near Levens

Nearest railway

Kendal

Refreshments

Plenty of choice in **Kendal**
Wheatsheaf PH ✿, **Brigsteer**
Punchbowl PH ✿✿, **Crosthwaite**
The Crown PH ✿, **High Newton**
Kings Arms PH ✿, Cavendish Arms PH ✿,
Pig and Whistle PH, **Cartmel**
Plenty of choice in **Grange-over-Sands**
Derby Arms PH, **Town End**
Gilpin Bridge Inn PH, **junction of A5074 and A590**
Hare and Hounds PH ✿✿, **Levens**
Strickland Arms PH ✿, **Sizergh**

To form a sixty mile loop, this ride can be linked most satisfactorily with route 9, which should be undertaken first, thus removing the climb over Scout Scar between Kendal and Underbarrow from both rides.

Places of interest

Cartmel 7
Ivy-clad walls, old shops and pubs surround the village square with its 18th-century market cross. The magnificent priory church, founded in 1188, has superb stained-glass windows and choir stalls carved with strange creatures. The 14th-century gate-house was once part of the priory

Levens Hall 16
Cones, corkscrews, pyramids and other curious shapes of fantastic 17th-century topiary gardens are maintained in their original forms. The grey-stone hall was built in 1250 around the peel tower but the building is mainly Elizabethan with superb plaster-work and carved woodwork. There is also a working steam engine collection

Sizergh Castle 19
The medieval hall and Elizabethan wings were added to the peel tower built in 1350. There are many portraits and relics of the Strickland family. Panelling, original fireplaces and windows are to be found in the tower museum and there are rock, rose and Dutch gardens in the grounds. The Queen's Room is named after Catherine Parr, the sixth wife of Henry VIII

Grange-over-Sands Meathop Levens Natland

1 With back to the Tourist Information Centre SA uphill onto Allhallows Lane towards a large chimney. After ½ mile, opposite the Riflemans Arms PH L 'Scout Scar, Brigsteer, Lyth'. Shortly, at X-roads SA onto Brigsteer Road

2 Easy to miss. Follow this road for 4½ miles climbing then descending through Brigsteer. 1½ miles after the Wheatsheaf PH in Brigsteer L 'Crosthwaite'. At T-j L 'Crosthwaite, Ulverston'. Shortly after the sign for Crosthwaite at start of village (near the Lyth Gallery) L opposite Guide Post Cottage 'Lancaster' then immediately R. (**Or** for link to route 9 L into Crosthwaite)

3 At X-roads with main road (A5074) SA 'Cartmel' '6 ft 6 ins width limit'

4 Climb then descend. 1½ miles after the last X-roads, at the bottom of a hill 1st R by a triangle of grass 'Bowland Bridge' then shortly 1st L 'Cartmel Grange'

➡ **page 76**

14 At T-j with A590 L 'Cumbria Cycleway' then 1st L onto A5074 'Windermere, Bowness'

15 Go past the Gilpin Bridge Inn, ignore the 1st left to Bowness and Windermere. Continue towards dual carriageway, take the next L just after a garage on the left 'Cumbria Cycleway'

16 At T-j after ¾ mile just after a bridge R 'Cumbria Cycleway' then at T-j after 50 yards by the Hare and Hounds PH L towards the church

17 At X-roads by Levens Methodist Church leave the Cumbria Cycleway and continue SA (your priority)

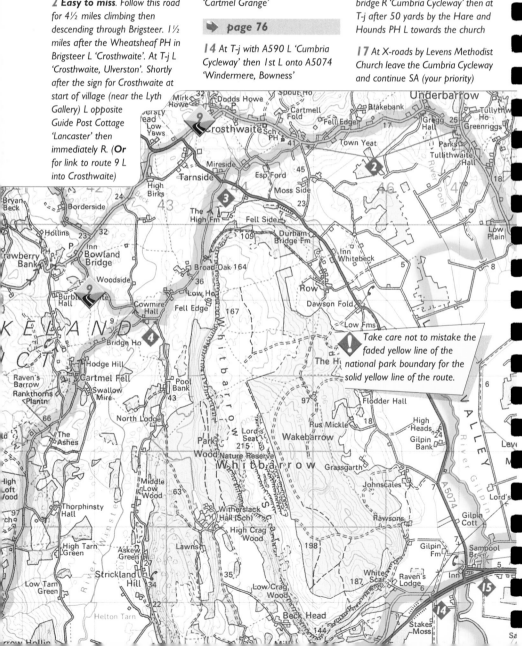

Take care not to mistake the faded yellow line of the national park boundary for the solid yellow line of the route.

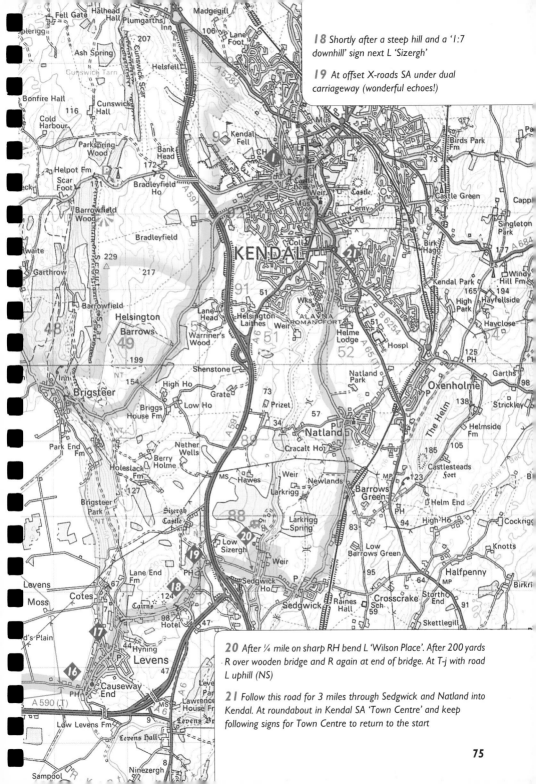

18 Shortly after a steep hill and a '1:7 downhill' sign next L 'Sizergh'

19 At offset X-roads SA under dual carriageway (wonderful echoes!)

20 After ¼ mile on sharp RH bend L 'Wilson Place'. After 200 yards R over wooden bridge and R again at end of bridge. At T-j with road L uphill (NS)

21 Follow this road for 3 miles through Sedgwick and Natland into Kendal. At roundabout in Kendal SA 'Town Centre' and keep following signs for Town Centre to return to the start

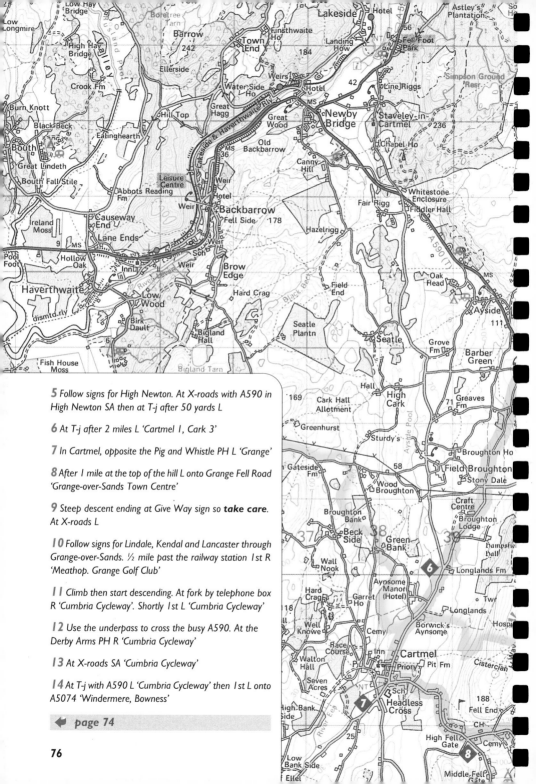

5 Follow signs for High Newton. At X-roads with A590 in High Newton SA then at T-j after 50 yards L

6 At T-j after 2 miles L 'Cartmel 1, Cark 3'

7 In Cartmel, opposite the Pig and Whistle PH L 'Grange'

8 After 1 mile at the top of the hill L onto Grange Fell Road 'Grange-over-Sands Town Centre'

9 Steep descent ending at Give Way sign so **take care**. At X-roads L

10 Follow signs for Lindale, Kendal and Lancaster through Grange-over-Sands. ½ mile past the railway station 1st R 'Meathop, Grange Golf Club'

11 Climb then start descending. At fork by telephone box R 'Cumbria Cycleway'. Shortly 1st L 'Cumbria Cycleway'

12 Use the underpass to cross the busy A590. At the Derby Arms PH R 'Cumbria Cycleway'

13 At X-roads SA 'Cumbria Cycleway'

14 At T-j with A590 L 'Cumbria Cycleway' then 1st L onto A5074 'Windermere, Bowness'

← **page 74**

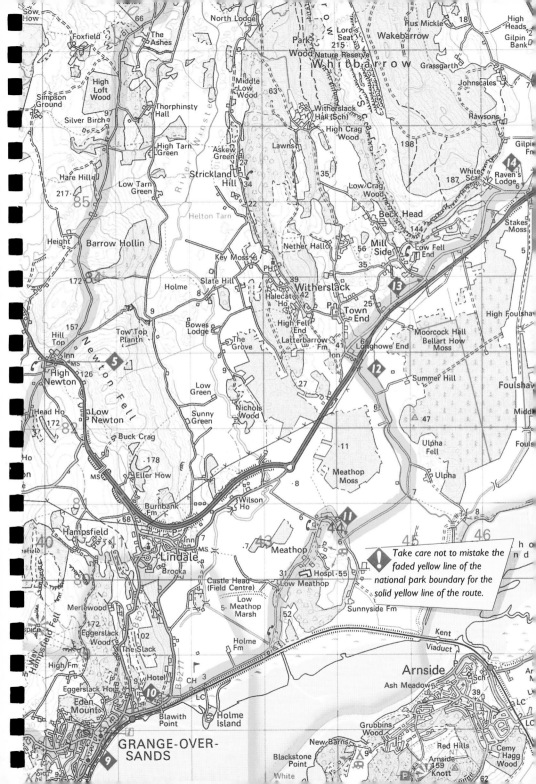

Take care not to mistake the faded yellow line of the national park boundary for the solid yellow line of the route.

North to Sedbergh from Kirkby Lonsdale, returning via the Lune Valley

The valley of the River Lune is the dominating feature of this ride linking the attractive settlements of Kirkby Lonsdale and Sedbergh. Soon after leaving Kirkby the route follows one of the tributaries of the Lune up the well-graded climb to the top of Barbondale, cutting through the western-

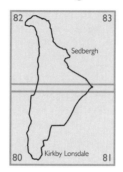

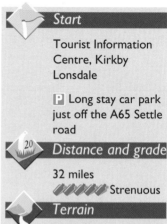

Start

Tourist Information Centre, Kirkby Lonsdale

P Long stay car park just off the A65 Settle road

Distance and grade

32 miles

Strenuous

Terrain

Steady 840 feet climb from the start along Barbondale. 290 feet climb from Sedbergh to the Height of Winder. 610 feet climb south from the crossing of the River Lune starting with an

most hills of the Pennines and offering fabulous valley views along Dentdale. After the climb to over 1000 feet, a steep descent takes you down into Dentdale with a delightful stretch along the River Dee. Sedbergh offers a wide variety of refreshments which you may well need before the next two climbs – first to the heights of Winder, then, having descended into the Lune Valley, a longer climb up to Fox's Pulpit. This second climb starts with two exceedingly steep sections near to the old railway viaduct. After Fox's Pulpit a long, invigorating descent takes you down to the valley floor but remember to conserve enough energy for the last, unexpected climb that soon follows. This whole section, along the western side of the Lune Valley, is wonderful cycling country.

Kirkby Lonsdale   Casterton   Barbon Low Fell   Barbondale   Gawthrop   Sedbergh

Snooty Fox PH 🍷🍷, Sun PH 🍷🍷, plenty of choice in **Kirkby Lonsdale**
Red Lion PH, Bull Hotel PH, Dalesman PH 🍷🍷, tea shops in **Sedbergh**

exceedingly steep section by the viaduct. Unexpected steep climb of 240 feet halfway along Lune Valley. Highest point – 1000 feet (300 mts) at the summit of Barbondale and also near Fox's Pulpit on the northern section of the ride. Lowest point – 130 feet (40 mts) Kirkby Lonsdale

Nearest railway

Wennington, 6 miles south of the start

Places of interest

Dent *(just off the route)* 6
Picturesque cobbled village overlooking the River Dee in Dentdale. Famous for its hand-knitted woollens, still produced by resident knitters at the nearby craft centre

Sedbergh 8
Lies beneath the domed peaks of the Howgill Fells where the Lune and Rawthey rivers meet. The playing fields of the public school, founded in 1525, flank the magnificent Norman church of St Andrew's

▼ Sedbergh

Howgill   Beck Foot   Fox's Pulpit   Killington   Kearstwick

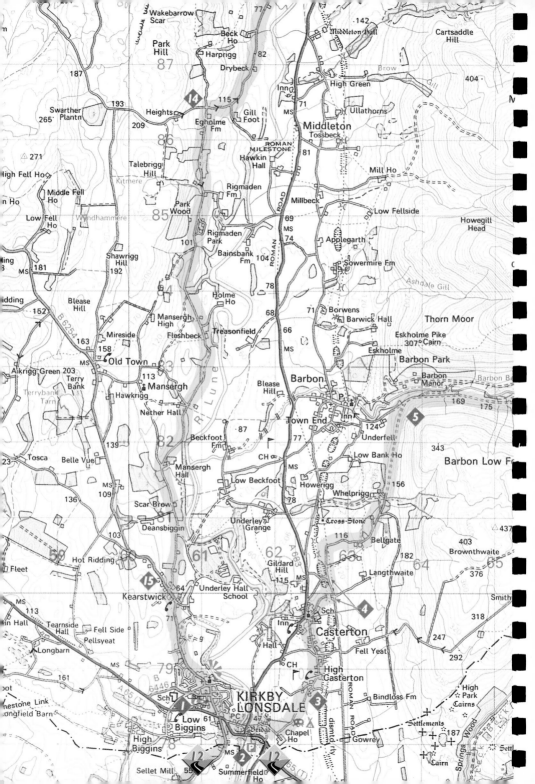

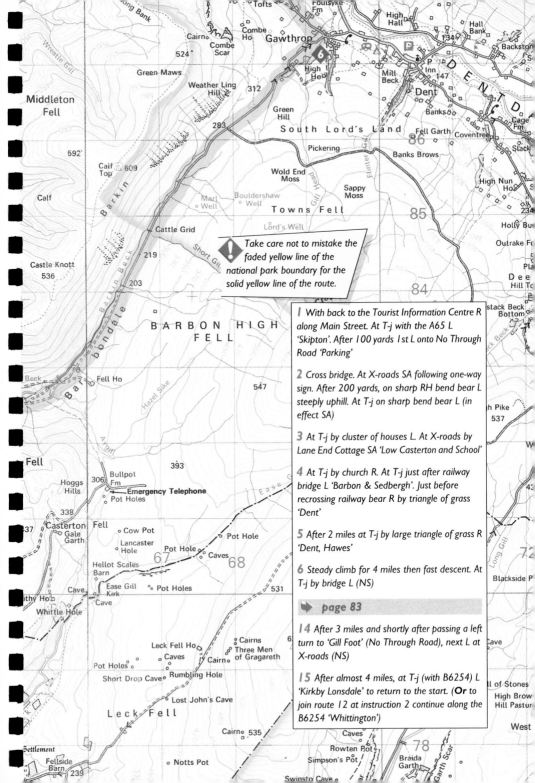

! Take care not to mistake the faded yellow line of the national park boundary for the solid yellow line of the route.

1 With back to the Tourist Information Centre R along Main Street. At T-j with the A65 L 'Skipton'. After 100 yards 1st L onto No Through Road 'Parking'

2 Cross bridge. At X-roads SA following one-way sign. After 200 yards, on sharp RH bend bear L steeply uphill. At T-j on sharp bend bear L (in effect SA)

3 At T-j by cluster of houses L. At X-roads by Lane End Cottage SA 'Low Casterton and School'

4 At T-j by church R. At T-j just after railway bridge L 'Barbon & Sedbergh'. Just before recrossing railway bear R by triangle of grass 'Dent'

5 After 2 miles at T-j by large triangle of grass R 'Dent, Hawes'

6 Steady climb for 4 miles then fast descent. At T-j by bridge L (NS)

➡ **page 83**

14 After 3 miles and shortly after passing a left turn to 'Gill Foot' (No Through Road), next L at X-roads (NS)

15 After almost 4 miles, at T-j (with B6254) L 'Kirkby Lonsdale' to return to the start. (**Or** to join route 12 at instruction 2 continue along the B6254 'Whittington')

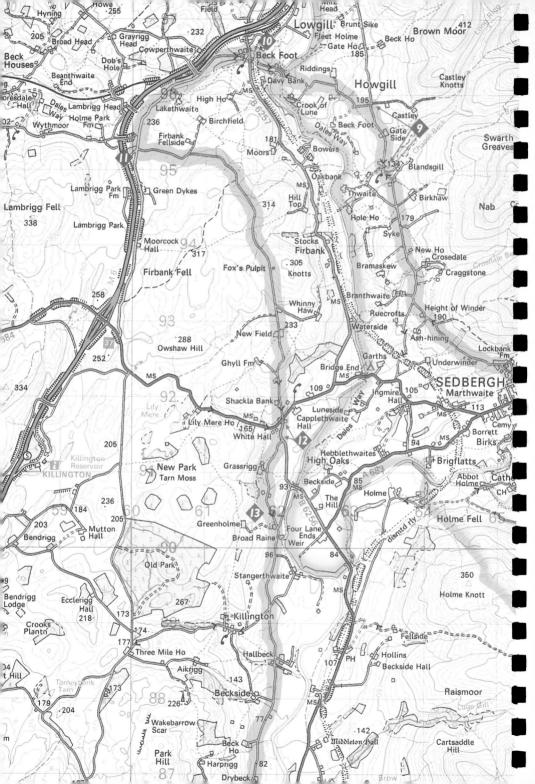

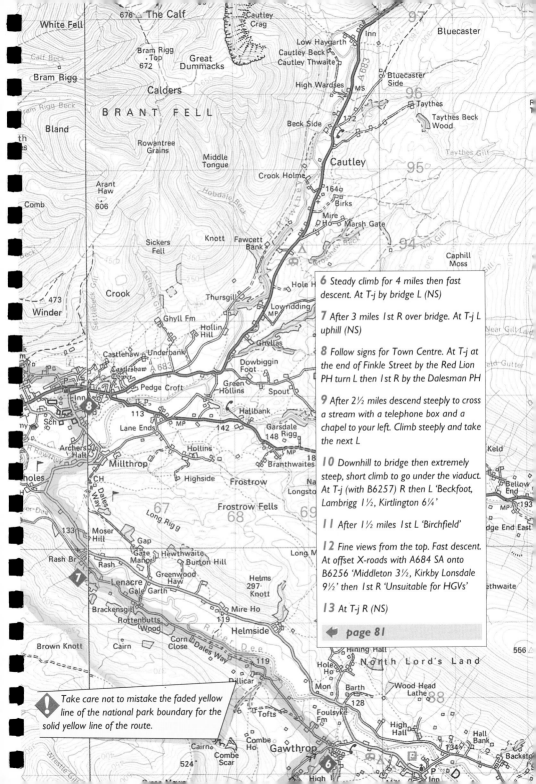

6 Steady climb for 4 miles then fast descent. At T-j by bridge L (NS)

7 After 3 miles 1st R over bridge. At T-j L uphill (NS)

8 Follow signs for Town Centre. At T-j at the end of Finkle Street by the Red Lion PH turn L then 1st R by the Dalesman PH

9 After 2½ miles descend steeply to cross a stream with a telephone box and a chapel to your left. Climb steeply and take the next L

10 Downhill to bridge then extremely steep, short climb to go under the viaduct. At T-j (with B6257) R then L 'Beckfoot, Lambrigg 1½, Kirtlington 6¼'

11 After 1½ miles 1st L 'Birchfield'

12 Fine views from the top. Fast descent. At offset X-roads with A684 SA onto B6256 'Middleton 3½, Kirkby Lonsdale 9½' then 1st R 'Unsuitable for HGVs'

13 At T-j R (NS)

← *page 81*

Take care not to mistake the faded yellow line of the national park boundary for the solid yellow line of the route.

12 South from Kirkby Lonsdale above the River Lune and east to Wray and Low Bentham

Start

Tourist Information Centre, Kirkby Lonsdale

P Long stay car park just off the A65 Settle road

Distance and grade

29 miles

Moderate

Terrain

420 feet climb from the River Keer near Capernwray south to the ridge above Aughton. 300 feet climb from the River Lune near Hornby to the hill between Wray and Low Bentham. 200 feet climb from Burton in Lonsdale to Leck. Highest point – 475 feet (149 mts) on the ridge above Aughton. Lowest point – 70 feet (21 mts) at the bridge over the River Lune near Hornby

Nearest railway

Wennington, 2 miles north of the route at Wray

*T*hree counties are visited during the course of this ride – Kirkby Lonsdale lies just inside Cumbria but you soon cross into Lancashire and stay in this county for most of the ride with the exception of a three mile section north of Low Bentham within North Yorkshire's boundaries. The ride heads south along the valley of the River Lune to Newton, after which quiet lanes take you out of the valley to Over Kellet before joining the magnificent ridge high above the valley bottom with wonderful views across to the moors to the east. The Lune is crossed at Loyn Bridge near to Hornby, the first of a succession of small villages along the course of the route, each with solid stone-built houses and a local hostelry. There is a last, lovely section through Ireby and Leck before a short, unavoidable two miles of the busy A65. The first half mile is the worst – you soon have a white line to separate you from the traffic on your return to the start.

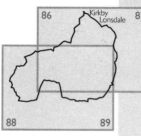

86   Kirkby Lonsdale   87

88   89

Kirkby Lonsdale   Whittington   Docker Park   Capernwray   Over Kellet

Kirkby Lonsdale 1

Georgian buildings and quaint cottages combine in the riverside 'capital' of the

▼ Devil's Bridge, Kirkby Lonsdale

Lune valley. The views from the churchyard were praised by Ruskin as 'naturally divine' and painted by Turner. There are two bridges over the River Lune, an ancient one called Devil's Bridge, supposedly built by Satan, and a new one built in 1932. It is said that when Satan put up his bridge, he claimed the first living thing to cross it – which turned out to be an old dog

Hornby 12

Gargoyles on the battlements of Hornby Castle grimace down on the village which is divided by the River Wenning. Below the castle, Hornby's main street leads down from the 19th-century Church of St Margaret to the three-arched stone bridge across the River Wenning. The street is bordered by Georgian houses and cottages and the Royal Oak Inn bears the names of its original owners, William and Emma Gelderd, with the date 1781

Refreshments

Snooty Fox PH♥♥, Sun PH♥♥, plenty of choice in **Kirkby Lonsdale** Dragons Head PH, **Whittington** Eagles Head PH, **Over Kellet** Castle Hotel PH, Royal Oak PH♥, **Hornby** New Inn PH, George and Dragon PH, **Wray** Punch Bowl Hotel PH, Sun Dial Inn PH, **Low Bentham**

Background picture:
Hornby Castle

Gressingham   Hornby   Wray   Low Bentham   Burton in Lonsdale

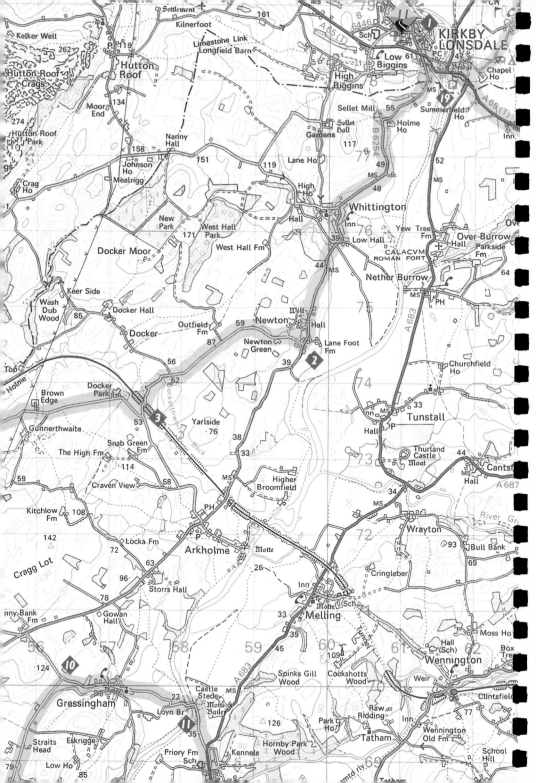

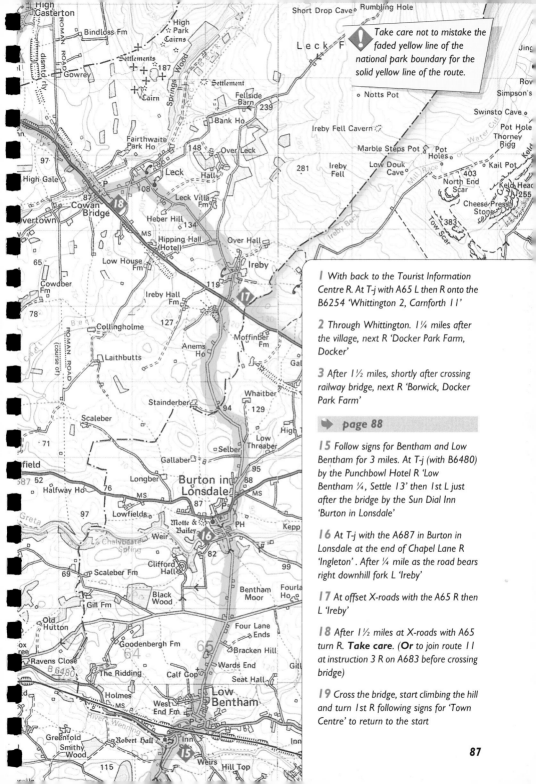

Take care not to mistake the faded yellow line of the national park boundary for the solid yellow line of the route.

1 With back to the Tourist Information Centre R. At T-j with A65 L then R onto the B6254 'Whittington 2, Carnforth 11'

2 Through Whittington. 1¼ miles after the village, next R 'Docker Park Farm, Docker'

3 After 1½ miles, shortly after crossing railway bridge, next R 'Borwick, Docker Park Farm'

➡ *page 88*

15 Follow signs for Bentham and Low Bentham for 3 miles. At T-j (with B6480) by the Punchbowl Hotel R 'Low Bentham ¼, Settle 13' then 1st L just after the bridge by the Sun Dial Inn 'Burton in Lonsdale'

16 At T-j with the A687 in Burton in Lonsdale at the end of Chapel Lane R 'Ingleton'. After ¼ mile as the road bears right downhill fork L 'Ireby'

17 At offset X-roads with the A65 R then L 'Ireby'

18 After 1½ miles at X-roads with A65 turn R. **Take care.** (**Or** to join route 11 at instruction 3 R on A683 before crossing bridge)

19 Cross the bridge, start climbing the hill and turn 1st R following signs for 'Town Centre' to return to the start

3 After 1½ miles, shortly after crossing railway bridge, next R 'Borwick, Docker Park Farm'

4 At T-j after 2½ miles L 'Capernwray, Arkholme'

5 After ¾ mile 1st R opposite church 'Capernwray House'

6 At X-roads (with B6254) in Over Kellet SA 'Nether Kellet 2'

7 After ¾ mile at the top of the hill opposite the neat stone wall of 'Challonaise' 1st L

8 At T-j L (NS) then 1st R (NS)

9 (Do not confuse with previous instruction!) At T-j R (NS) then 1st L 'Aughton'

10 Superb views into Lune Valley. At T-j after 3 miles R 'Gressingham ½, Hornby 2'

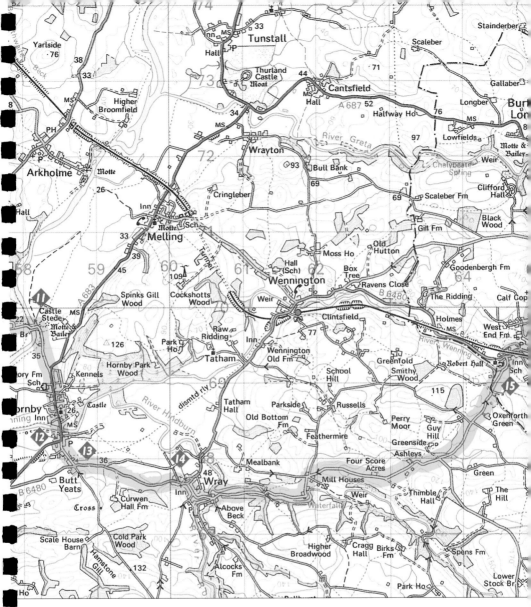

11 Cross bridge over River Lune. At T-j with A683 R 'Lancaster'

12 Through Hornby. Cross bridge over river. On sharp RH bend next L 'Bentham 6¼, Wray 1¼'

13 At X-roads with B6480 L 'Wray, Bentham'.

14 Shortly after the New Inn in Wray 1st R 'Higher Tatham, Lowgill'

15 Follow signs for Bentham and Low Bentham for 3 miles. At T-j (with B6480) by the Punchbowl Hotel R 'Low Bentham ¼, Settle 13' then 1st L just after the bridge by the Sun Dial Inn 'Burton in Lonsdale'

← page 87

South from Hawkshead to the southern end of Lake Windermere, returning via Coniston Water

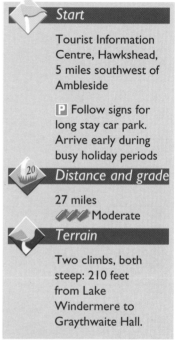

Heavy tourist traffic in the heart of the Lake District makes most roads among the central fells unsuitable for leisure cycling at all but the quietest times of the day or year. This ride goes as close to the central fells as possible

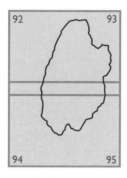

Start

Tourist Information Centre, Hawkshead, 5 miles southwest of Ambleside

P Follow signs for long stay car park. Arrive early during busy holiday periods

Distance and grade

27 miles

Moderate

Terrain

Two climbs, both steep: 210 feet from Lake Windermere to Graythwaite Hall.

on lightly used roads. However, even here it is best to avoid the busiest times of year. Starting at Hawkshead, the ride follows the eastern side of first Esthwaite Water then Lake Windermere and the lake is occasionally glimpsed through the trees. A steep climb onto the ridge above the lake takes you past Graythwaite Hall then Bobbin Mill, the sole survivor of the local bobbin factories. A descent into the unexpected flat and tidal Rusland Valley is followed by a climb over the hill into the valley of the River Crake which drains Coniston Water. This is the loveliest stretch of the ride with spectacular views across Coniston Water to the fells behind. There are no black arrows on the map but the climb from the end of the lake to the B5285 and on to High Cross is the longest and most sustained of the ride. The good side of this is that you are left with a fine, fast descent back to the start.

▶ *Estwaitewater*

Hawkshead

Near Sawrey

Graythwaite Hall

Finsthwaite

Bouth

Hawkshead 1

A medieval village with a maze of alleys. The church and the courthouse are 15th-century. William Heelis had his solicitor's office in Thimble Hall when he married Beatrix Potter and the Hall now houses an exhibition of her life and work

Hill Top 3

Scenes from Peter Rabbit come alive in the 17th-century farmhouse that inspired Beatrix Potter's work. She bought it as her retreat in 1905 and it is now preserved by the National Trust

Stott Park Bobbin Mill 6

The sole survivor of the local bobbin factories. Opened in 1835 and still in working order, it is now a museum of social and industrial history

Brantwood 13

The Coniston home, built in 1797, of the Victorian artist and writer John Ruskin from 1872 to 1900. The study, dining room and bedroom are much as he left them, full of drawings and artistic treasures; the grounds include a nature trail

Refreshments

Kings Arms PH, *Queens Head*, *plenty of choice in* **Hawkshead**
Tower Bank Arms PH, **Near Sawrey**
Sawrey Hotel PH, **Far Sawrey**
White Hart PH, **Bouth**
Royal Oak PH, **Spark Bridge**

510 feet from Coniston Water to High Cross above Hawkshead. Highest point – 655 feet (197 mts) at High Cross, above Hawkshead. Lowest point – sea level at the crossing of Rusland Pool near Bouth

Nearest railway

Windermere, 3 miles from the route at Far Sawrey (via the ferry)

Spark Bridge — High Nibthwaite — Brantwood — Hawkshead Hill

1 With back to the Tourist Information Centre SA. At T-j after 50 yards bear R 'Grizedale 3, Newby Bridge 8'

2 *Easy to miss.* After 2 miles 1st L 'Sawrey 1, Ferry 3'

3 At T-j (with B5285) R 'Ferry'

4 Shortly after the Sawrey Hotel, next R 'Cunsey'

5 After 3 miles at T-j by telephone box L 'Lakeside 2¾, Newby Bridge 3¾'

➡ **page 94**

13 Follow for 7 miles along the lakeside. Superb views. 1½ miles after passing Brantwood House 1st R 'Hawkshead'

14 Steep climb. At T-j with B5285 R 'Hawkshead 2, Windermere by ferry'

15 Climb then descend. At T-j R on B5285 'Windermere by ferry 6, Hawkshead 1½'

16 After ½ mile on sharp LH bend bear R by the filling station 'No vehicles except access'. **Walk** the short pedestrianised section to return to the start

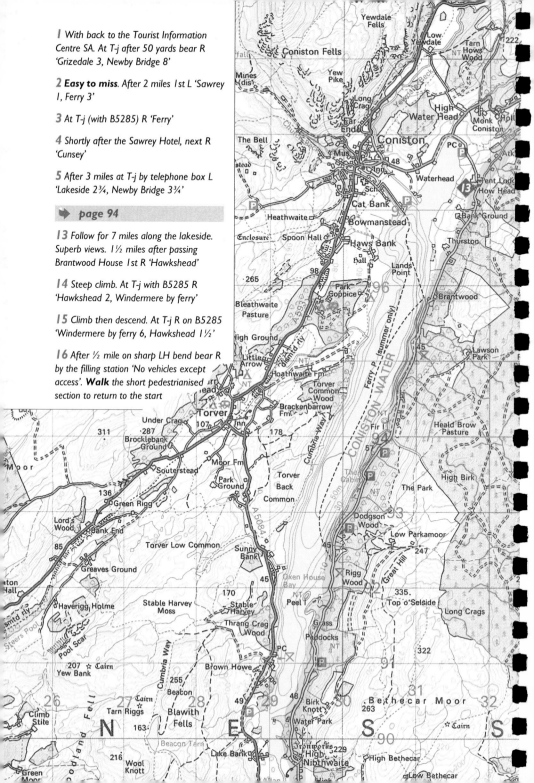

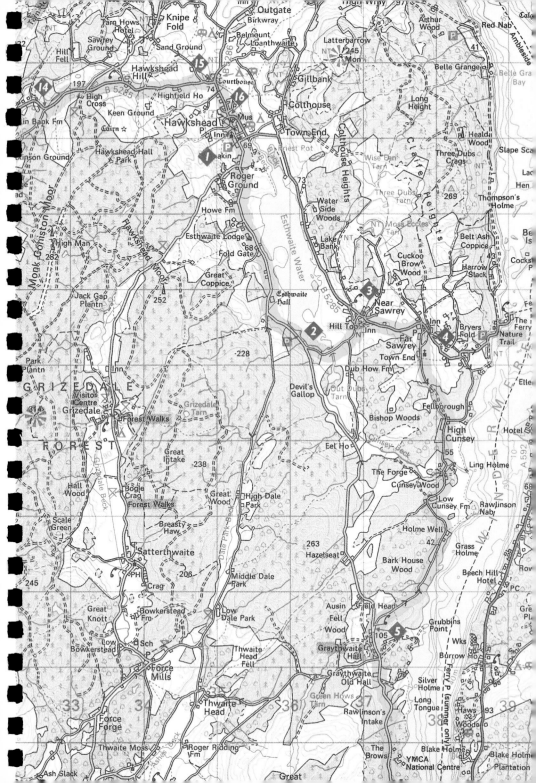

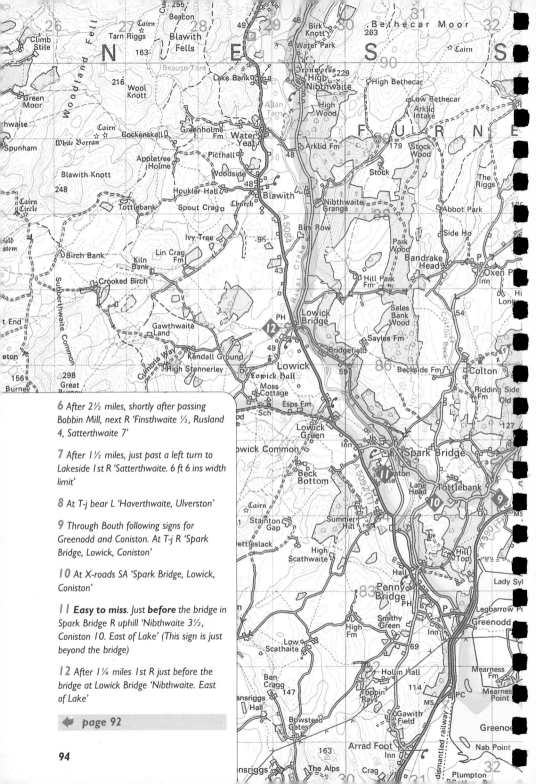

6 After 2½ miles, shortly after passing Bobbin Mill, next R 'Finsthwaite ½, Rusland 4, Satterthwaite 7'

7 After 1½ miles, just past a left turn to Lakeside 1st R 'Satterthwaite. 6 ft 6 ins width limit'

8 At T-j bear L 'Haverthwaite, Ulverston'

9 Through Bouth following signs for Greenodd and Coniston. At T-j R 'Spark Bridge, Lowick, Coniston'

10 At X-roads SA 'Spark Bridge, Lowick, Coniston'

11 **Easy to miss**. Just **before** the bridge in Spark Bridge R uphill 'Nibthwaite 3½, Coniston 10. East of Lake' (This sign is just beyond the bridge)

12 After 1¼ miles 1st R just before the bridge at Lowick Bridge 'Nibthwaite. East of Lake'

← *page 92*

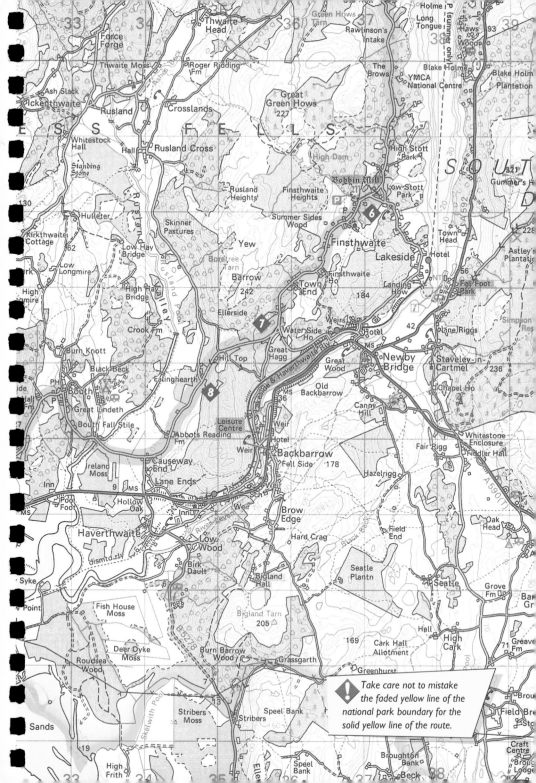

Take care not to mistake the faded yellow line of the national park boundary for the solid yellow line of the route.

14 Over steep fells to Ravenglass northwest from Broughton in Furness

Start

The square, Broughton in Furness, 10 miles southwest of Coniston

P In the square in Broughton in Furness

Distance and grade

34 miles

Highly strenuous

Terrain

Hilly, with 3 major climbs and two shorter ones. 230 feet north from Broughton at the start. 730 feet from Broughton Mills to the pass over Dunnerdale Fells. 630 feet from Ulpha to the pass over Birker Fell

This is the toughest road ride in the book with over 3000 feet of climbing, at times very steep. It takes in the little-visited southwestern corner of the Lake District, starting from the attractive, solid village of Broughton in Furness. The first three miles present few problems enabling you to appreciate the quintessential Lakeland beauty of the valley of the charmingly-named River Lickle with its glades, stonewalls, streams and stone hamlets. Soon after the pub in Broughton Mills the first major hill is encountered. A fast descent to the River Duddon at Hall Dunnerdale is followed by a gentle section along the valley floor. Make the most of it! The 1 in 4 sign at the bottom of the hill tells no lies: the first section is very steep. The open moorland of Birker Fell is traversed leading to the easy middle section in the valleys of the Rivers Esk and Mite. You descend to the sea at Ravenglass, crossing a footbridge over the estuary next to the railway line. Ravenglass was much loved by smugglers in centuries past. An unavoidable three mile section on the busy A595 must be endured before the final, and hardest challenge up over Corney Fell.

Broughton in Furness · Lower Hawthwaite · Broughton Mills · Hall Dunnerdale · Ulpha · Birker Fell · Eskdale Green

(including a very steep 1:4 section at the start). 260 feet climb from Ravenglass to Muncaster Castle. 1330 feet climb from crossing the River Esk to the pass over Thwaites Fell with some very steep sections. Highest point – 1330 feet (400 mts) on Thwaites Fell. Lowest point – sea level at Ravenglass

Nearest railway

Foxfield, 1½ miles south of the route at the start or Ravenglass (on the route)

Places of interest

Broughton in Furness 1
The village has a market overlooking the Duddon estuary. The Market Square has stone-slab stalls and a 1766 clock. Broughton Tower is a 14th-century peel tower, incorporated into the 18th-century house

Ravenglass 10
Lies on an estuary where three rivers – the Esk, the Mite and the Irt – enter the sea, and for a long while its sheltered position made it an important harbour. The Romans used it and, in the 2nd century, built the large fort of Glannaventa on the cliffs above. In the 18th century, Ravenglass was much used as a base for smuggling contraband tobacco and French brandy from the Isle of Man. The century-old miniature railway was once used to carry minerals and now takes tourists on a scenic seven mile trip up Eskdale

Muncaster Castle 11
Home of the Pennington family since the 13th century, it was a sanctuary for Henry VI during the Wars of the Roses. There is an owl aviary and rhododendron gardens

Refreshments

Plenty of choice in **Broughton in Furness**
Blacksmith Arms PH, **Broughton Mills**
King George IV PH♥, Bower House
Inn PH♥♥, **Eskdale Green**
Ratty Arms PH♥, **Ravenglass**

Most sheep are stupid; those that live on Thwaites Fell on the long fast descent back to the start are not only stupid but also suicidal and likely to leap out of a ditch to throw themselves under your wheels without any provocation – resist the temptation to break the land speed record on this stretch and never lose your concentration.

Ravenglass   Broad Oak   Corney Fell   Thwaites Fell   Duddon Bridge

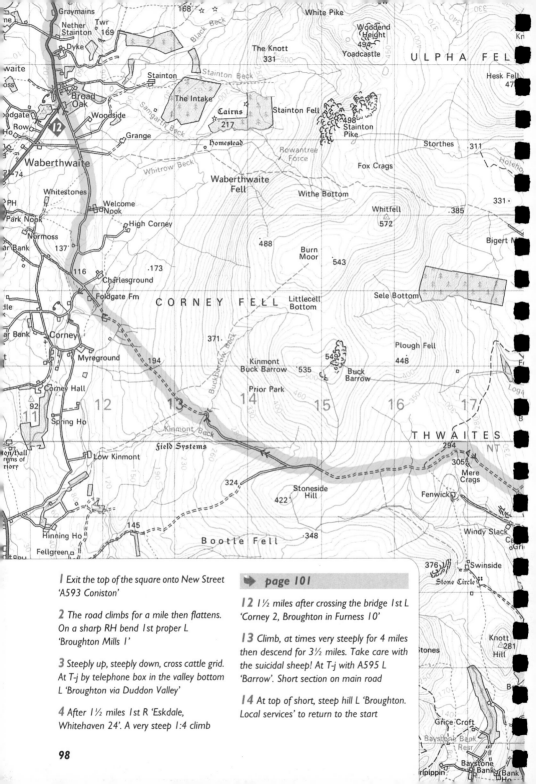

1 Exit the top of the square onto New Street 'A593 Coniston'

2 The road climbs for a mile then flattens. On a sharp RH bend 1st proper L 'Broughton Mills 1'

3 Steeply up, steeply down, cross cattle grid. At T-j by telephone box in the valley bottom L 'Broughton via Duddon Valley'

4 After 1½ miles 1st R 'Eskdale, Whitehaven 24'. A very steep 1:4 climb

➡ **page 101**

12 1½ miles after crossing the bridge 1st L 'Corney 2, Broughton in Furness 10'

13 Climb, at times very steeply for 4 miles then descend for 3½ miles. Take care with the suicidal sheep! At T-j with A595 L 'Barrow'. Short section on main road

14 At top of short, steep hill L 'Broughton. Local services' to return to the start

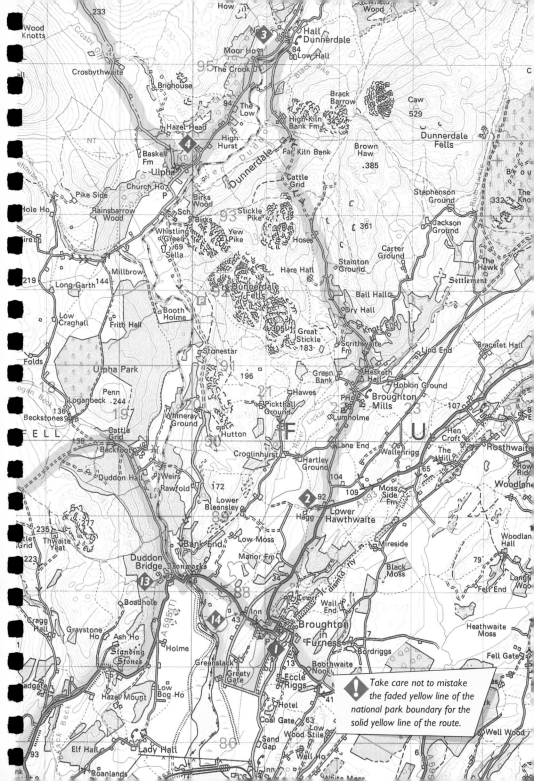

Take care not to mistake the faded yellow line of the national park boundary for the solid yellow line of the route.

Take care not to mistake the faded yellow line of the national park boundary for the solid yellow line of the route.

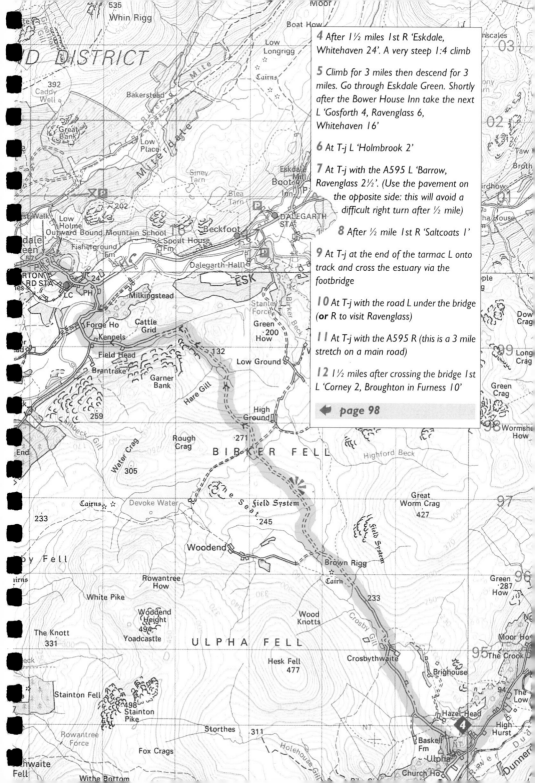

4 After 1½ miles 1st R 'Eskdale, Whitehaven 24'. A very steep 1:4 climb

5 Climb for 3 miles then descend for 3 miles. Go through Eskdale Green. Shortly after the Bower House Inn take the next L 'Gosforth 4, Ravenglass 6, Whitehaven 16'

6 At T-j L 'Holmbrook 2'

7 At T-j with the A595 L 'Barrow, Ravenglass 2½'. (Use the pavement on the opposite side: this will avoid a difficult right turn after ½ mile)

8 After ½ mile 1st R 'Saltcoats 1'

9 At T-j at the end of the tarmac L onto track and cross the estuary via the footbridge

10 At T-j with the road L under the bridge (**or** R to visit Ravenglass)

11 At T-j with the A595 R (this is a 3 mile stretch on a main road)

12 1½ miles after crossing the bridge 1st L 'Corney 2, Broughton in Furness 10'

← **page 98**

Tour of the Caldbeck and Uldale Fells from Bassenthwaite

A classic ride at the northern edge of the Lake District, starting from the attractive village of Bassenthwaite and climbing steadily for 1300 feet first on road then on a good stone-based track past the delights of Dash Waterfalls. The gradient is steep enough for some short pushing sections. Skiddaw House used to be an old shepherd's hut and is now a youth hostel. The next section is slow and may be boggy and / or rough. Once the track improves you are rewarded with a very fine descent all the way to the improbably situated Quakers coffee shop in Mosedale, a very welcome stop. The second climb is on road as far as Calebreck. Unfortunately the old mining road contouring the northern edge of the Caldbeck Fells is not a right of way, which is a pity as it would be an ideal track for off-road riding. Instead you must descend to Hesket Newmarket before climbing back up to Fell Side. There is one last off-road section between the farms at Howburn and Longlands. The views of Skiddaw along the final road section are magnificent and a gentle descent down to Bassenthwaite is a well-deserved reward at the end of the ride.

Start

The Sun PH, Bassenthwaite, 6 miles north of Keswick

P No specific car park. Please ask for permission if you use the pub car park or alternatively park along the tree-lined avenue in the village of Bassenthwaite

Distance and grade

24 miles

Strenuous

Terrain

In general good surface on quiet lanes or stone-based tracks. One boggy / rough section for about 1½ miles northeast from Skiddaw House. Two main climbs – 1300 feet from Bassenthwaite to above Dash Waterfalls, parts of which will require pushing, 600 feet of

Bassenthwaite   Dead Crags   Skiddaw House   Roundhouse   Mosedale

climbing in two sections between Hesket Newmarket and Longlands. Highest point – 1630 feet (490 mts) above Dash Waterfalls. Lowest point – 330 feet (100 mts) at the start in Bassenthwaite

Nearest railway

Penrith, 12 miles east of the route at Mosedale or Aspatria, 8 miles northwest of the route at Bassenthwaite

Places of interest

Bassenthwaite *1*
There are traces of Roman and Norse settlements around the village

Hesket Newmarket *9*
The open sided market building on the village green survives from days of sheep and cattle trading

Caldbeck *(just off the route)* *10*
John Peel was buried here after falling from his horse in 1854, aged 78. The river-powered woollen mills once produced grey cloth for Peel's hunting coats. The wheel still turns on the restored 18th-century Priests Mill

Skiddaw *14*
The mountain is one of only four peaks in England that rise to over 3000 feet; the other three are also in the Lake District – Scafell, Scafell Pike and Helvellyn

Refreshments

The Sun PH ✿ ✿, **Bassenthwaite**
Quaker Coffee House, **Mosedale**
Mill Inn PH ✿, **Mungrisdale** *(just off the route south of Mosedale)*
Old Crown PH ✿ ✿, **Hesket Newmarket**

▼ *Mosedale*

Hesket Newmarket   Branthwaite   Longlands   Orthwaite

1 With back to The Sun PH turn L then 1st R over the bridge

2 Climb steadily. At T-j R 'Keswick 8'

3 Descend to the stream and start climbing. After ¾ mile, shortly after the brow of the hill L onto tarmac lane 'Public Bridleway. Skiddaw House and Threlkeld via Dash Falls'

4 Climb on tarmac through several gates. After 1 mile 1st major track R by a cairn of stones 'Bridleway via Dash Falls. Skiddaw House. Threlkeld'

5 Gradient steepens. Some short pushing sections. Past falls, over the brow then descend and climb to Skiddaw House. Just before the house L downhill by wall on grassy slope

6 This section is in parts boggy and for the next 1½ miles you will be faced with a mixture of cycling and pushing. The surface improves then turns to tarmac

7 At T-j with road L

8 1½ miles after passing through Mosedale, just past a chevron sign turn L onto fell road

9 At T-j at bottom of hill L 'Hesket Newmarket ½, Caldbeck 2'

10 At the end of the village, on a sharp RH bend, bear L between houses (NS)

11 After 1½ miles, at top of hill, turn L 'Fell Side, Branthwaite, Green Head'

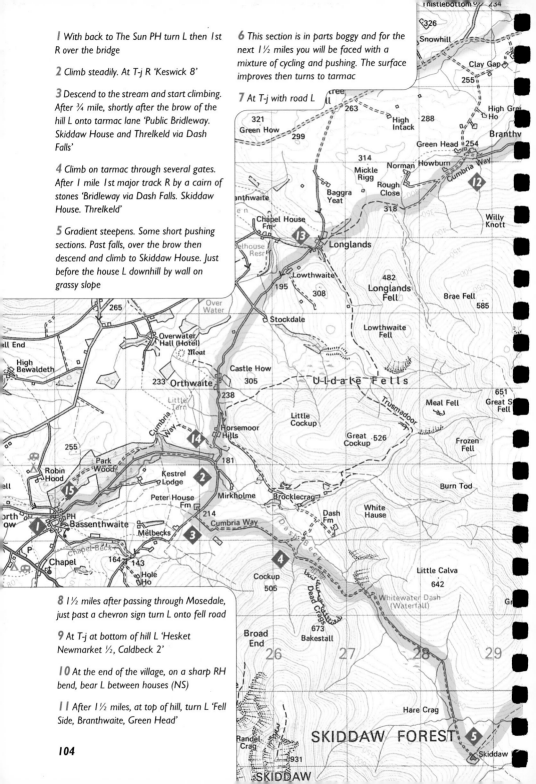

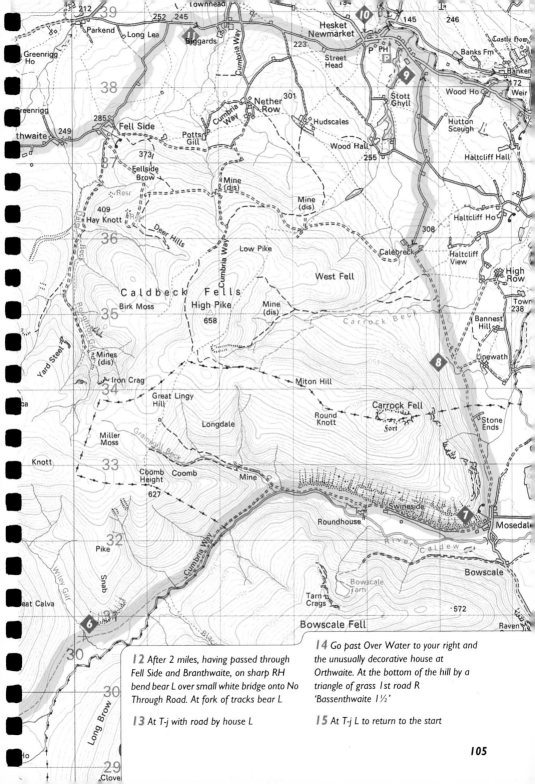

12 After 2 miles, having passed through Fell Side and Branthwaite, on sharp RH bend bear L over small white bridge onto No Through Road. At fork of tracks bear L

13 At T-j with road by house L

14 Go past Over Water to your right and the unusually decorative house at Orthwaite. At the bottom of the hill by a triangle of grass 1st road R 'Bassenthwaite 1½'

15 At T-j L to return to the start

2 Along the Allerdale Ramble east from Cockermouth

Starting from the handsome town of Cockermouth the ride heads east on roads along the valley of the River Derwent for almost seven miles, passing the attractive house at Hewthwaite Hall and heading towards ever closer views of the fells lying to the east, notably Binsey, the Uldake Fells and the great bulk of Skiddaw. The off-road riding starts at Irton House with a short section of fields and gates before the going improves on good tracks through forestry. The route descends to the road near Castle Inn and joins the course of the Allerdale Ramble which it follows all the way back to Cockermouth, starting with a stretch alongside the River Derwent which may be muddy in parts after wet weather. The longest climb of the ride and the best descent starts after the crossing of the River Derwent near Isel. Almost 500 feet of ascent through woods then fields bring you to the top of Watch Hill with the long, grassy descent back to Cockermouth spread out before you.

Start

Earl Mayo's statue, High Street, Cockermouth

P Several pay and display car parks in Cockermouth

Distance and grade

15 miles

Easy/moderate

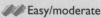

Terrain

A short section near to the River Derwent may become muddy after wet weather. 330 feet climb from crossing the River Derwent to the start of the off-road section at Irton House. 470 feet climb from the river up to the top of Watch Hill. Highest point – 700 feet (210 mts) at the top of Watch Hill. Lowest point – 140 feet (41 mts) at the start

Nearest railway

Maryport, 7 miles northwest of Cockermouth

Cockermouth   Hewthwaite Hall   River Derwent   Irton House

▶ *The River Derwent*

Places of interest

Cockermouth 1
William Wordsworth was born in a
Georgian house at the end of the main
street. There are the remains of a largely
14th-century castle at the junction of the
Cocker and Derwent rivers

Refreshments

Brown Cow PH ●, plenty of choice
*in **Cockermouth***
*Castle Inn PH, **Kilnhill***

Castle Inn

River Derwent

Watch Hill

1 With back to the Bush PH (near to the statue) R along the main street following signs for the Sports Centre up Castle Gate

2 At the edge of town 1st major L onto Isel Road 'Hospital, Isel 3'

3 After 3 miles 1st road L 'Blindcrake 1¾, Sunderland 2¼'. Cross bridge then immediatley R 'Sunderland, Bewaldeth'

4 Ignore 1st right on sharp LH bend (No Through Road). Take next road R 'Bewaldeth'

5 Under pylons, SA at X-roads (your priority) then shortly after brow of hill R onto track towards Irton House Farm 'Public Bridleway. Castle Inn'. Opposite 1st

house on right turn L through gate (blue arrow) aiming for corner of yard

6 Through gate and turn L following fence to the end of the field. Exit field via gate and keep fence to your right. At the end of this field turn R through gate to continue on a course at right angles to previous direction

7 Soon join better track. Follow this past ruin and through gate onto stone track. At X-roads of tracks L through Forestry Commission gate onto forest road

8 At fork stay on upper LH track

9 At T-j with road R for ¼ mile then on sharp LH bend R onto No Through Road (to the R of Hotel Entrance)

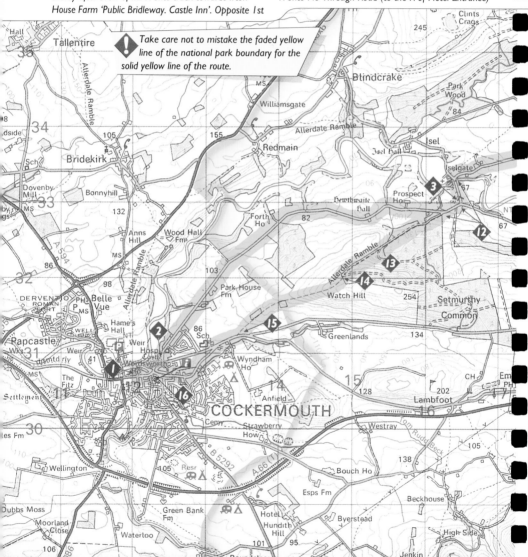

Take care not to mistake the faded yellow line of the national park boundary for the solid yellow line of the route.

10 As tarmac drive swings right bear L (in effect SA) through bridlegate 'Public Bridleway to Isel'

11 Follow this track, at times excellent and at times muddy, in the same direction and through farm . At road bear L (in effect SA)

12 At T-j L over bridge 'Cockermouth'. Climb steeply. At T-j R 'Cockermouth 3¼'. After ¼ mile near brow of hill bear L through wide wooden gate onto broad stone track

13 At fork of tracks at edge of deciduous wood bear R uphill

14 Exit wood via green metal gate on to grassy track climbing through field

15 Climb then superb, long, grassy descent. At T-j with road R then 1st road L just past drive to Wyndham House

16 At T-j in the centre of Cockermouth L to return to the start

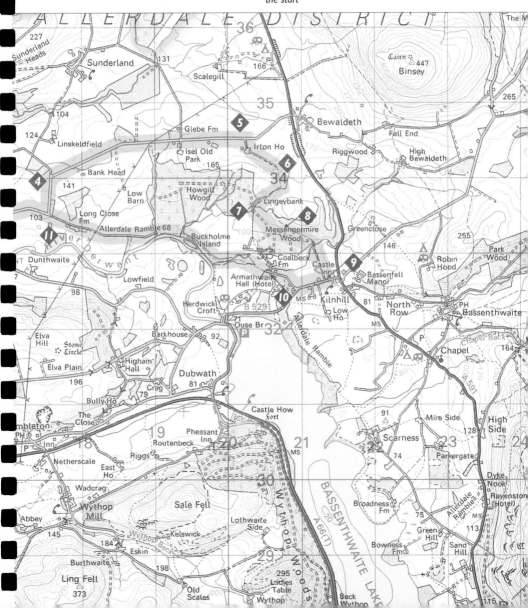

North from Loweswater over Mosser Fell

Distance and grade

14 miles

 Easy / moderate

Terrain

Almost all the ride is on metalled surfaces. With the exception of a ½ mile section in fields near the end, the off-road riding is on stone-based tracks. Three climbs: 400 feet from Loweswater to the high point on Mosser Fell; 300 feet from Mosser Mains to the highpoint on Whin Fell; 230 feet along the B5289 to the start of the last off-road section. Highest point

Although this ride spends the majority of its length on metalled roads, the lanes in question have at their start signs with 'Unsuitable for motors' or 'Unfit for cars' which means that you will have them to yourself. The other benefit of this is that the ride is an all-year round route which will hardly deteriorate after wet weather or in the winter. The ride starts from the bottom of Scale Hill at the north end of Crummock Water and in the first section there are fabulous views to savour southeast down the Buttermere valley towards the very heart of the Central Fells. Nearer to hand lies the dramatic lump of Melbreak rising almost 1500 feet above Crummock Water. Loweswater is almost circumnavigated first on tracks through woodland then along the lakeside road before taking a sharp left turn signposted with that most encouraging of invitations for the off-road cyclist – 'Unfit for cars'. A steep climb takes you up onto Mosser Fell and through outlying farms before another 'Unsuitable for motors' sign leads you east to Low Lorton. A tiny lane through Lorton Vale beneath the towering slopes of Gasgale Crags sets you up for the last off-road section and the final downhill through woodland back to the start.

Loweswater

Waterend

Mosser

– 800 feet (240 mts) on Mosser Fell. Lowest point – 240 feet (71 mts) at the crossing of the River Cocker near to Lorton

Nearest railway

Workington, 10 miles west of the route at Waterend

Refreshments

Kirkstile Inn PH 🍴🍴, **Loweswater** Coffees and teas at **the Grange Country House Hotel** (at the northern end of Loweswater) Wheatsheaf PH, **Low Lorton** (just off the route)

Places of interest

The Lortons 8

Lorton Hall is partly a 15th-century peel tower, built as a refuge for the villagers against raiding Scots during the Border wars. The Jennings brewery in Cockermouth started off in what is now the village hall in High Lorton. At the rear stands a yew tree under which the founder of the Quaker movement, George Fox, preached pacifism to a large crowd that included Cromwellian soldiers. William Wordsworth in his poem Yew Trees wrote:

'There is a yew tree, pride of Lorton Vale
Which to this day stands single, in the midst
Of its own darkness, as it stood of yore'

▼ Loweswater

Low Lorton

Brackenthwaite

1 Exit Car Park turn L, cross bridge then 1st L 'Lowpark ½, Highpark ¾'

2 At T-j by Kirkstile Inn bear R (in effect SA) uphill. At T-j with road L then after 300 yards at brow of hill 1st L 'Public Bridleway'

3 At fork of tracks bear R past small parking area. At fork of tracks in wood take either track – they link up. Climb to Hudson Place and bear R onto tarmac

4 At T-j with road opposite Grange Hotel R

5 After 1 mile, in the wood, sharply L back on yourself 'Mosser. Unfit for cars'

6 Steep climb. Up over brow and down through Mossergate Farm. ¼ mile after going through Mosser Mains 1st R over small stone bridge 'Unsuitable for motors'

7 At T-j R. Cross bridge. At T-j R then L 'Keswick 8½'

8 1st R at X-roads 'Hopebeck 1'

9 At T-j with B5289 L 'Buttermere 4, Loweswater 2' then 1st L 'Buttermere 4, Crummock Water'

10 Climb steadily through the wood. ¼ mile after the end of the wood, just before house ahead, R through wooden bridlegate 'Public Bridleway'

11 Through gates continuing in same direction. At offset X-roads with more major track SA downhill. At T-j R to return to the car park

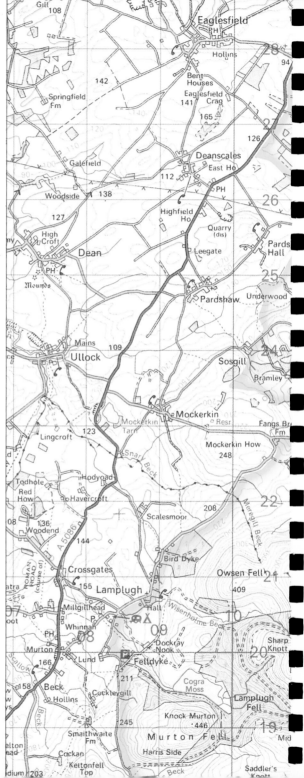

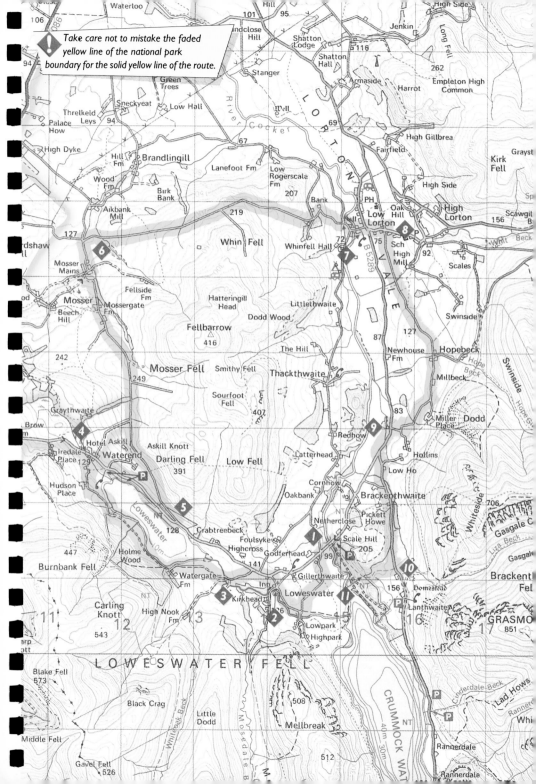

Take care not to mistake the faded yellow line of the national park boundary for the solid yellow line of the route.

4 Two loops from Eskdale Green between Muncaster Fell and Wast Water

Start

Irton Road Station, Eskdale Green (on the Ravenglass and Eskdale railway). Eskdale Green is off the A595 half-way between Whitehaven and Barrow-in-Furness

P As above

Distance and grade

23 miles (two loops of 11½ miles)
Moderate

Terrain

The tracks are predominantly stone-based but there may be some short pushing sections on the stretch through the forest on the northern part of the route. There is a 2 mile section running alongside the Ravenglass railway that may be boggy in parts. 600 feet climb from

Between the sea and the western slopes of the high fells lies an area of farms and woodlands with fine views towards the high hills and a good quantity of fine bridleways. This ride describes a figure of eight with the two loops linking near to Santon Bridge, to the southwest of Wast Water. For convenience of parking the route starts at Eskdale Green. Several short sections of bridleway are linked before a longer climb takes you east through forest setting up a fine descent, at first technical then grassy back down to the road. It looks from the map as though there should be a good loop around the back of Wast Water but the author found this track too steep, rocky, boggy or vague for the purposes of this book. However, the detour alongside Wast Water to Wasdale Head is well worth making for the dramatic views and atmosphere of being at the very heart of the fells. The route continues in a southwesterly direction towards Muncaster Fell which is almost encircled by the course of the route. There is a short rough / boggy section near to the miniature railway but the track on the southern side of the fell is superb all the way back to the start with fine views southeast to Ulpha Fell.

Eskdale Green

Santon Bridge

Whin Garth

crossing the River Bleng near Hall Bolton to the top of the forestry section near Hollow Moor. 430 feet climb from the railway to Chapel Hill on Muncaster Fell. Highest point – 760 feet (226 mts) in the forestry at the northern end of the ride. Lowest point – 25 feet (9 mts) south of Muncaster Fell

▲ Wasdale Head and Great Gable

Nearest railway

Ravenglass, 1 mile from the route at Muncaster Castle

Refreshments

Bower House Inn PH 🍺, George IV PH 🍺, **Eskdale Green**
Bridge Inn PH, **Santon Bridge**
Strands Hotel PH 🍺, The Screes PH 🍺, **Nether Wasdale**
Ratty Arms PH 🍺, **Ravenglass** (just off the route)

Places of interest

Ravenglass (just off the route) 26
Lies on an estuary where three rivers – the Esk, the Mite and the Irt – enter the sea, and for a long while its sheltered position made it an important harbour. The Romans used it and, in the 2nd century, built the large fort of Glannaventa on the cliffs above. In the 18th century, Ravenglass was much used as a base for smuggling contraband tobacco and French brandy from the Isle of Man. The century-old miniature railway was once used to carry minerals and now takes tourists on a scenic seven mile trip up Eskdale

Muncaster Castle 26
Home of the Pennington family since the 13th century, it was a sanctuary for Henry VI during the Wars of the Roses. There is an owl aviary and rhododendron gardens

Nether Wasdale

Santon Bridge

Watermill

Chapel Hill

1 Out of the car park, turn R. At T-j with the road L

2 After ½ mile, after Bower House Inn, next road L 'Holmbrook 3'

3 **Easy to miss**. Shortly after passing 1:6 downhill sign and after a RH bend, turn R onto track in wood 'Bridleway'

4 Climb on single track through wood. At T-j with more major forestry track bear L

5 Climb then descend. At the end of a sharp RH bend at the bottom of the hill, shortly after the track starts climbing again L onto broad track

6 At T-j with road L

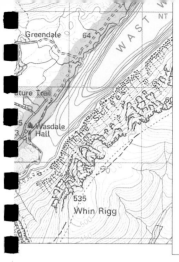
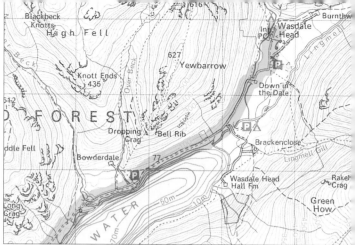

7 Cross bridge, go past the Bridge Inn PH. After 1 mile 1st L by triangle of grass 'Holmbrook 2'

8 After ¾ mile, shortly after wood starts on left 1st R onto driveway to Wardwarrow Farm 'Public Bridleway'

9 After ½ mile 1st track R then after 100 yards L onto grassy track along the edge of woodland

10 At T-j with better track bear R (in effect SA). Follow track as it swings R by house

11 At X-roads with road SA onto stone track 'Public Bridleway Hall Bolton, Bolton Head'

12 With cattle grid and houses ahead bear L downhill

13 Cross bridge, ignore turnings to left and right. At T-j with road L

14 After ¾ mile at brow of hill R 'Public Bridleway. Cathow Bridge'

15 Steady climb over 2 miles with forestry on one or both sides. Short sections where you will have to push

16 At the end of the wood where the walls spread out, cross stream via wooden bridge and follow grassy track parallel with RH wall as the

latter swings round in a wide arc until you are running downhill parallel with the stream

17 The track follows the RH wall as it swings L downhill to cross stream and become more distinct. Stony, technical descent becomes fast, grassy descent. At T-j with road L over cattle grid

18 After ½ mile 1st track R 'Little Ground. Ghyll Farm'. At fork of tracks by gate bear L 'Bridleway'

19 At T-j with road R then L 'Santon Bridge 2, Drigg 6'. (**Or** turn L at road for thoroughly recommended detour along the edge of Wast Water to Wasdale Head)

20 At T-j after 2 miles L 'Eskdale, Broughton 14' then 1st R 'Irton ¾, Ravenglass 5'

21 At brow of hill after 1 mile, 1st road L by post box 'Eskdale Green 2½, Broughton 13½'

22 After ½ mile at bottom of hill by collection of farm buidings turn R 'Sandbank. Public Bridleway'

23 Cross two fields. 100 yards before hillside turn R alongside stone wall. Through gate at end of field and across next field in same

direction. From the gate at the end of this field diagonally L to a gate in the far LH corner

24 Follow railway line with the fence to your left. At times a rough push. Keep eye out for bridlegate to the L to cross tracks and continue in the same direction, with the line now to your right

25 At times narrow and muddy. It improves, becoming broad, stone track. Shortly after sign for 'Mill and Road' to the right sharply L back on yourself 'Bridleway. Castle'

26 Steep climb (push). Follow 'Bridleway' and 'Permitted Bridleway' signs for the castle. At X-roads of tracks beyond gate L uphill. At T-j with road sharply L back on yourself 'Public Bridleway. Muncaster Fell via Fell Lane'

27 Easy to miss. Shortly after brow of hill, leave main gravel track and take 1st grassy track to the R 'Public Bridleway. Lower Eskdale'

28 Fine descent. At T-j L

29 After 1½ miles, with farm buildings to the left, turn L by fir trees. Follow past Forest How back to the start

From Eskdale Green across to the Duddon Valley and back over Birker Fell

One of two off-road rides in the book which involves a sustained push, this one of some forty minutes from the bottom of Hardknott to the top of the pass between the valleys of the rivers Esk and Duddon beneath Harter Fell. There is a chance to warm up for this with a four mile section of delightful, rideable off-road running parallel with the road and river although there must be some sort of record for the number of gates that need to be opened along this stretch. The push climbs 850 feet on a straightforward stony track then across the roots of recently cleared forestry before joining a splendid forestry track that descends to the road running alongside the beautiful River Duddon. You may well be tempted by the attractions of the Newfield Inn at Seathwaite before girding your loins for the steep road climb up over Birker Fell and back down to the start.

Start

George IV PH, at the eastern end of Eskdale Green, 6 miles east of Gosforth. (Gosforth is halfway between Whitehaven and Barrow-in-Furness on the A595)

P Go past George IV PH following signs for Ulpha and Broughton. Cross bridge. There is a large layby just past the bridge on the right

Distance and grade

19 miles

⚜⚜⚜⚜⚜ Strenuous

Terrain

The section alongside the River Esk is rideable. From the road at the bottom of Hardknott to the pass is mainly pushing on a well-defined stony track then across a short, rough stretch of cleared forestry. Two

Eskdale Green

Dalegarth Hall

Brotherilkeld

Harter Fell

Hinning House Close

major climbs: 850 feet from the road to the pass beneath Harter Fell, 630 feet from Ulpha to the top of the road over Birker Fell. Highest point – 1150 feet (345 mts) below Harter Fell. Lowest point – 80 feet (25 mts) at the start

Nearest railway

Ravenglass, 6 miles west of Eskdale Green

▲ *Seathwaite*

Places of interest

River Duddon Valley 10
Its magnificent scenery is immortalized by Wordsworth in no fewer than 35 individual sonnets. His poem 'Excursion' describes the village of Seathwaite and its 18th-century parson, Robert Walker

Ravenglass and Eskdale Railway 1
Established in 1875 to carry iron ore, this narrow gauge railway known as 'La'al Ratty' has been revived to carry passengers through seven miles of countryside between Dalegarth in Eskdale to Ravenglass on the coast

Refreshments

George IV PH🍷*, Bower House Inn PH*🍷*,* **Eskdale Green**
Newfield Inn PH🍷*,* **Seathwaite**

Seathwaite

Ulpha

Birker Fell

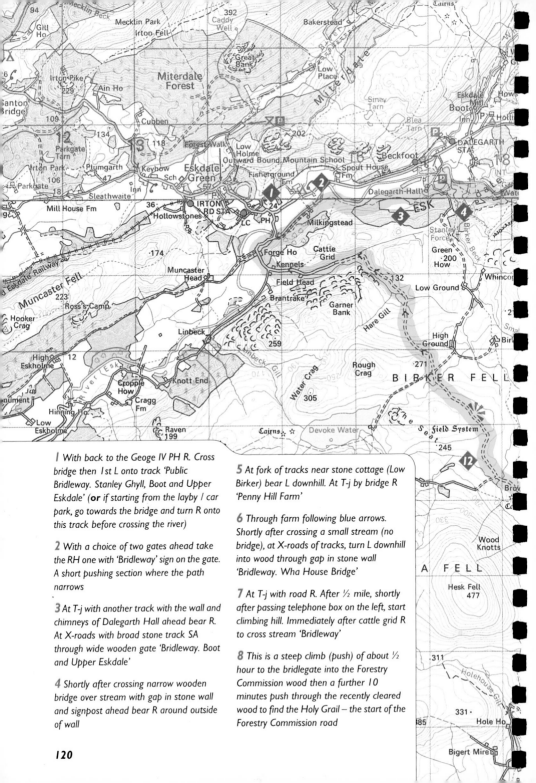

1 With back to the Geoge IV PH R. Cross bridge then 1st L onto track 'Public Bridleway. Stanley Ghyll, Boot and Upper Eskdale' (**or** if starting from the layby / car park, go towards the bridge and turn R onto this track before crossing the river)

2 With a choice of two gates ahead take the RH one with 'Bridleway' sign on the gate. A short pushing section where the path narrows

3 At T-j with another track with the wall and chimneys of Dalegarth Hall ahead bear R. At X-roads with broad stone track SA through wide wooden gate 'Bridleway. Boot and Upper Eskdale'

4 Shortly after crossing narrow wooden bridge over stream with gap in stone wall and signpost ahead bear R around outside of wall

5 At fork of tracks near stone cottage (Low Birker) bear L downhill. At T-j by bridge R 'Penny Hill Farm'

6 Through farm following blue arrows. Shortly after crossing a small stream (no bridge), at X-roads of tracks, turn L downhill into wood through gap in stone wall 'Bridleway. Wha House Bridge'

7 At T-j with road R. After ½ mile, shortly after passing telephone box on the left, start climbing hill. Immediately after cattle grid R to cross stream 'Bridleway'

8 This is a steep climb (push) of about ½ hour to the bridlegate into the Forestry Commission wood then a further 10 minutes push through the recently cleared wood to find the Holy Grail – the start of the Forestry Commission road

120

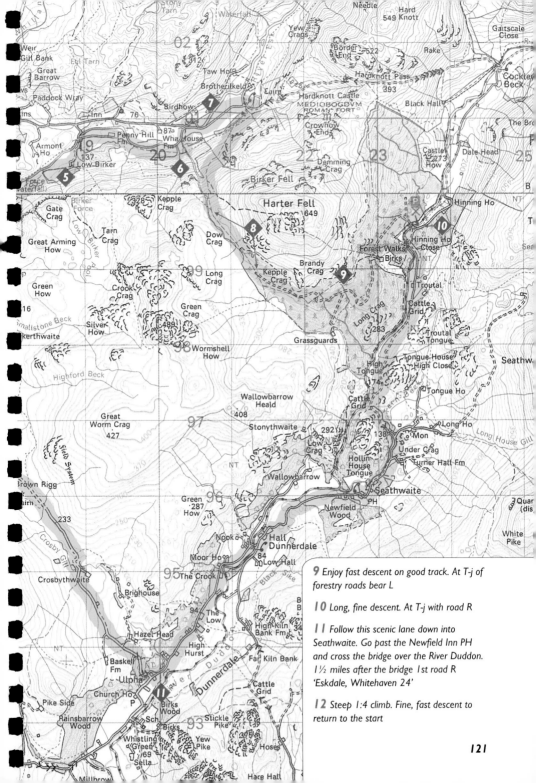

9 Enjoy fast descent on good track. At T-j of forestry roads bear L

10 Long, fine descent. At T-j with road R

11 Follow this scenic lane down into Seathwaite. Go past the Newfield Inn PH and cross the bridge over the River Duddon. 1½ miles after the bridge 1st road R 'Eskdale, Whitehaven 24'

12 Steep 1:4 climb. Fine, fast descent to return to the start

Sawrey and Claife Heights at the northwest corner of Lake Windermere

This is a small, perfectly-formed ride that has most of the ingredients that one would ever wish to find in an off-road trip: good quality tracks with regular waymarking, rideable climbs and fast descents, wide-ranging views and a long flat off-road section by a lake to finish. All this and a bike-friendly ferry crossing of the lake to take you to the start of the ride. The ferry is a commercial concern running every fifteen minutes non-stop from morning to late evening and it is one of the greatest cycling pleasures to ride past the line of cars to get to the head of the queue. The ferry only takes five minutes and is cheap and easy to use. The route climbs from Far Sawrey up onto Claife Heights past three small tarns. From here the views are magnificent. A fast forestry road drops you near to Wray Castle from which point there is a superb lakeside track running all the way back to the ferry. This ride could easily be linked to the signposted routes in the Forestry Commission land in Grizedale Forest.

Start

Car parks either side of the ferry from Bowness-on-Windermere

P Use the long stay (slipway) pay and display car park on the way to the ferry at the south end of Bowness

Distance and grade

10 miles
Easy

Terrain

Excellent tracks throughout. One steady 500 feet climb from the start up onto Claife Heights. Highest point – 650 feet (195 mts) near to Wise Een Tarn. Lowest point – Lake Windermere 140 feet (41 mts).

Nearest railway

Windermere, 2½ miles north of the ferry at Bowness

▶ Lake Windermere

Far Sawrey

Wise Een Tarn

High Wray

Refreshments

Plenty of choice in
Windermere *and*
Bowness
The Sawrey Hotel PH,
Far Sawrey

Places of interest

Bowness *1*
Resort on Lake Windermere with quaint, narrow streets and 15th-century church. The World of Beatrix Potter Exhibition includes 3-D tableaux and videos

Hill Top, Near Sawrey *2*
Scenes from Peter Rabbit come alive in the 17th-century farm that inspired Beatrix Potter's work

Three Dubs Crags

1 Cross on the ferry to the west coast. Let the cars go by. After 1 mile, just after the Sawrey Hotel, R onto No Through Road 'The Glen'

2 Cross cattle grid and after 100 yards bear L onto track. At T-j at the top of track bear R 'Public Bridleway. Claife Heights'

3 Follow main track and blue arrows past farms into forest to the brow of the hill and descend on better track

4 Follow good forestry track and signs for Hawkshead. Continue on main track. At signpost no. 10 follow 'Bridleway. Wray'

5 Long descent. At T-j with road by High Wray Farm R

6 50 yards before the turrets of Wray Castle turn R sharply back on yourself onto track 'Public Bridleway' (not the track to the church)

7 Follow this lakeside track past Belle Grange all the way back to the B5285. At T-j with road L to return to the ferry

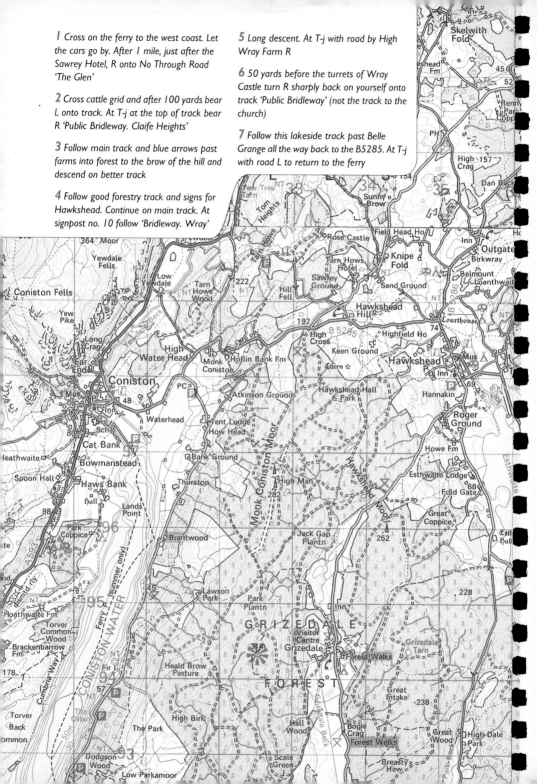

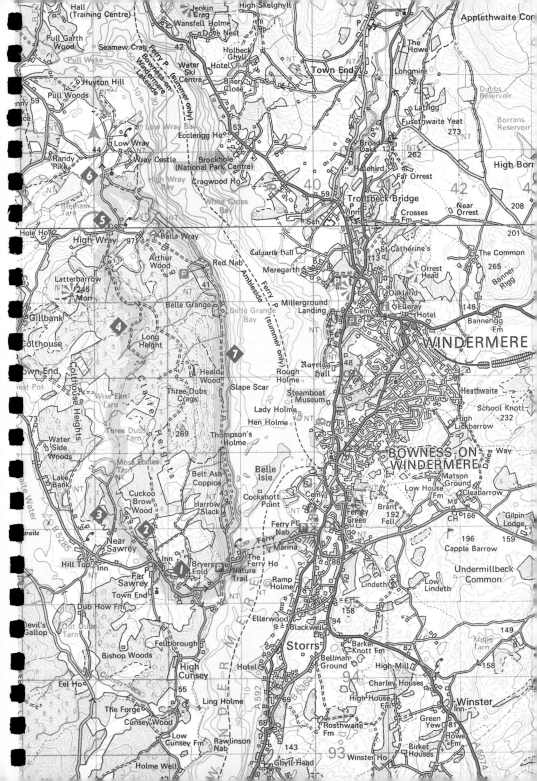

Tracks and green lanes east of Lake Windermere

Start

The Punch Bowl PH, Crosthwaite, 5 miles west of Kendal

P By the church at the eastern end of Crosthwaite

Distance and grade

24 miles   Moderate

Terrain

Almost all the route is on good quality tracks, many of which are unclassified roads which turn from tarmac to track with great frequency. 400 feet climb from the River Gilpin south of Crosthwaite to the highest point of the bridleway beneath Whitbarrow. 700 feet climb from the River Winster west of Witherslack to the the farm at Height. Highest point – 750 feet (225 mts) on the road just beneath Gummer's How. Lowest point – 25 feet (9 mts) at the crossing of the River Winster near to Witherslack

Nearest railway

Windermere, 4 miles north of the route near Winster

*E*ast of Lake Windermere lies a tangled web of lanes, green lanes, old county roads, byways and bridleways that offer some very fine year-round cycling away from the seething hordes in the central fells. Heading south from Crosthwaite the ride soon finds the delightful track which runs from Row in an arc west then south beneath Whitbarrow. A climb up to Witherslack Hall is rewarded with a long, leisurely descent through woodland down to the road. Nothing so far prepares you for the brutal, unrelenting climb up onto Newton Fell, a total of almost 700 feet with the first 500 feet within the first mile! Once gained the height is more or less maintained on a series of unclassified roads running towards Gummer's How then north towards Winster. Two excellent pubs lie just off the route at Strawberry Bank and Bowland Bridge, although this will involve losing some height. Green lanes, bridleways and tiny roads lead you back to the start at Crosthwaite.

Crosthwaite   Row   Park Wood   Witherslack   River Winster

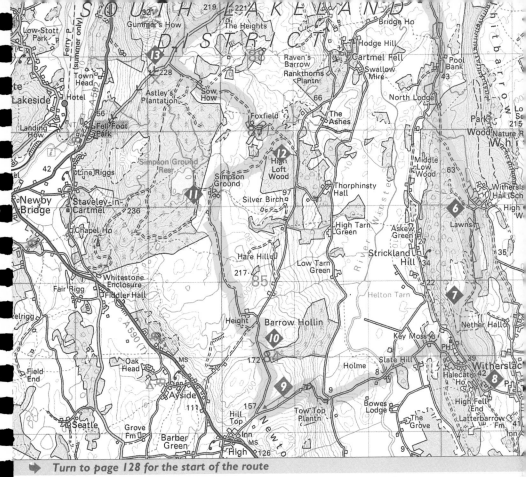

➡ **Turn to page 128 for the start of the route**

6 After 2½ miles, at end of wood opposite large stone barn on left at brow of hill, R onto track 'Public Bridleway. Knot Wood, Halecat'. At fork by house bear R

7 At end of stone track bear R uphill away from the wall to the left on indistinct grassy track which soon becomes more obvious. Aim for gate in the middle of the far wall

8 Superb descent through woodland. At T-j with road sharply R back on yourself then after ½ mile 1st road L 'Newton, Cartmel Fell, Halecat'

9 Follow signs for High Newton up very steep hill. At T-j R 'Cartmel Fell, Kendal 12'

10 After short descent and climb 1st road L at top of hill (through gate) then 1st R 'Simpson Ground only'

11 At fork near to the house at Simpson Ground bear L uphill through gate. At end of tarmac bear R alongside wall 'Public Right of Way'

12 At T-j with tarmac L. Through farm (Foxfield) and onto track

13 Through next farm onto tarmac. At T-j with road R

➡ **page 128**

High Loft Wood

Gummer's How

Hartbarrow

Scorrs

Gilpin Mill

1 With back to the Punch Bowl PH L, then just past the Village Hall on the right L down track by village signboard and house called 'Oak Lea'

2 At T-j with road L then after 300 yards R onto track through Esp Ford (near 'Aspen' sign) 'Public Bridleway'

3 At T-j with main road (A5074) L then after ¾ mile 1st road R 'The Row'

4 **Easy to miss**. Through Row on tarmac lane which becomes track. Climb steadily then descend. Track narrows as it runs along the side of the woodland to your left. Keep eye out for bridgegate to R in wall / fence into field and towards farm

5 Aim for the upper end of the farm. Descend on track through farm. At T-j with road L

← page 127

14 **Easy to miss**. Fast descent. Once out of forest, opposite Lightwood Guest House on the right, L onto narrow road (NS)

15 At T-j L (NS)

16 Shortly after passing left turn to Low and High Moor How, with two road turns to the right in quick succession, take the 2nd R 'Bowness' then 1st R onto road between stone gate posts (NS)

17 Tarmac becomes track. As track swings sharp R towards farm and gate with 'Private' sign on it bear L onto grassy track and alongside wall. Through gate keeping wall to your right and woodland to your left

18 At 'Ghyll Head' signpost R towards road. At X-roads with road SA '6 ft 6 ins width limit' onto track. At X-roads with next road SA 'Green Lane'

19 Tarmac turns to track. At T-j with road R (NS) then L (NS). Do not lose control!

20 On sharp LH bend by a sign for 'Crosthwaite' 1st R (in effect SA)

21 Follow in same direction towards barn with black doors. Bear L downhill then 1st R opposite house

22 Follow path alongside stream. At T-j by farm L then R onto road

23 At T-j after 1½ miles L to return to the start

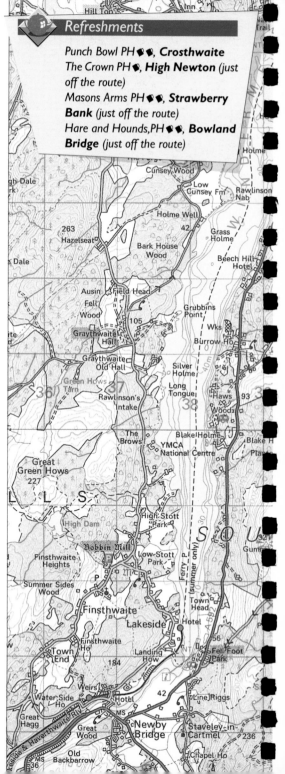

Refreshments

Punch Bowl PH ♥♥, **Crosthwaite**

The Crown PH ♥, **High Newton** (just off the route)

Masons Arms PH ♥♥, **Strawberry Bank** (just off the route)

Hare and Hounds, PH ♥♥, **Bowland Bridge** (just off the route)

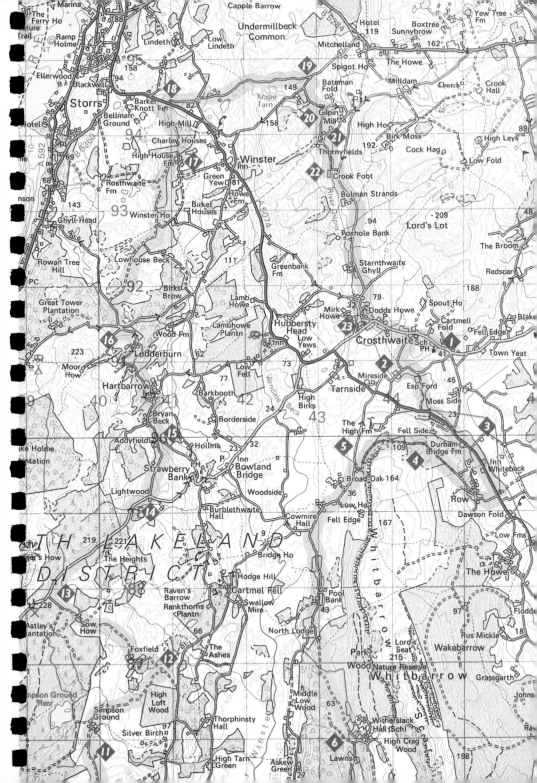

8 Burneside and the Garburn Pass between Kentmere and Troutbeck

*T*his is the second of the off-road rides in the book that involves a sustained push – this one lasts about half an hour from Kentmere to the top of the Garburn Pass. The reward is a long, fine descent with magnificent views of the central fells. Garburn Pass lies at the heart of the ride: at the start there is a steady climb alongside the River Kent from Burneside to Bowston and Hagg Foot and up over Staveley Head Fell past outlying farms before a fine descent down into Kentmere. The climb up to the Garburn Pass is straightforward on a stony track. A climb of one mile is compensated by a descent of almost four down to cross the busy A591, the road carrying most of the traffic into the heart of the Lakes. This main road is avoided in favour of quiet gated roads and a final green lane before the return to Burneside.

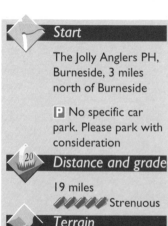

Start

The Jolly Anglers PH, Burneside, 3 miles north of Burneside

P No specific car park. Please park with consideration

Distance and grade

19 miles

///// Strenuous

Terrain

There is a grassy section which is well-signposted from Staveley Head Fell down into Kentmere. The track over Garburn Pass is all

Burneside   Staveley Head Fell   Long Houses   Kentmere   Garburn Pass stone-based although the ascent is a push and there may be short sections on the descent where you need to walk. 630 feet climb from Bowston to the top of Staveley Head Fell. 950 feet climb from Kentmere to the Garburn Pass. Two climbs of 200 feet to the south of the A591. Highest point – 1500 feet (450 mts) at Garburn Pass. Lowest point – 170 feet (51 mts) at the start

Nearest railway

Burneside

Refreshments

Jolly Anglers PH, **Burneside**

Places of interest

Troutbeck *(just off the route)* 12
This dispersed, picturesque settlement is worth visiting for its many surviving farmhouses and cottages, which are usually grouped around wells. The best conserved of them all is Townend, a 17th-century farmhouse now owned by the National Trust. Its interior decoration is uncommonly intact, with carved and dated fittings and furnishings. Dating and initialing was evidence of the Lakelanders' pride in their great prosperity after the mid-17th century, when their poor economy improved with cattle grazing and industrial sidelines in metals and stocking-knitting

Lake Windermere *(seen from the route)* 15
Windermere is a busy lake, with the resort town of Bowness-on-Windermere centrally located on its eastern shore. Steamers, yachts, pleasure boats and a chain ferry are some of the craft that can regularly be seen from the fells overlooking the lake. On the wooded Belle Isle, just opposite Bowness, a cylindrical mansion, built in 1774, pokes its roof up through the tree tops

Dubbs Reservoir

Heaning

New Hall

Rather Heath

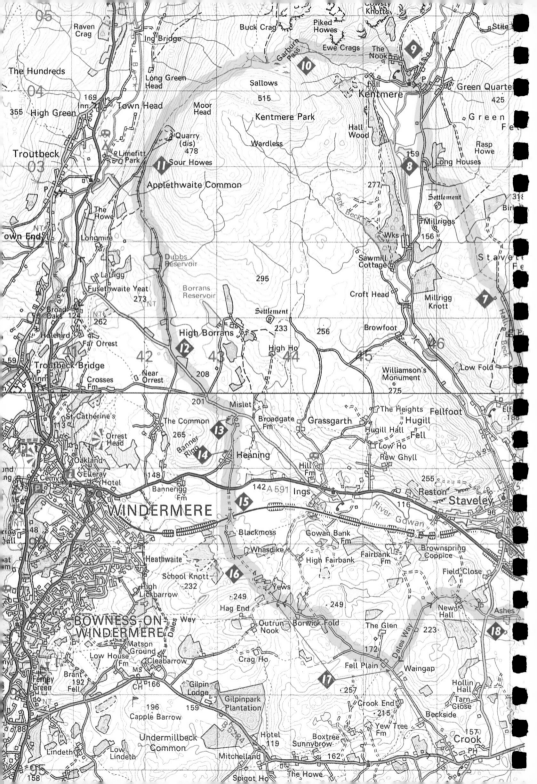

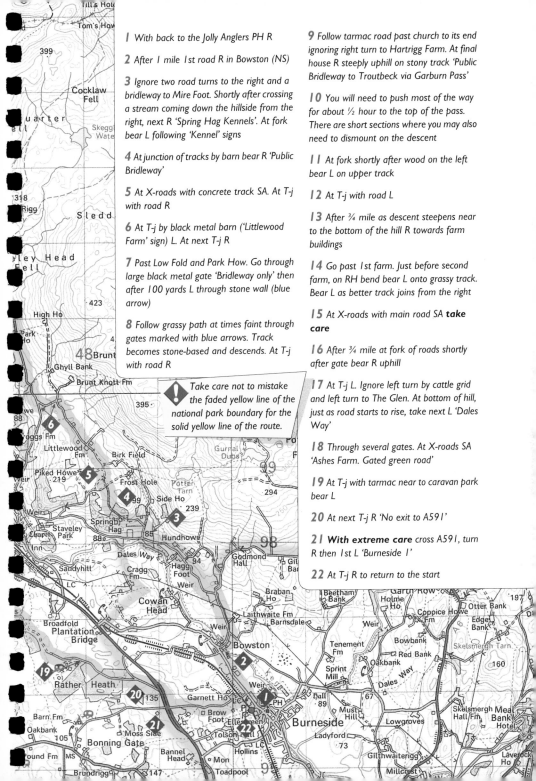

1 With back to the Jolly Anglers PH R

2 After 1 mile 1st road R in Bowston (NS)

3 Ignore two road turns to the right and a bridleway to Mire Foot. Shortly after crossing a stream coming down the hillside from the right, next R 'Spring Hag Kennels'. At fork bear L following 'Kennel' signs

4 At junction of tracks by barn bear R 'Public Bridleway'

5 At X-roads with concrete track SA. At T-j with road R

6 At T-j by black metal barn ('Littlewood Farm' sign) L. At next T-j R

7 Past Low Fold and Park How. Go through large black metal gate 'Bridleway only' then after 100 yards L through stone wall (blue arrow)

8 Follow grassy path at times faint through gates marked with blue arrows. Track becomes stone-based and descends. At T-j with road R

⚠ Take care not to mistake the faded yellow line of the national park boundary for the solid yellow line of the route.

9 Follow tarmac road past church to its end ignoring right turn to Hartrigg Farm. At final house R steeply uphill on stony track 'Public Bridleway to Troutbeck via Garburn Pass'

10 You will need to push most of the way for about ½ hour to the top of the pass. There are short sections where you may also need to dismount on the descent

11 At fork shortly after wood on the left bear L on upper track

12 At T-j with road L

13 After ¾ mile as descent steepens near to the bottom of the hill R towards farm buildings

14 Go past 1st farm. Just before second farm, on RH bend bear L onto grassy track. Bear L as better track joins from the right

15 At X-roads with main road SA **take care**

16 After ¾ mile at fork of roads shortly after gate bear R uphill

17 At T-j L. Ignore left turn by cattle grid and left turn to The Glen. At bottom of hill, just as road starts to rise, take next L 'Dales Way'

18 Through several gates. At X-roads SA 'Ashes Farm. Gated green road'

19 At T-j with tarmac near to caravan park bear L

20 At next T-j R 'No exit to A591'

21 **With extreme care** cross A591, turn R then 1st L 'Burneside 1'

22 At T-j R to return to the start

West from Kirkby Stephen over the fells of Smardale and Crosby Garrett to Great Asby

Start

Start of Silver Street (Soulby Road) Kirkby Stephen, 10 miles east of M6, Junction 38

P Just off Silver Street (Soulby Road)

Distance and grade

22½ miles

Moderate / strenuous

Terrain

Well-drained earth / grass tracks over parts of Smardale and Crosby Garrett Fells and also west from Whygill Head. 750 feet climb from Kirkby

Between the Lake District and the Pennines, north of the Howgills and south of the Eden Valley lies an area of sparsely-populated gently rolling fells with a plethora of bridleways where it is possible to plan several loops. This ride uses as a base the attractive town of Kirkby Stephen with lots of tea-shops and pubs to look forward to upon your return. It climbs southwest over Smardale Fell crossing the lovely stone bridge over Scandal Beck. From Brownber the route skirts the flanks of Nettle Hill before one of the best descents in the whole book down to Crosby Garrett. The course of the ride lies westwards along grassy tracks from Whygill Head. Great Asby is a charming, unspoilt village and offers the only refreshment stop on the whole route. There is a last section of off-road before a five mile stretch of the Cumbria Cycleway through Soulby and back to the start.

Kirby Stephen   Waitby   Smardale Bridge   Brownber   Crosby Garrett

Stephen to the top of Smardale Fell; 350 feet from the crossing of Scandal Beck to the high point on Nettle Hill; 270 feet climb from Water Houses west to Maisongill. Highest point – 1100 feet (330 mts) on Smardale Fell. Lowest point – 500 feet (150 mts) in Soulby

Nearest railway

Kirkby Stephen station lies 2 miles south of the town

Refreshments

Kings Arms PH, *White Lion PH*, *plenty of choice in* **Kirkby Stephen** *Three Greyhounds PH*, **Great Asby**

Places of interest

Kirkby Stephen I
Brightly painted shops and old coaching inns huddle among attractive cobbled squares above the Eden valley. Inside the 13th-century St Stephen's church is the shaft of the unique 10th-century cemetery cross of Loki, the Danish Devil. The Market Square is surrounded by an ancient collar of cobblestones which mark the area used until 1820 for bull baiting – a sport which ceased after a disaster when a bull broke free

Crosby Garrett II
Ancient records show that the village was once called Crosby Gerard, although no one seems to know who Gerard was! Crosby means farmstead with a cross. In the early days of Christianity, communities without churches made do with simple wood or stone crosses

Nettle Hill II
Nettles had various uses including dye for local wool and are a sign of earlier human settlement. These hills are covered with cairns and hut circles

Great Asby

Soulby

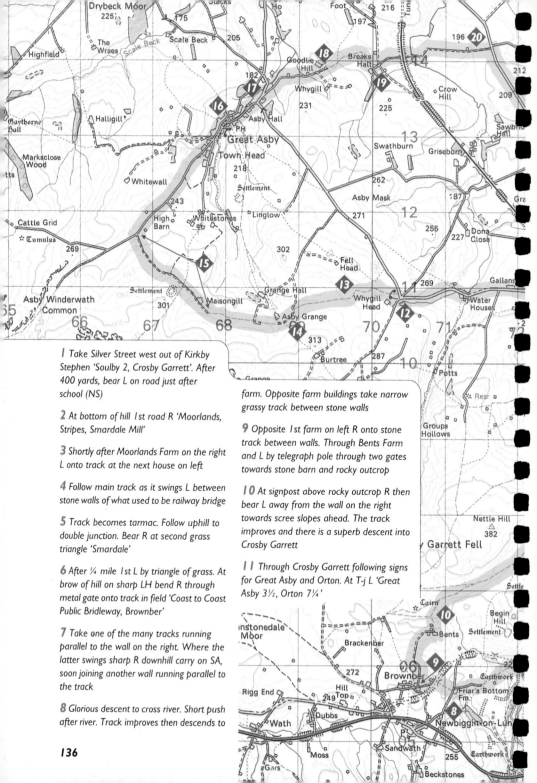

1 Take Silver Street west out of Kirkby Stephen 'Soulby 2, Crosby Garrett'. After 400 yards, bear L on road just after school (NS)

2 At bottom of hill 1st road R 'Moorlands, Stripes, Smardale Mill'

3 Shortly after Moorlands Farm on the right L onto track at the next house on left

4 Follow main track as it swings L between stone walls of what used to be railway bridge

5 Track becomes tarmac. Follow uphill to double junction. Bear R at second grass triangle 'Smardale'

6 After ¼ mile 1st L by triangle of grass. At brow of hill on sharp LH bend R through metal gate onto track in field 'Coast to Coast Public Bridleway, Brownber'

7 Take one of the many tracks running parallel to the wall on the right. Where the latter swings sharp R downhill carry on SA, soon joining another wall running parallel to the track

8 Glorious descent to cross river. Short push after river. Track improves then descends to farm. Opposite farm buildings take narrow grassy track between stone walls

9 Opposite 1st farm on left R onto stone track between walls. Through Bents Farm and L by telegraph pole through two gates towards stone barn and rocky outcrop

10 At signpost above rocky outcrop R then bear L away from the wall on the right towards scree slopes ahead. The track improves and there is a superb descent into Crosby Garrett

11 Through Crosby Garrett following signs for Great Asby and Orton. At T-j L 'Great Asby 3½, Orton 7¼'

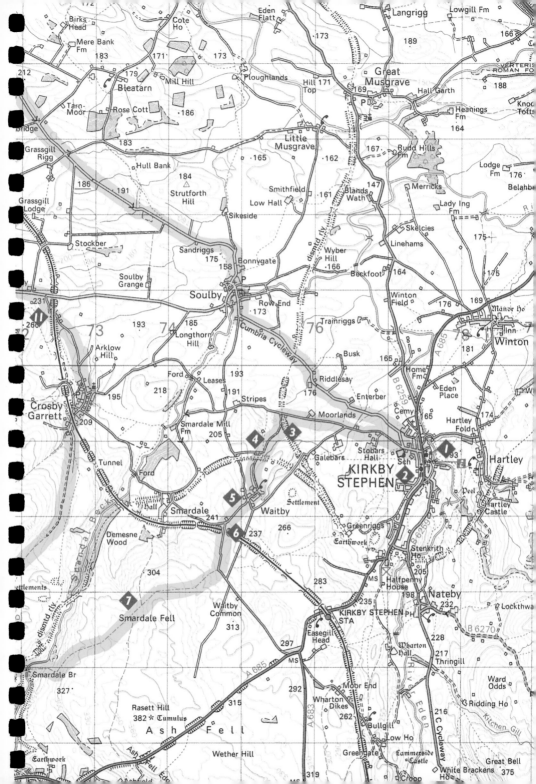

Above Ullswater from Askham and over Askham Fell

10

A short, delightful ride with some magnificent views of Ullswater. Askham is one of those time-stood-still villages with solid stone houses and two good pubs. A steady climb takes you onto the far side of Heughscar Hill where the views of Ullswater are breathtaking. You soon cross the course of High Street, a Roman Road that runs south over a mountain of the same name and down into Troutbeck. High Street makes one of the more challenging 'expedition' style off-road rides in the Lake District which require lots of pushing, some carrying and some sustained technical descents. The track over Askham Fell is a dream, as are the tiny lanes through Scalegate and Scales Farm and down through Hullockhowe to Bampton. A quiet road above the valley of the River Lowther delivers you back to Askham.

Start

The Post Office & Stores in Askham, 5 miles south of Penrith

P No specific car park. Please show consideration

Distance and grade

12 miles

Easy / Moderate

Terrain

Excellent tracks over Askham Fell, short rough section near to Heltondale Beck. The lanes are all but free of traffic. 350 feet climb from Askham to the track over Heughscar Hill above Ullswater. Highest point – 1150 feet (345 mts) on Kid Moor south of Scales Farm. Lowest point – 550 feet (165 mts) at the crossing of the River Lowther south of Askham

Nearest railway

Penrith, 5 miles north of Askham

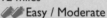

Askham

Askham Fell

Dale House

Askham 1
Immaculate village on the steep wooded bank of the River Lowther. The upper green has fine views to Lowther Castle and the Pennines. There is an ancient stone circle and burial sites on Askham Fell

Refreshments

Queens Head PH 🍺, Punch Bowl PH 🍺 🍺, **Askham**
St Patrick's Well PH 🍺, **Bampton**
Crown and Mitre PH, **Bampton Grange**

Roman Road (High Street) 9
It is thought that the road linked the fort at Brougham, south of Penrith, with the fort at Ambleside. The line it takes is remarkably straight along the fell ridges

Lowther (just off the route) 14
The fairy-tale facade of towers, turrets and battlements is the only remnant of the 19th-century castle which was demolished in 1957. Lowther Park was created in 1283 for the estate's deer and is now a country park with nature trails, children's entertainments, rare breeds and red deer whose ancestors roamed the original deer park

▼ A steamer by the pier at Pooley Bridge on Ullswater

1 With back to the Post Office R uphill 'Ullswater'. After 300 yards 1st L 'Celleron'

2 Ignore 1st bridleway to the left. Go past wood on left and climb to brow of hill. Turn L onto tarmac drive over cattlegrid 'Public Bridleway'

3 Follow main track as it swings L uphill towards trees on the horizon. At a stone barn leave main track and turn R onto grassy track 'Public Bridleway'

4 Diagonally L across field following cairns under telephone lines. The track improves and superb views of Ullswater open up

5 At X-roads of tracks at the bottom of hill L 'Bridleway. Helton'

6 At T-j with road R

7 Through farms following bridleway signs. Cross stream and bear L downhill then diagonally R across field to gate in far RH corner. Follow upstream to cross via small stone bridge

8 Follow arrow through gate by ruin. Stay close to the RH wall at the lower edge of the field. Exit via gate and turn L steeply uphill following track around the perimeter of the wall

9 Join better track near barn and bear R towards telegraph poles. At T-j with road R

10 Through several gates. At T-j L

11 Fine descent. At T-j with more major road by telephone box R. Follow signs for Bampton Grange then Shap over two bridges into the village

12 At the end of the village 1st road L 'Knipe, Whale'

13 After 1 mile turn R by a telephone box through gate 'Whale, Lowther'

14 At T-j after 2½ miles R 'Askham, Lowther, Penrith' to return to the start

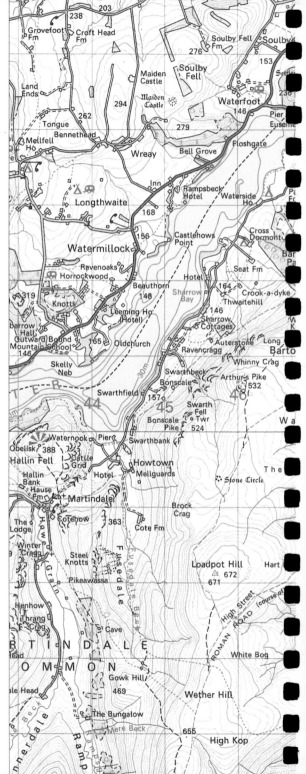

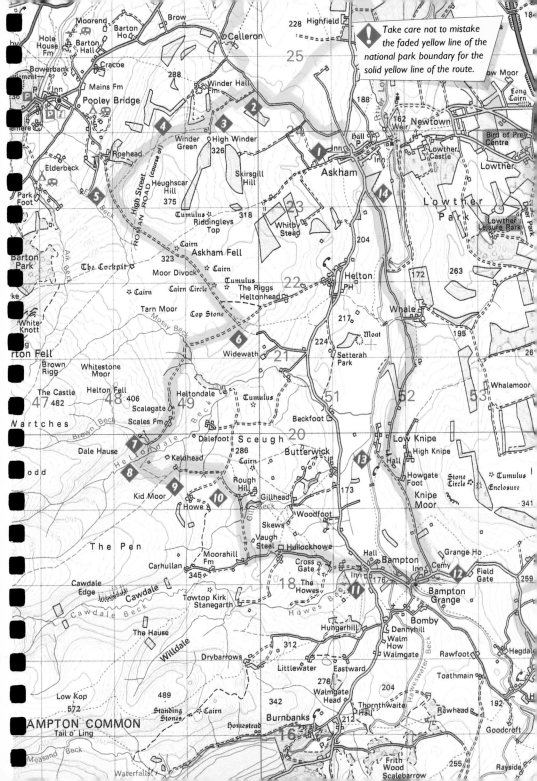

Take care not to mistake the faded yellow line of the national park boundary for the solid yellow line of the route.

Cycle
TOURS

The Ordnance Survey Cycle Tours series

Around Birmingham
Avon, Somerset & Wiltshire
Berks, Bucks & Oxfordshire
Cornwall & Devon
Cumbria & the Lakes
Dorset, Hampshire & Isle of Wight
East Anglia – South
Gloucestershire and Hereford & Worcester
Kent, Surrey & Sussex
Southern Scotland

The whole series is available from all good bookshops or by mail order direct from the publisher. Payment can be made by credit card or cheque/postal order in the following ways

By phone

Phone through your order on our special *Credit Card Hotline* on *01933 414000*. Speak to our customer service team during office hours (9am to 5pm) or leave a message on the answer machine, quoting your full credit card number plus expiry date, your full name and address and reference T503N73C

By post

Simply fill out the order form opposite and send it to:
Cash Sales Department, Reed Book Services, PO Box 5, Rushden, Northants, NN10 6YX

Cycle TOURS

I wish to order the following titles

T503N73C

Title	Price	Quantity	Total
Around Birmingham ISBN 0 600 58623 5	£9.99		
Avon, Somerset & Wiltshire ISBN 0 600 58664 2	£9.99		
Berks, Bucks & Oxfordshire ISBN 0 600 58156 X	£9.99		
Cornwall & Devon ISBN 0 600 58124 1	£9.99		
Cumbria & the Lakes ISBN 0 600 58126 8	£9.99		
Dorset, Hampshire & Isle of Wight ISBN 0 600 58667 7	£9.99		
East Anglia – South ISBN 0 600 58125 X	£9.99		
Gloucestershire and Hereford & Worcester ISBN 0 600 58665 0	£9.99		
Kent, Surrey & Sussex ISBN 0 600 58666 9	£9.99		
Southern Scotland ISBN 0 600 58624 3	£9.99		

Postage and packing free　　　　　　　　　　　Grand total ▢

Name _____ (block capitals)

Address _____

_____ Postcode

I enclose a cheque/postal order for £ ▢ made payable to **Reed Book Services Ltd**

or please debit my ☐ Access ☐ Visa ☐ American Express ☐ Diners account

number ▢▢▢▢ ▢▢▢▢ ▢▢▢▢ ▢▢▢▢

by £ ▢ expiry date ▢▢ ▢▢ _____ Signature

GETTING READY
TO SHAPE UP

1

GETTING READY
TO SHAPE UP

THIS SECTION AIMS TO:

give an introduction to weight problems, outline the *Shape-Up* approach, and help you to plan carefully the changes you want to make.

It will help you to:

- ☑ make an honest assessment of how motivated you are to make changes

- ☑ learn some new skills to help you change your eating and activity habits more effectively

- ☑ set the stage for the rest of the *Shape-Up* programme, and

- ☑ consider the things that might get in the way of you making changes.

WEIGHT CONCERNS

Our expanding nation

In Britain – as in most other developed countries – we have been getting fatter, especially in the last 20 years. The kind of life we live these days makes it easy for this to happen. We have a greater number of foods available to us than at any other time in history, and we are more inactive than we have ever been. Nowadays, most people's jobs involve very little physical exertion compared with previous generations. We use our cars more and more, and our homes are full of appliances which save us from physical work. We're also surrounded by lots of tempting foods that are available at all hours. So is it surprising that our weight is increasing?

How your weight can affect your health

Being overweight increases your risk of a range of health problems such as:

- ☑ diabetes
- ☑ hypertension (high blood pressure)
- ☑ coronary heart disease
- ☑ stroke
- ☑ osteoarthritis, and
- ☑ cancer.

Obesity reduces life expectancy by, on average, nine years. In England, obesity is responsible for 9,000 premature deaths each year.

Why are some people more overweight than others?

Food is an essential and enjoyable part of our lives. Our bodies need food to be able to function, and food often plays an important role in family and social occasions.

Being overweight is the result of an imbalance between energy coming into the body from food, and energy spent in physical activity and in keeping the body working (metabolism).

When people eat more than they need to, the excess weight is stored on the body as fat. We live in a society where high calorie, convenience foods are available at relatively low prices, and where people don't need to do very much physical activity, so it's very easy for there to be an imbalance.

In order to lose weight, you need to reverse this imbalance so that you take in less energy from food and use up more energy by being active. In *Shape-Up* sections 2, 3 and 4 you will learn more about these steps.

There are many reasons which contribute to people becoming overweight. For example:

Genetic factors

Weight problems tend to run in families. It is easy to just 'blame our genes', but it is also common for unhealthy habits to be passed on within a family. Studies on children who have been adopted at birth show that weight is influenced by genes as well as lifestyle. This doesn't mean that people with overweight parents are bound to become overweight, but they may have to work harder to avoid becoming overweight – by making special efforts to eat healthily and be active.

Glands

Some overweight people believe that they have a problem with their glands – for example an underactive thyroid. In fact only about 5% of overweight people suffer from this. If you're in doubt, ask your doctor. However, whatever the answer, you will find that you still need to change your lifestyle in order to change your weight.

Metabolism

Your 'metabolic rate' is the rate at which your body uses energy. If you have a slow metabolic rate, you will use up less energy to do an activity. If you have a high metabolic rate you will use more energy to do the same activity. Research has shown that people with lower metabolic rates tend to gain more weight over their lifetime. So people with a lower metabolic rate may need to eat slightly less than others to avoid gaining weight.

Ageing

On average, people put on between one and two pounds (about 0.5kg to 1kg) a year from their 20s to their 60s. This could be due to

"The first time I went to a slimming club I did really well, but then I gradually put everything back on – all 3 stones that I'd lost. So now I want to try making smaller, more permanent changes and see what happens."

a slower metabolism associated with ageing. However, people also tend to become less physically active as they get older, and sometimes don't cut down enough on what they eat to compensate for this.

Is 'slimming' the answer to being overweight?

The traditional approach to weight control has been 'slimming'. People go on a diet that restricts what they eat and they lose weight.

At the start of a slimming regime people usually feel optimistic, and if they start losing weight quite quickly, they are very pleased. However, sooner or later weight loss slows down or stops. This can be frustrating and people often abandon their diet at this point. Even more demoralising is the fact that most people find that they can't keep off the lost weight for long. And some may put on even more weight than they lost in the first place so that, as time goes on, they are starting at a higher and higher weight.

Many people find it hard to stick to their diet, and usually blame themselves rather than question the approach. This self-blame can make people feel worse about themselves – 'a failure' – and they may be all the more vulnerable to the next diet fad. And yet, although slimming diets are often not effective in the long term, they are more popular than ever.

How do you know if you're overweight?

Waist size

Waist size is a useful guide. The distribution of body fat in different parts of the body varies from person to person. In general, women are more likely to deposit fat on their hips and thighs, while men are more likely to have more fat in their abdomen (around their middle).

Fat around the middle is more likely to increase the risk of heart disease. People with an apple shape (fatness around the waist and stomach) have a greater risk of heart disease than pear-shaped people (fatness around the hips).

Of course, people come in many different shapes. It can be difficult deciding where your waist is, and the waistline of clothes can be very low or quite high. The simplest way of deciding where to measure your waist is by measuring around your body 2.5cm (1 inch) above your navel.

- For **women**, a waist size over 80cm (32 inches) indicates an increased risk to health, and over 88cm (35 inches) indicates a substantial risk to health.
- For **men**, a waist size over 94 cm (37 inches) indicates an increased risk to health, and over 102 cm (40 inches) indicates a substantial risk to health.

Body mass index (BMI)

Another way of checking if you're overweight is by finding out your body mass index, or BMI. For any particular height there is a range of acceptable healthy weights. Calculating BMI is a way of describing the degree of a person's overweight.

$$BMI = \frac{weight \quad (in \; kilos)}{height^2 \quad (in \; metres)}$$

To work out your BMI you need to know your weight in kilos and your height in metres. Take your weight (in kilos) and divide it by the square of your height in metres (m^2).

Example:
For a person weighing 80 kilos and with a height of 1.68 metres, the calculation would be:

$$\frac{80 \; (kilos)}{1.68 \; (metres) \times 1.68 \; (metres)} = BMI \; 28.3$$

A person with a BMI over 25 is overweight.
A person with a BMI over 30 is obese.

What weight should you aim for?

In the past, you might have been given an 'ideal weight' to aim for. Nowadays, experts prefer to recommend a healthy **range** of weight for your height. They are also paying more attention to what people can realistically achieve. Why?

Research shows that many people manage to lose around 10-20 pounds, but few lose more than that. Fortunately, losing that amount of weight – even if it doesn't match people's 'ideal' weight –

still produces enormous benefits to health. Keeping the weight off in the longer term will greatly reduce the risk of disease. At *Shape-Up* we find that it is better to recommend aiming for a manageable weight loss and to emphasise keeping the weight off, rather than advising people to get down to their ideal weight which they may struggle to do and often fail to achieve.

If you're aiming to lose weight, a gradual weight loss of 1-2 pounds (0.5kg to 1kg) per week is recommended.

_MY TARGET WEIGHT

The right target for you may be just to maintain your current weight. Preventing further weight gain will improve long-term health and is in itself an achievement.

If you are aiming for weight loss, we recommend that you set a realistic target of between 5-10% of your present weight. You may think that you should lose more than this, but research shows that maintained weight loss of 5-10% can reduce the risk of heart disease, diabetes, stroke and some cancers. It is also enough to make people feel better overall.

My current weight _____ **Date** _____

My target weight in three months' time _____

Once you have achieved an initial modest weight loss and have kept the weight off for a time, you can always aim to lose another smaller amount of weight.

THE SHAPE-UP APPROACH TO WEIGHT MANAGEMENT

The *Shape-Up* approach holds that weight control is about learning. The programme not only teaches you what to eat for successful weight control, but also teaches you ways of putting that information into practice. **It is this focus on helping you change your behaviour that makes *Shape-Up* unique.**

But learning takes time. The habits that have led you to become overweight took time to develop. Changing them to healthier habits will also take time. *Shape-Up* teaches you how to use 'behaviour change techniques' to help you develop habits that will lead to weight loss.

"I still have to change my eating. So isn't *Shape-Up* just another diet?"

The use of behaviour change techniques is what makes *Shape-Up* different from typical 'diets'. On a typical diet, you are asked to change many things in one go – eat different foods, eat less, and throw yourself into exercise routines. For many people, each one of these changes is difficult enough. If you have to change everything at once, you may only manage for a while and then falter. This is the first problem with many diets: too many changes at once.

The best way to make changes is to concentrate on making one change at a time and make sure that it becomes a habit before you move on to the next change. So *Shape-Up* asks you to focus on changing one aspect of your lifestyle at a time, in the hope that you will be more likely to succeed in making a more permanent change towards a healthier lifestyle. Think about it: you're more likely to be successful with New Year's resolutions if you just set yourself one resolution and make that a habit before you move on to another resolution, rather than trying to achieve ten resolutions at the same time.

It's up to you how long you take to work through the suggested changes. There is little sense in putting a time limit on developing a lifetime's habits. The important thing is to try and do things in the order we suggest.

In *Shape-Up*, you are encouraged to try out different strategies, to value even small achievements, and to work on making lasting changes, rather than quick fixes that you can't keep up for long.

The *Shape-Up* 3-step plans

The *Shape-Up* programme contains two 3-step plans – one for healthy eating and one for physical activity. These give you a guide to which behaviours to change, and in which order. As you will see, completing each step in turn will set the stage for success in the later steps.

The *Shape-Up Healthy eating plan*
The three steps in the *Shape-Up Healthy eating plan*, shown in section 2, are:
- ☑ Step 1: Keep to a regular eating pattern
- ☑ Step 2: Get a healthier balance of foods
- ☑ Step 3: Cut down the quantity.

The *Shape-Up Activity plan*
The three steps in the *Shape-Up Activity plan*, shown in section 3, are:
- ☑ Step 1: Reduce the amount of time you spend sitting down
- ☑ Step 2: Increase lifestyle activity
- ☑ Step 3: Do more organised activity and sports.

A FEW NEW IDEAS ABOUT BEHAVIOUR CHANGE

In the *Shape-Up* programme we believe that, in order to make permanent changes to your eating and activity habits, you need three things:

- ☑ knowledge
- ☑ skills, and
- ☑ motivation for change.

Knowledge

You may already know what kind of changes you should aim for – for example to become more active, or to eat more fruit and vegetables – but often people are unsure of how to go about making the changes, or what opportunities there are to enable them to carry out their plans. *Shape-Up* will help you with this.

Skills

To be successful in changing your lifestyle, it will help if you develop some new skills. For example, it might help if you learn the skill of being more assertive when offered unnecessary food, or learn how to cope with low moods which can trigger 'comfort eating'. It's also helpful to keep a record or diary of what you eat and how much activity you do. Your diaries will help you learn what situations, moods or thoughts affect the kinds of food you eat and how much you eat, and what helps you stick to your plans and what undermines them.

"If only I had the willpower."

People sometimes talk about willpower as if it's a personal trait that people are born with – as if some people have it and some don't. Other people talk about willpower as if it is something that comes and goes of its own accord. So you might hear someone say, "I lost a lot of weight last year but I don't have the willpower this time." It is as if willpower is something magical: just wait for it to come and don't bother with the planning, organising and practising that are needed in order to achieve change.

Psychologists think that willpower isn't something you are born with or without; nor is it magical – it's a skill. Psychologists who specialise in behaviour change have spent decades looking at 'self-control' and they have shown that it is a skill that can be learned. *Shape-Up* shows you how to increase your self-control. By thinking ahead, setting yourself achievable targets and planning your routine around them, you will find that your confidence in your ability to change will grow and grow.

Motivation for change

So, how motivated are you to change?

Psychologists think of motivation as a combination of:

- the value **you** attach to the desired change, and
- your **confidence** that the desired change can be achieved.

How valuable is change for you?

This depends on how much you stand to gain by losing weight versus how much effort you have to make to get there (the costs).

The personal benefits of losing weight are often high – for example, feeling better, looking great or buying new clothes. But unfortunately the 'costs' of achieving change can also be high – for example, having to eat less of some of your favourite foods, creating problems for feeding other members of the family, or exercising when you don't feel like it. The changes now start to look more difficult, but being realistic is a great way to begin.

So, on the one hand it might be really important to you to have a lower weight but, on the other hand, it may also be important for you to have your favourite food when you feel like it. The conflict between your competing desires, and the accompanying frustration, will often lead people to seek out solutions that falsely promise both – lose weight and eat what you like (a marketing strategy that is now familiar to many people).

On the next page are examples of what some people think are the advantages and disadvantages of changing their lifestyle to control their weight. Have a look at these and then fill in the empty boxes at the bottom of page 17, giving your own advantages and disadvantages.

EXAMPLE

CHANGING MY LIFESTYLE

A Advantages	B Disadvantages
- More energy - Wider range of clothes available - Day-to-day tasks will be easier - Reduced risk of heart disease - Reduced risk of diabetes	- Increasing physical activity will be hard - Going without favourite foods is uncomfortable - Pressure from other people - Eating less than others in social situations - Frustration of constantly having to think about what I eat

NOT CHANGING MY LIFESTYLE

C Disadvantages	D Advantages
- Weight will continue to go up - Increased lethargy - Greater risk to health - More difficulty buying clothes that I want - More difficulty getting out and about	- Eat what I like - No need to exercise - Don't have to prepare special meals - Won't be given a hard time by others - Don't have to think about food all the time

Now fill in your own chart.

CHANGING MY LIFESTYLE

A Advantages	B Disadvantages

NOT CHANGING MY LIFESTYLE

C Disadvantages	D Advantages

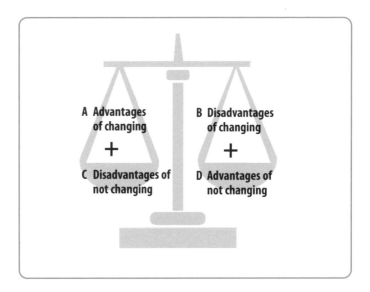

The chart you have just filled in on page 17 shows that motivation comes from the value you place on conflicting aspects of your lifestyle. When the things in sections A and C are more important to you than those in B and D, your own motivation for changing lifestyle will be high. But when B and D look more important than A and C, then change is going to be much less appealing.

How confident are you that you can change?
Your confidence in being able to change your behaviour is a combination of:

- ✓ past experience
- ✓ getting support from the right people
- ✓ getting positive feedback
- ✓ observing other people's attempts, and
- ✓ perhaps most importantly, practice!

Throughout the *Shape-Up* programme we show you ways of building up your confidence in your ability to make long-term changes to your lifestyle.

PAVING THE WAY

A 'cognitive behavioural' approach to change

The *Shape-Up* programme uses techniques from 'cognitive behavioural therapy' to help you change your lifestyle and control your weight. 'Cognitive' is to do with how you think and feel. 'Behavioural' is to do with how you behave, or what you actually do.

The cognitive behavioural approach helps you to identify patterns of thinking, feeling and behaving that are unhelpful to you. You will learn skills to help you change the thoughts and feelings that reduce your ability to change your behaviour. This in turn will increase your confidence and motivation to make and sustain permanent lifestyle changes.

Cognitive behavioural therapy is not a miracle cure, but experts consider it the most successful and comprehensive approach to managing weight.

Three techniques used in cognitive behavioural therapy are particularly useful for people who want to control their weight. These are:

- ✔ self-monitoring
- ✔ effective goal-setting, and
- ✔ rewarding your effort and achievements.

You will be using these techniques throughout the *Shape-Up* programme, so it's important that you begin by learning about each one.

SELF-MONITORING

This means keeping careful track of:

- ✔ what you eat
- ✔ how active you are, and
- ✔ your weight.

Monitoring what you eat

In *Shape-Up* we recommend that you monitor what you eat by keeping a food diary. We explain more about this on page 22.

Why monitor what you eat?

☑ Monitoring gives you a clear record of what you actually eat.

☑ It gives you accurate information about your eating patterns and draws your attention to things you might not have noticed before.

☑ It makes you more aware of what you eat, when you eat, and what causes you to eat more than planned.

☑ Later on, when you compare the way you eat with how you eat now, it will help you see how well you've done.

☑ Research on people who are trying to lose weight shows that people who self-monitor are more likely to succeed in losing weight and maintaining weight loss.

☑ Some people find it painful to own up to what they have eaten, but in facing up to reality, you may already have won half the battle.

If eating is a difficult area for you, the thought of writing down what you eat might seem daunting. Some people may feel a sense of shame over what they eat. This is what Pat said:

"For ages, I wouldn't co-operate with keeping a diary. When I finally did, I knew why. The broken biscuits had to go on the record. The olives and cubes of cheese while preparing meals had to go on the record. Finishing off the kids' plates had to go on the record. Snacks going round in the office had to go on the record. Glasses of wine in the evening had to go on the record. It was very traumatic to look at my total consumption. But in the end, I knew why I was overweight and I did something about it."

In a war, the first rule of combat is 'Know your enemy'. Although some people are daunted by the task of keeping a food diary every day, most come to see it as extremely useful in helping them control their weight:

"I found the food diaries very helpful for showing patterns. There are pre-menstrual times when I eat more, so I can think about managing that time a bit better."

"I welcomed the food diary because it's very easy for me to forget what I put in my mouth, and that's my greatest problem."

Monitoring how active you are

It can be difficult to keep a record of exactly how much activity you do, so we recommend that you use a pedometer to record the number of steps you do each day. We explain more about using a pedometer on page 78.

You will also need to keep a record of any episodes of physical activity of at least moderate intensity that you do for at least 10 minutes continuously – for example, brisk walking, cycling, moderate housework (such as scrubbing the floor), or gardening. 'Moderate intensity' means activity that makes you feel warm and breathe harder than usual.

Monitoring your weight

Why monitor your weight?

☑ It will increase your awareness of the effects of eating and activity on your weight.

☑ It will help you to see if the changes you are making to your lifestyle are having a positive effect on your weight.

☑ It acts as a reminder of the progress you are making while following the *Shape-Up* programme.

☑ If you are putting on weight, it allows you to review the changes you have made and focus on important areas for change sooner rather than later.

☑ It will help you to manage and maintain your weight loss in the future.

We also recommend that you keep a regular record of your weight. A gradual weight loss of 1 to 2 pounds (0.5kg to 1kg) per week is recommended. There may be some weeks when you lose more weight than this, or your weight may stay the same, or you may gain weight. There may be a number of different reasons for this, such as being unwell, or if there was a special occasion during the week. To avoid a feeling of failure, it is best to look at the changes in weight over a few weeks, rather than looking at one week in isolation. This will enable you to identify a **pattern** in your weight changes. It is also helpful to use any weight changes as a learning tool – and in the *Shape-Up* programme we show you some ideas for doing this.

How often should I weigh myself?

Regular weighing is an incentive for some people as it provides feedback on the progress they have made and spurs them on. For others, stepping onto the scales can be an upsetting event, which they may dread from week to week.

Since different people have different thoughts about weighing themselves, you need to consider how **you** feel about weighing yourself. We recommend no less than once a week and no more than once a day. Many people find daily weighing is good because it becomes a habit like brushing your teeth and stops being something to worry about. Of course, on any one day, things like water retention can affect weight, but if your weight goes up for several days in a row, you know that you need to take action.

STARTING TO MONITOR

To help you with self-monitoring, you can use the *Shape-Up Diary* (shown on the next page) and the *Shape-Up Weight change record* (shown on page 24). These will help you check your progress.

Shape-Up Diary

Start filling in your *Shape-Up Diary* now. There's a blank diary on page 145. (You'll be filling in lots of diaries, so we suggest you make some enlarged photocopies of the blank diary, or print out some copies of the blank diary from www.weightconcern.org.uk. Or you can just write up your diaries in a notebook, keeping to the outline of the *Shape-Up Diary*.)

At first, fill in the diary without trying to change your eating or activity habits too much. We recommend that you complete a *Shape-Up Diary* for seven consecutive days. Remember – it's important to chart weekdays and the weekend days.

Write down the times when you eat and all the food and drinks you have, and the activity you do, each day. Try to record as you go along rather than at the end of the day. People's memories are not like photographs, and inaccurate records will not help you. A sample filled-in diary is shown on the next page. **Please remember to keep your diary as you'll need to refer to it later.**

In this column, write down the actual time you eat or drink anything.

SHAPE-UP **DIARY**

Date 7 July

Day Saturday

FOOD AND DRINK

In this column, write down **everything** you eat or drink. This includes any milk in your tea, spreads on bread, oil used for cooking, crisps with drinks, and even biscuit crumbs! Every morsel and sip contribute to your daily intake.

What did you eat or drink?

Time	
8.15am	1 slice of wholemeal toast with butter and jam
	1 cup of tea with milk and 1 sugar
10am	jam doughnut
	1 cup of coffee with milk and 1 sugar
12.15pm	bowl of tinned tomato soup
	1 white roll and butter
	glass of orange juice
	packet of crisps
3pm	1 cup of tea with milk and 1 sugar
	Licked the bowl of pineapple upside-down cake
5.30pm	I was making for dessert
	Tested a spoonful of spaghetti bolognese I was making for dinner
6pm	2 pieces of bread and 1 glass of wine while cooking
6.15pm	Spaghetti bolognese, garlic bread and salad
7pm	1 glass of wine
	2 pieces of pineapple upside-down cake with custard
10pm	Glass of milk and 4 biscuits before bed

ACTIVITY

Did you do any physical activity of at least moderate intensity today that lasted at least 10 minutes? 'Moderate intensity' means activity that makes you feel warm and breathe harder than usual. ☑ YES ☐ NO How long did you do it for?

If YES … What did you do?

15 minutes each way = 30 minutes

Walked to and from the shops

In this section of the diary you can include any form of physical activity that makes you feel warm and breathe harder. This can include walking, cycling, moderate housework, gardening and DIY, as well as organised sport and exercise.

WEIGHT 14 stones 7 pounds

Pedometer count: 4,700

See page 78 for more about pedometers.

Using the *Shape-Up Weight change record*

You can use the *Shape-Up Weight change record* on page 150. Each day or each week, record your weight and fill in the rest of the record too.

Think about the changes that you have made to your lifestyle this week. These can be positive changes which have resulted in weight loss. Or you may need to think about reasons why your weight has gone up. You may want to look back at your **Shape-Up Diary** to help you answer the questions.

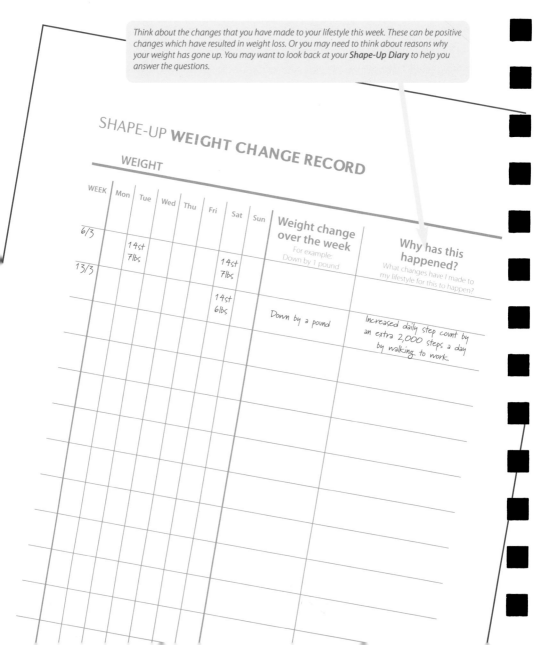

SHAPE-UP **WEIGHT CHANGE RECORD**

WEIGHT

WEEK	Mon	Tue	Wed	Thu	Fri	Sat	Sun	Weight change over the week For example: Down by 1 pound	Why has this happened? What changes have I made to my lifestyle for this to happen?
6/3		14st 7lbs							
13/3						14st 7lbs			
						14st 6lbs		Down by a pound	Increased daily step count by an extra 2,000 steps a day by walking to work

EFFECTIVE GOAL-SETTING

If you have participated in other weight loss programmes, you have probably been asked to set yourself a target weight. But you can't guarantee yourself a certain weight any more than you can guarantee a certain blood pressure or cholesterol reading. All you can do is to change what you do to help you move closer to your aim.

In *Shape-Up*, goals are set not in terms of **weight change** but in terms of **behaviour change**, that is, what you actually do. For example, a goal might be to eat breakfast, or to rehearse helpful thoughts in preparation for a tempting situation, or to walk the dog after dinner. Throughout the programme, you will be asked to set yourself 'sub-goals' (or steps) that lead towards a main goal. Look at the example in the box below.

Shape-Up goal – An example

Simon is a *Shape-Up* participant. He had always felt that the important goal for him was to cut down on the amount of fat in his food. Through keeping a food diary, he identified that his regular fat intake was coming from meat, from fat added to vegetables and to salads, from spreads on bread, and from milk in his tea. Simon enjoyed eating foods with a high fat content. He had previously tried to cut down but succeeded for only a short time: *"After eating 'bland meals' for about six weeks, I got really fed up and, I suppose, lapsed back to old habits."*

This time, however, Simon took **one small step at a time, starting with the most achievable**. He set himself a series of sub-goals, and tackled these one at a time. The process took several months, and this is the sequence that he remembers:

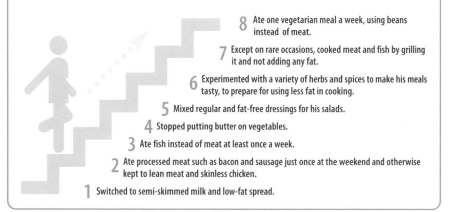

8 Ate one vegetarian meal a week, using beans instead of meat.

7 Except on rare occasions, cooked meat and fish by grilling it and not adding any fat.

6 Experimented with a variety of herbs and spices to make his meals tasty, to prepare for using less fat in cooking.

5 Mixed regular and fat-free dressings for his salads.

4 Stopped putting butter on vegetables.

3 Ate fish instead of meat at least once a week.

2 Ate processed meat such as bacon and sausage just once at the weekend and otherwise kept to lean meat and skinless chicken.

1 Switched to semi-skimmed milk and low-fat spread.

The principles of goal-setting
Try to make your goals 'SMART'.

for Specific
What we can learn from Kate:
"I had all the right intentions, but I was just a bit vague. I mean, to eat healthily was all very well, but it didn't commit me to anything specific. So I pinned myself down and specifically targeted eating more fruit. I ate fruit between meals to help me not overeat during mealtimes."

for Measurable
This means you need to be able to assess how far you have reached your goal. If you make a goal like 'I'll be more active', you won't know when you have succeeded. A measurable goal would be 'I'm going to spend 30 minutes a day either walking or swimming, at least twice a week.'

for Achievable
No more New Year resolutions that never get started, or falter after two weeks! Set realistic goals by aiming for small, specific steps and then work gradually towards your main goal. Carole did exactly that:
"I knew I needed to control my chocolate intake. I also knew that dropping it completely would be unrealistic. I went from two bars a day to one bar, and now I'm down to a low-calorie option every other day."

for Relevant
Don't try and change something just because everybody else says you should. If it isn't relevant to you, you're unlikely to stick with it. Brian said:
"For years my doctor went on about my weight. But my weight is stable and I feel fit because I'm on my feet a lot and I go to the gym and I don't have a family history of heart disease. My goal is to keep to my physically active lifestyle. It's not that I don't listen to what people say; I just don't think it would stick."

for Time-specific
Give yourself a realistic time frame for your goal. Changing eating behaviour – permanently – will take a while, because it means changing lifelong daily habits.

SHAPE-**UP** section 1

An example of a SMART goal

Here's another example of a SMART goal, and the steps needed in order to reach that goal.

My goal is:

To eat a total of five portions of fruit and vegetables every day.

I will take the following steps:

1. To buy more fruit and fewer biscuits when I shop and to take a piece of fruit to work each day.
2. To drink a small glass of pure fruit juice with breakfast every day.
3. To start evening meals with a small salad.
4. To try one new recipe every week, using different kinds of fruit and vegetables – fresh, frozen, canned or dried.
5. To have some dried fruits after my meal instead of a dessert.

_SMART goals

On the left below are some common responses people give when they are asked to set a goal. They reflect vague hopes or good intentions. On the right they are translated into SMART goals.

Vague goals	SMART goals
"I won't eat any more chocolate."	*"I'll ring Mum tonight and ask her to bring me something else other than chocolate when she next comes."*
"I'm going to get really fit in the new year."	*"I'll go swimming after work every Monday and review it after two months."*
"I'll eat more healthily in the next few months."	*"I'll eat a piece of fruit each day and if I succeed for two weeks, I'll increase it to two."*
"I'll make myself stick to my gym routine somehow."	*"Next time I don't feel like going to the gym, I'll remind myself at least once that I always feel better after going."*

Now try and translate the next four vague goals into SMART goals:

Vague goals	SMART goals
"I'm going on a health kick for a bit."	

Vague goals	SMART goals
"I'm going to lose a stone in the next month."	
"My wife nags me about my weight. I'll do what I can when I come back from my trip."	
"I'm avoiding all fatty foods."	

Goal-planning exercise

Throughout the *Shape-Up* programme you will be invited to set yourself goals. To further strengthen your habit of setting SMART goals, think of one small goal for yourself, plan it in as much detail as possible and then fill in the *Shape-Up Goalsheet* on the next page. There are examples to show what is meant for each section but please write down what is relevant to you.

Later on in the *Shape-Up* programme you'll be asked to choose two or three 'SMART' goals to start with. Once you've decided on each goal, this is what you'll need to do:

- Complete a *Shape-Up Goalsheet* for the goal (see page 152).
- Enter the goal in your *Shape-Up Log* on page 154.
- Review your goals periodically to see how you've got on, and rate your success in your *Shape-Up Log*.
- Maintain what you have achieved and think about setting the next goal to build towards your overall aim.

SHAPE-UP GOALSHEET

Remember to make your goals:
Specific **M**easurable **A**chievable **R**elevant **T**ime-Specific

Examples:
- To change to skimmed milk.
- To eat five portions of fruit and vegetables a day.
- To eat breakfast every day.

MY GOAL IS:

_____
_____
_____
_____

The review date might be, for example, a week after you set yourself the goal.

Review date:

Today's date:

Enter your goal and the date into your *Shape-Up Log* on page 154.

I will take the following steps:

Examples:
- Change my order with the milkman.
- Keep a fruit bowl at work.
- Set my alarm half an hour early.

1 _____

2 _____

Examples: *Going out in the evening, work schedule, partner pushing food on me. I'll overcome these by: rehearsing saying no, warning partner ahead of time.*

3 _____

4 _____

I have thought about and/or planned for the following:

Examples: *My friend at work, my sister. They could: praise me each time I succeed; not comment and leave it to me; ask me how I've done at the end of the week.*

☐ Things that could get in my way and how I will overcome them
☐ People who might be able to help
☐ Time I'm going to give it
☐ How and when I'm going to review my goal
☐ How I will reward myself if I succeed.

Example: *Review my diary at the end of two weeks.*

Write about the outcome in your *Shape-Up Log* (see page 154).

Examples: *The next CD in a series, see a film, a long soak in the bath uninterrupted by family. (See the next page for more about rewards.)*

REWARDS

Rewards make it more likely that you will achieve your goals. We all use rewards in everyday life to make us do things – for example promising ourselves that we can have a cup of tea once we've done the washing up.

For every goal that you set during *Shape-Up*, you should plan to receive a reward for when you achieve it. Rewards should not be food or drink, and they need not be expensive. Below are some suggestions from other *Shape-Up* participants:

- ✔ Time to yourself
- ✔ A small gift voucher that can be saved up for a bigger treat
- ✔ A new CD
- ✔ A new item of make-up
- ✔ A magazine
- ✔ A day out with a friend
- ✔ A trip to the cinema or theatre or to an art gallery
- ✔ Someone else doing the washing up while you're at the gym
- ✔ A long soak in the bath without interruptions
- ✔ A plant or a bunch of flowers
- ✔ A star on your calendar or in your diary.

✎_How I will reward myself for reaching my goals
Add your own ideas here.

_____
_____
_____
_____

You've now learned about self-monitoring, effective goal-setting and rewarding your efforts and achievements. So you're now ready to move on to another section. Go to either section 2 *The Shape-Up Healthy eating plan*, or section 3 *Getting more active*.

THE SHAPE-UP
HEALTHY
EATING PLAN

2

THE SHAPE-UP
HEALTHY
EATING PLAN

THIS SECTION AIMS TO:

offer you the current scientific
information about food and nutrition,
and guide you through a 3-step plan
that will help you control your weight.

2

It will help you to:

- ☑ increase your understanding of the link between nutrition, health and weight

- ☑ keep to a regular eating pattern

- ☑ get a healthier balance of foods, and

- ☑ gradually adjust the quantity of food you eat.

This section contains the *Shape-Up 3-step Healthy eating plan*. The three steps are shown below. It's important to work through these steps in this order. We suggest that you spend a few weeks on each step – making small changes gradually. Once you feel that a step has become part of your life, move on to the next one.

If you need to lose weight, the bottom line is that you'll need to eat fewer calories. Cutting down the **quantity** of food you eat is usually the most difficult change to make, yet it is often suggested at the beginning of a weight loss programme. In *Shape-Up*, we suggest you do this last. This is because, if you put a few things in place first, you are more likely to succeed in cutting down.

The Shape-Up 3-step Healthy eating plan

Step 1 Keep to a regular eating pattern.

Step 2 Get a healthier balance of foods.

Step 3 Cut down the quantity.

SHAPE-UP **STEP 1**
KEEP TO A REGULAR EATING PATTERN

What happens in Step 1?
In Step 1 you will look at:

- ✔ your current eating pattern
- ✔ why it's important to keep to a regular eating pattern, and
- ✔ the importance of eating breakfast.

LOOKING AT YOUR CURRENT EATING PATTERN

Keeping to a regular eating pattern is the foundation on which you can build other healthy eating habits.

Following the same eating pattern every day is an essential first step in breaking free from the vicious cycle of dieting and overeating. Before you go any further, take a look at what your eating pattern is like at the moment.

✎_What's my eating pattern?
Below is a list of different eating patterns. Put a tick next to the pattern which applies to you. (You can tick more than one.)

- ☐ *1* I try to restrict the overall amount of food I eat. If I feel I have eaten my daily quota of calories in the morning, I eat nothing for the rest of the day until I'm starving and then have a huge meal before bedtime.
- ☐ *2* I try to eat only when I'm hungry. So I end up eating at different times every day.
- ☐ *3* I eat at roughly the same times each day.
- ☐ *4* I try to put off eating for as long as possible in the day – for example, not starting to eat until late in the day – but then I eat more or less constantly until I go to bed.
- ☐ *5* I do nearly all of the above in rotation.
- ☐ *6* I have eating habits that defy any patterning.
- ☐ *7* I always intend to eat regularly, but am often unable to because of having to work late or unexpected meetings.

If you already follow the same eating pattern from day to day –
that's if you have ticked number 3 – all the better! You may want to
go straight to *Shape-Up* Step 2 on page 40. If not, carry on reading.

WHY IT'S IMPORTANT TO KEEP TO A REGULAR EATING PATTERN

What does 'a regular eating pattern' mean?
Whether you like to eat two or five times a day, the important thing is
to stick to a pattern and try to eat at roughly the same times each day.

Why is it important?
Keeping the same pattern of meals from day to day will help to
ensure that you don't get too hungry and that your body can learn
when your next meal will be due.

Following the same eating pattern is a very important part of
dealing with overeating. However, if you haven't eaten like this for
some time, or if you never have, it will require effort. Here are some
of the reasons people give for not following the same eating pattern
from day to day:

*"I tend to give in and eat when I really want to, so it must help if I skip the
calories when I don't have the urge to eat."* Jackie

*"My shift changes every couple of weeks, so eating at the same times is
out of the question."* Jo

Why keep to the same eating pattern?
It means that:
- ✓ you'll find it easier to stop eating at the end of your meal
- ✓ you'll find that you're ready to eat at mealtimes
- ✓ you'll be less likely to think about food in between meals, and
- ✓ you won't need to resort to high fat snacks because of missed
  meals.

It will also help you have:
- ✓ a more stable blood sugar
- ✓ improved concentration and reduced fatigue

☑ greater and more consistent energy levels, and

☑ a lower blood cholesterol level.

Getting started

To start with, concentrate mainly on *when* you eat rather than *what* you eat.

Sometimes it's tempting to run away with a good idea. For example, you might have thought of changing the times you eat, eating more healthy foods, and eating a smaller quantity all at once. DON'T! We have all come up with the perfect plan which we then abandon after two days. Making too many changes all at once increases your chance of not changing anything at all.

For the moment, concentrate on eating a variety of foods which you feel 'at home' with, but keep to the same pattern each day.

Using your *Shape-Up Diary*

Keeping a *Shape-Up Diary* (see page 23) can help you to find out if you keep to the same eating pattern each day. It will also help you to identify at which times you find it difficult to keep to the same eating pattern each day, and the reasons why you find it difficult.

A WORD ABOUT BREAKFAST

Why is breakfast important?

Breakfast is important for several reasons:

- First thing in the morning, the body is low on energy reserves and needs fuel (from food) to get going.
- Research has shown that people who don't eat breakfast miss out on many vital nutrients such as calcium and B vitamins. And if you don't have breakfast, it's difficult to get enough of these nutrients during the rest of the day.
- Eating breakfast can improve memory and ability to retain information.
- Research has shown that adults who skip breakfast tend to have higher cholesterol levels, and so may be at a greater risk of developing heart disease.
- Research shows that adults who eat breakfast are less likely to be overweight than those who skip breakfast.

People who eat breakfast regularly – on at least four or more days a week – are more likely to be successful at maintaining weight loss.

Breakfast ideas

- ✓ Breakfast cereal with semi-skimmed or skimmed milk. Avoid sugar-coated cereals and go for high-fibre versions – for example, bran-based cereals, oats or porridge, weetabix, muesli or bran flakes.
- ✓ Toast with low fat spread, marmite, jam, marmalade, honey, pure fruit spread, or a mashed banana.
- ✓ For variety, try a toasted bagel or muffin, or a couple of crumpets with your choice of topping.
- ✓ Porridge made with semi-skimmed or skimmed milk.
- ✓ Low fat yogurt with a selection of fresh or dried fruit, such as raisins, banana and apple. You could also add a few nuts for extra flavour and texture.
- ✓ A bowl of mixed fresh fruit.
- ✓ Toast with baked beans, tinned tomatoes or grilled mushrooms.
- ✓ Toast with scrambled or poached eggs.
- ✓ Try cereal bars if you have to have breakfast on the move. You'll need to check the food labels to make sure that they are not too high in fat or sugar. (See page 95 in section 4 for more information on food labels.)

Healthy eating tips for breakfast

- ✓ Try using wholemeal or granary bread for toast, rather than white bread.
- ✓ Try having your toast without spread, especially when you have a moist topping such as beans or eggs.

GOAL

In this section we have talked about why keeping to a regular eating pattern and eating breakfast are so important. Now you can start setting yourself some goals.

Look back to your *Shape-Up Diary* (or just think back to a day last week) and decide how you can organise things so that you can eat at about the same times each day. Or, if you don't already have breakfast regularly, you might want to concentrate on having breakfast regularly. Here are some examples of SMART goals:

- ✓ 'I will eat breakfast on at least three weekday mornings this week.'
- ✓ 'I will make or buy a healthy sandwich for lunchtime, on at least four days over the next week.'
- ✓ 'I will eat my evening meal at roughly the same time every day, on every weekday for the next month.'
- ✓ 'On every morning for the next week I will plan at what time I'm going to eat my two allotted healthy snacks for the day.'

Fill in a *Shape-Up Goalsheet* (see page 152) and then write your goal in the *Shape-Up Log* on page 154.

Once you've learned the habit of eating regularly, it's time to move on to Step 2.

SHAPE-UP **STEP 2**
GET A HEALTHIER BALANCE OF FOODS

What happens in Step 2?
In Step 2 you will look at changing the **balance** of foods you eat, in order to achieve a healthier diet.

What are you aiming for?
You're aiming to achieve the balance of different types of foods as shown in the *Balance of Good Health* below.

The Balance of Good Health

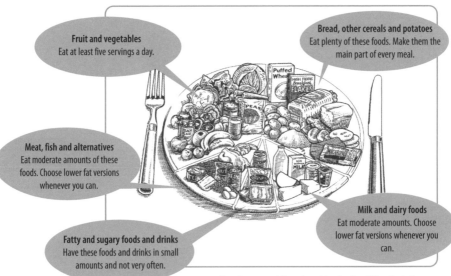

Based on material produced by the Food Standards Agency.

The *Balance of Good Health* plate above shows the types and proportion of foods you need to eat to achieve a well-balanced and healthy diet. It is based on the following five food groups:

- Bread, other cereals and potatoes
- Fruit and vegetables
- Meat, fish and alternatives
- Milk and dairy foods
- Fatty and sugary foods.

As you can see, although healthy eating will mean eating more of certain foods and less of others, you don't have to give up any single food or drink completely. A healthy eating plan includes the correct balance of foods from the four main food groups every day – the first four listed above – plus a small allowance for extras from the 'fatty and sugary foods' group.

Remember though, that all foods and drinks, and snacks as well as meals, count towards the balance of what you eat. You don't have to include food choices from all five food groups at every meal. Just use the plate as a guide to how much the different foods should contribute to your total food intake over a day or a week.

Eating towards the proportions shown on the *Balance of Good Health* plate will make sure you get the right balance of vitamins and minerals as well as starch and fibre, while keeping your fat and sugar intake down. This will not only help you keep your weight down, but also reduce your risk of heart disease, some cancers, and dental problems, as well as keeping your bowels healthy.

Choose mainly from the healthier foods that you enjoy. But it's fine to have a treat now and again.

The basic message is …

☑ Choose most of your foods from:
   – the 'bread, other cereals and potatoes' group, and
   – the 'fruit and vegetables' group.

☑ Have smaller amounts from:
   – the 'meat, fish, and alternatives' group, and
   – the 'milk and dairy foods' group
   and choose lower-fat versions of these whenever you can.

☑ Have tiny amounts of 'fatty and sugary foods'.

☑ Choose options that are lower in salt whenever you can.

BREAD, OTHER CEREALS AND POTATOES

Eat plenty of these foods. Make them the main part of every meal.

Foods in this food group include: bread, potatoes, rice, pasta, noodles, oats, crackers, breakfast cereals, couscous, maize, cornmeal, yams and chapattis.

What do these foods contain?

These foods contain:

- **Starchy carbohydrate**, which provides energy.
- **Insoluble fibre** – especially in wholegrain varieties. This is important for healthy bowels.
- **Soluble fibre** – in oats. This can help reduce blood cholesterol levels and improve blood sugar levels.
- **Vitamins**, especially vitamin B which is essential for growth and a healthy nervous system.
- **Minerals**, especially calcium which is important for strong teeth and bones, and iron which is important for making healthy red blood cells.

What are carbohydrates?

Carbohydrates are the body's main source of energy. Carbohydrates are divided into refined and unrefined carbohydrates.

Refined carbohydrates are foods that have been altered by processing, so that the fibre-containing parts (the bran and the germ) have been removed. Examples of refined carbohydrates are white bread, sugary cereals, and pasta and noodles made from white flour.

Unrefined carbohydrates consist of the whole grain (the bran and the germ) and so are higher in fibre than unrefined sources. These foods make you feel fuller for longer. Examples include wholegrain rice, wholemeal bread and porridge oats.

Which foods to choose – Making healthier choices

- ☑ Choose wholegrain bread such as wholemeal or granary bread more often than white varieties.
- ☑ Eat more wholemeal pasta instead of white pasta.
- ☑ Eat more brown rice instead of white rice.
- ☑ Eat wholegrain breakfast cereals such as porridge, weetabix or bran flakes more often than lower fibre cereals such as cornflakes or sugar-coated or honey-coated varieties.
- ☑ Use some wholemeal flour in cooking.
- ☑ Eat new potatoes in their skins.
- ☑ Use more wholewheat crackers, rye crackers and crispbreads.
- ☑ If you make bread products such as bread rolls or chapattis, use wholemeal flour. You may find it more acceptable to use half wholemeal and half white flour to start with.

What is the 'glycaemic index' of foods?

Carbohydrates are not all equal. They are broken down and absorbed by the body at different rates and have different effects on your blood sugar level. This is also known as the *glycaemic index* (GI) of a food.

Foods with a *high glycaemic index* – high-GI foods – are broken down more quickly and cause a rapid rise in blood sugar. Examples of high-GI foods are white bread, sugar, sweets, sugary drinks and potatoes.

Foods with a *low glycaemic index* – low-GI foods – are broken down more slowly and cause a slower rise in blood sugar. Examples of low-GI foods are pasta, sweet potatoes, basmati rice, pulses, beans, nuts, lentils, wholegrain cereals, vegetables and fruit (such as apples, apricots, peaches and pears).

Choosing low-GI foods

Choosing foods with a lower glycaemic index can help to keep your blood sugar levels more stable. This is particularly beneficial for people with diabetes. Everyone can probably benefit from including more low-GI foods in their diet, as this may reduce the risk of developing heart disease or diabetes. But other foods can be part of healthy eating too. (Being too rigid can make it harder to stick to your healthy eating plan.)

Aim to include the following low-GI foods into your diet:
- pasta
- wholegrain such as wholegrain breakfast cereals, granary bread, and crackers with grains
- sweet potatoes, yam
- basmati rice
- pulses, such as lentils, beans and chickpeas
- nuts
- fruits, such as apples, apricots, peaches, pears, plums, bananas, cherries and grapefruit
- vegetables, such as sweetcorn, carrots and peas.

FRUIT AND VEGETABLES

Eat at least 5 servings of fruit and vegetables a day.

Choose from fresh, frozen, or canned fruit and vegetables. And don't forget fruit juice* and occasionally some dried fruit. Add some to each meal or snack, from breakfast to bedtime. It's important to have as wide a variety as possible of different fruits and vegetables. (See page 63 for information on how much counts as one serving.)

---

* Only one of the five portions a day should be fruit juice. (Remember that many fruit juices are a concentrated source of natural sugar, so they are high in calories.)

What do these foods contain?

Fruit and vegetables provide:

- **Antioxidant vitamins C, E and beta-carotene** which may help protect you against heart disease and certain types of cancer.
  Good sources of vitamin C: oranges, blackcurrants, green and red peppers, strawberries, grapefruit, kiwi fruit, cabbage, peas, tomato juice, fresh parsley, pineapple.
  Good sources of vitamin E: spinach, broccoli, Brussels sprouts, blackberries, watercress.
  Good sources of beta-carotene: carrots, spinach, red peppers, mango, spring greens, cabbage, broccoli, tomatoes, apricots, sweet potatoes, cantaloupe melon.
- **B vitamins**, especially folic acid (particularly in green leafy vegetables) which is essential for the development of red blood cells.
- **Soluble fibre and some carbohydrate**.

Fruit and vegetables are also naturally low in fat. This makes them an excellent snack food or addition to any meal.

How to eat more fruit and vegetables

- ☑ Add chopped fresh or dried fruit to breakfast cereal.
- ☑ Have a bowl of fresh fruit salad for breakfast.
- ☑ Have fruit as a between-meal snack.
- ☑ Have fruit rather than other snacks and desserts.
- ☑ Have a bowl of salad with a meal.
- ☑ Have a vegetable-based meal instead of a meat-based one.
- ☑ Eat a bowl of home-made vegetable soup.
- ☑ Experiment and treat yourself to more exotic fruits such as kiwi or mango, instead of sweets.
- ☑ Add root vegetables such as carrots, leeks and parsnips to casseroles, stews or soups, or eat them as part of a meal.
- ☑ Add chopped vegetables such as onions, peppers, courgettes, sweetcorn and mushrooms to your meals.
- ☑ If you have a ready-made meal, add extra vegetables or salad to it.

If the thought of chopping and preparing fruit and vegetables puts you off, try these ideas:

- ☑ Use frozen vegetables or fruit. Frozen fruits and vegetables can be higher in nutrients than fresh, as they are frozen straight away. They are also handy to keep in the freezer and reduce wastage as you can take just the amount you need.
- ☑ Thaw some frozen berries and add them to breakfast cereals, yogurts or other desserts.

MEAT, FISH AND ALTERNATIVES

Eat moderate amounts of these foods. Choose lower fat versions whenever you can.

This group includes meat, fish, and 'alternatives' such as eggs, nuts and nut butter, pulses such as peas, beans and lentils, seeds, quorn and tofu.

Lower fat choices from this food group include: lean meat, chicken, turkey, fish, eggs, tofu, quorn, beans and lentils.

Aim to have fish twice a week, including oily fish once a week. Examples of oily fish include fresh or tinned mackerel, salmon, pilchards, herring, sardines and fresh tuna steaks. Tinned tuna does not count as oily fish. Oily fish helps stop blood clotting and protects against coronary heart disease and stroke.

Important information about oily fish

The Food Standards Agency has recommended a maximum amount of oily fish that should be eaten. Above these amounts there are health concerns regarding the level of toxins in the fish. The maximum amounts are given below. A portion of oily fish is defined as 140g.

- Men, boys and women past childbearing age can eat up to 4 portions of oily fish a week.
- Girls, women of childbearing age, pregnant women and breastfeeding women can eat up to 2 portions of oily fish a week.
- Pregnant women, women intending to become pregnant, and children should avoid eating swordfish, shark or marlin, and should have no more than two tuna steaks or four cans of tuna a week, due to toxin levels.

If you eat fish regularly, choosing from a wider variety of fish can help reduce the environmental impact. You might also like to make sure you are buying fish which is being sustainably sourced. Be careful not to eat too much crab, sea bream, sea bass, turbot, halibut and rock salmon, as these fish may also contain toxins.

Fish contains vitamin A. If you take additional vitamin supplements or fish oil, you may need to check that you are not having more than your daily maximum recommended amount of vitamin A. For more details, see www.eatwell.gov.uk.

What do meat, fish and alternatives contain?

- **Protein** – for new tissue formation, and growth and repair of damaged tissues.
- **Iron** – for healthy red blood cells.
- **B vitamins** – especially B_{12}, which helps with the development of red blood cells and in maintaining a healthy nervous system.
- **Zinc** – important for the immune system.
- **Magnesium** – an essential component of all cells.
- **Soluble fibre** – Beans, lentils and peas are also rich in soluble fibre. This helps to reduce blood cholesterol levels and improve blood sugar levels.

Which foods to choose – How to eat enough from this food group

☑ Include one serving of meat or fish or an alternative at lunch, and one at dinner. (See page 64 for information on serving sizes.)

☑ Use meat or fish as a flavouring – for example in strips or small chunks in casseroles or stir-fry dishes – rather than having large chunks.

☑ Alternatives to meat include:
- beans (on toast or with a jacket potato)
- eggs (for example, boiled and sliced in a sandwich, or scrambled or poached on toast)
- nut roast
- beany casserole
- peanut butter (on crackers)
- mackerel, pilchards or tuna mashed with cottage cheese or low fat cream cheese to make a pâté
- tofu or quorn in a casserole or stir-fry
- soya mince in a bolognese sauce
- dhals
- pulses in curries – for example chickpeas or lentils
- soups containing pulses, such as pearl barley, lentils or butter beans
- hummous in a sandwich with salad, or as a dip for raw vegetables. (Watch out for the fat content of hummous if shop-bought; try to buy lower fat varieties where possible.)

Which foods to choose – Making healthier choices

It is important that you eat adequate amounts from the 'meat, fish and alternatives' food group to ensure that you are getting enough protein. But foods which are high in protein may also be high in fat, so choose lower fat alternatives wherever possible. Below are some examples of healthier alternatives to choose.

Fish

☑ Fish canned in water or brine is a lower fat alternative to fish canned in oil. (Water is better, as brine contains a lot of salt.)

☑ Soak salted fish overnight and boil in plenty of water before cooking. Eat salted fish only occasionally as it will still contain a lot of salt even if it has been soaked and boiled.

Meat

- Buy the leanest cuts of meat you can afford, or trim off the fat and keep portions small (about 100g or 3.5 ounces).
- Avoid processed meat products such as burgers, sausages, pies and meat pâtés if possible.
- Choose meats with as little visible fat in the meat as possible.
- Beef has less fat than lamb. Chicken has less fat than duck or goose.
- Choose breast of chicken or poultry rather than legs or wings (ie the white meat rather than dark meat), and remove the skin.

Alternatives (for example pulses, eggs, tofu, soya)

- If you eat meat, try to have at least two meat-free meals a week, to reduce the overall amount of fat you eat.
- If you don't eat meat, you are in a good position to be eating healthily, as long as you plan your diet carefully. Don't rely on quick-to-prepare foods such as cheese or processed vegetarian sausages or burgers as these can contain a lot of fat. Try to include a mixture of alternatives to meat to ensure you get all the goodness that your body needs, while not having too much fat.
- Choose pulses such as beans, lentils, chickpeas and peas more often. They have lots of nutritional benefits: they are high in soluble fibre, they lower blood cholesterol levels, are a good source of protein and are low fat. Pulses are available canned. They can be easily added to casseroles, soups, salads and mince dishes. When buying them in cans it's preferable to choose ones with no sugar or salt added.
- Choose soya products (such as tofu), or quorn, or nuts and seeds for other meat-free meals.
- Use beans or tofu instead of meat for casseroles and stir-fries.
- Combine meat alternatives with grains (bread, pasta, rice, cereals) to provide an excellent source of protein.

MILK AND DAIRY FOODS

Eat moderate amounts. Choose lower fat versions whenever you can.

Foods from this group include milk, cheese, yogurt and fromage frais.

Milk and dairy foods are necessary to improve bone and dental health and to help prevent osteoporosis (brittle bones). One in three women and one in ten men are at risk of osteoporosis.

What do these foods contain?

- **Calcium** – Generally, low fat products in this group contain more rather than less calcium.
- **Protein** – Milk and dairy foods contain all the essential amino acids (protein building blocks) in the correct proportions.
- **Vitamin B_{12}** – an essential nutrient for the development of healthy cells, functioning of the nervous system and for helping the body process protein and fat into a useable source of energy.
- **Vitamin A** – essential for maintaining healthy skin and hair, and for eyesight.
- **Vitamin D** – essential for bone and tooth development and for helping the body to absorb calcium.

Which foods to choose – How to eat enough from this food group

- ✓ Have a glass of milk to drink.
- ✓ Have a pot of low fat yogurt as a dessert or snack.
- ✓ Use natural yogurt or fromage frais as the base of a dip for vegetable sticks.

☑ Add small amounts of low fat cheeses to salads, sandwiches or pizzas.

Which foods to choose – Making healthier choices

☑ Use semi-skimmed or skimmed milk instead of full fat milk.

☑ Use low fat or reduced fat spreading cheese instead of full fat versions.

☑ Eat low fat cottage cheese instead of other cheeses.

☑ Eat medium fat cheese (such as edam, gouda, feta, camembert or reduced fat cheddar), rather than full fat cheese (such as cheddar, gorgonzola or stilton).

☑ Eat low fat versions of yogurt, fromage frais, quark and curd cheese instead of cream or crème fraîche. Half fat crème fraîche contains less fat than the regular variety, but use it sparingly as it is still fairly high in fat.

☑ Eat foods that contain only low or medium fat dairy products – for example low fat custard, or soups made with skimmed milk, rather than full fat versions.

☑ Eat hard cheeses such as cheddar or stilton less than once a week.

☑ Full fat dairy products, such as condensed and evaporated milk, are high in fat and should be avoided where possible.

☑ Mix plain low fat yogurt with fruit yogurt to reduce fat and sugar.

If you don't eat milk and dairy foods, you need to get alternative sources of calcium. The following foods contain reasonable amounts of calcium:

- calcium-fortified soya milk
- bread
- tinned sardines (with the bones)
- tinned salmon (with the bones)
- sesame seeds
- tahini paste (made from sesame seeds)
- figs
- almonds
- shelled prawns
- broccoli
- cauliflower
- spinach
- tofu
- red kidney beans.

FATTY AND SUGARY FOODS

Eat these foods in small amounts and not too often.

This food group includes:
- fats such as butter, margarine, spreading fats, low fat spread, oils, ghee, lard, mayonnaise, oily salad dressing, gravy and savoury sauces, and
- other fatty and sugary foods such as sugar, jam, honey, biscuits, cakes, puddings, chocolate, sweets, pastries, ice cream, cream, pork pies, sausage rolls, crisps and other savoury snacks.

What do these foods contain?

Fat in the diet is a major problem as far as heart disease, high blood cholesterol and weight gain are concerned. Some fat is essential, but too much of it can affect your health. This is especially true of saturated fats.

Unlike starchy carbohydrates (such as bread, cereals and potatoes), **sugar** contains only empty calories with no vitamins, minerals or fibre for your health. Cravings for sweet foods are often caused by low blood sugar. Responding by eating a lot of sugary foods causes a rapid rise in blood sugar and energy which is followed by a rapid drop to a level even lower than the original low. This is often accompanied by a low mood. If this happens it is better to satisfy cravings with a starchy carbohydrate (such as bread) or fruit (such as a banana) which will give you a more stable, prolonged release of energy.

Which foods to choose – Making healthier choices
Fats
Choose monounsaturated or polyunsaturated oils and spreads (such as olive, rapeseed, sunflower or safflower oils), instead of saturated fats like butter or palm oil.

Sugar and sweeteners
- ☑ Use sugar-free desserts and whips.
- ☑ Choose canned fruit in juice instead of syrup.
- ☑ Choose sugar-free jellies.
- ☑ Choose reduced fat, reduced sugar rice pudding.
- ☑ Choose fat-free ice cream.
- ☑ Try reduced sugar or pure fruit spreads, jams and preserves.

Sweeteners
Sweeteners are calorie-free sugar substitutes and are available in different types and different forms – tablets, granulated and liquid.

The government's Committee on Toxicity has set what it calls an 'Acceptable Daily Intake', abbreviated as ADI. The ADI for an adult weighing nine and a half stones (60kg) is 300mg of saccharin, 540mg of acesulfame and 2,400mg of aspartame. If you use sweeteners, use a variety of different types to minimise the risk of exceeding the ADI.

How to eat less fatty and sugary foods
Fats
- ☑ If you use butter or full fat margarine, use less. Sometimes we use it through habit and you can soon get used to not having it at all.
- ☑ Use a low fat spread instead of a full fat one or butter. Make sure you use it sparingly as it still contains a lot of fat.
- ☑ If you're using a moist sandwich filling, don't use any spreading fats.
- ☑ Use a minimum of fat or oil in cooking. (Grill, bake, dry roast, stew, pressure cook, casserole, microwave, boil, poach or steam.)
- ☑ It's easier to control the amount of oil you use in cooking if you measure it with a spoon rather than just pouring it into the pan. Or use a spray oil instead.

- ☑ Drain off any excess fat or oil after cooking. After cooking fried foods, put them briefly on a paper towel, to absorb some of the oil.
- ☑ Eat fewer chips and roast potatoes and have them less often.
- ☑ If you do have chips, use oven chips rather than frying chips. (If you are making chips yourself, cut them thick and straight and fry them in an oil that is high in unsaturates, such as sunflower or rapeseed oil. Change the oil frequently.) Or, try oven-baked potato wedges instead.
- ☑ Eat baked potatoes without any butter or margarine.
- ☑ Use fat-free dressings.
- ☑ Eat salad without a dressing. Use lemon juice and pepper instead. Or make salad dressings with natural yogurt, fromage frais, herbs, spices, tomato juice, vinegar or lemon juice rather than using oil, mayonnaise or salad cream.
- ☑ Eat cooked vegetables without added butter or margarine.
- ☑ Ghee is very high in fat and should be kept to a minimum.
- ☑ Try not to add fat to chapattis, either before or after cooking.
- ☑ Oven-baked tandoori dishes are lower in added fat than fried dishes.
- ☑ Avoid adding coconut milk or cream to dishes, as these are high in fat and calories. Reduced fat coconut milk is available, but it is still high in fat so use it sparingly.
- ☑ Avoid adding condensed milk to drinks or dishes, as it is high in fat.
- ☑ Use a fat replacer for some baking – for example Lighter Bake prune purée (available in supermarkets).

Other fatty and sugary foods
- ☑ Instead of snacks like crisps, pakora, samosa, chocolate, chevda, sev, cakes, sweet pastries, biscuits and croissants, try:
    - grain bread, currant buns, scones, crumpets or fruitbreads (without added spread)
    - wholegrain bread with a low fat dip such as yogurt with cucumber
    - a piece of fruit or raw vegetable
    - plain popcorn, sprinkled with paprika
    - breadsticks, wholegrain crackers, crispbreads or rice cakes.

- ☑ Choose pizza with more vegetables and less cheese or meat topping.
- ☑ Avoid processed meat products such as pies and sausages.
- ☑ Non-fried chapattis and rotis are a good low fat alternative to fried breads such as parathas, naan, puries and bhaturas.
- ☑ Avoid rich sauces and gravies.
- ☑ Instead of butter, margarine and cream, have fromage frais or yogurt.
- ☑ Eat less creamy sauce on pasta, noodles or rice. Choose vegetable-based sauces – such as a tomato sauce – instead.
- ☑ Eat lightly boiled or steamed or baked vegetables more often than vegetables fried or served in creamy sauces.
- ☑ Choose low fat ice cream or frozen yogurt rather than full fat ice cream.
- ☑ Choose wholegrain cereals rather than those coated with sugar or honey.
- ☑ Gradually cut down the amount of sugar you add to cereal, or use calorie-free artificial sweeteners instead.
- ☑ Gradually reduce the amount of sugar you add when cooking.
- ☑ Stew fruit in fruit juice or half juice and half water, rather than sugar syrup.
- ☑ Use fruit tinned in natural juice rather than in syrup.
- ☑ Eat natural yogurt, diet yogurt or low fat yogurt instead of other yogurts. (But check how much sugar the yogurt contains.)
- ☑ Instead of sponge or pastry puddings, choose fruit-based desserts like summer fruit meringue or fruit crumble made with more fruit and less crumble. (These are still quite high in sugar, so they're not everyday foods.)

For information on food labels to help you to make healthier food choices, see page 95 in section 4.

DRINKS

Drink 6-8 cups of non-alcoholic liquid each day, and limit sugary and alcoholic drinks.
Everyone should aim to have at least 6-8 cups of fluid a day – a total of 1.5 litres (2.5 pints) a day. This can include some tea and coffee, but water is one of the most thirst-quenching drinks.

Fruit juices diluted with water, or sugar-free squashes, are also thirst-quenching and are better than sugary squashes as far as losing weight is concerned.

Fizzy and sugary drinks should be limited, as sugar contains empty calories (with no helpful nutrients, vitamins or minerals) which will contribute to weight gain and can cause tooth decay.

Cutting down on sugary drinks

☑ Avoid, or gradually cut down on, the amount of sugar you use in tea or coffee.

☑ Drink more water.

☑ Drink water, pure fruit juice diluted with water, sugar-free squashes, sugar-free soft drinks and slimline mixers instead of sugary drinks where possible.

☑ Choose unsweetened fruit juice instead of 'fruit juice drinks' which are mostly made with sugar. (But limit the amount that you drink, as one small glass of unsweetened juice contains about 50kcal.)

☑ Avoid high energy drinks – either milk-based or glucose-based – as these contain a lot of calories.

Alcohol

Alcoholic drinks are very high in calories, so if you want to lose weight you'll need to consider reducing the amount you drink. Alcohol also increases your appetite: some people tend to notice that they eat more when they drink alcohol. Watch out for high calorie nibbles like nuts and crisps. On the next page we show the calorie content of some alcoholic drinks.

How many calories are there in alcoholic drinks?

The percentages in brackets show the alcohol strength ('ABV' or alcohol by volume).

Drinks	kcal
1 pint strong cider (8.5%)	574
1 pint strong ale	409
1 pint draft beer (3.5%)	182
1 alcopop (275ml bottle)	180
1 glass (50ml) cream liqueur e.g. Baileys	165
1 alcoholic cocktail (eg. a bloody Mary)	120
½ pint sweet cider	119
1 small glass (125ml) sweet white wine	118
½ pint dry cider (5%)	102
1 flute (125ml) of champagne (12.5%)	95
½ pint lager	90
1 small glass (125ml) red wine	85
1 gin and tonic (25ml gin)	85
1 small glass (125ml) dry white wine (12%)	83
1 glass (50ml) port	79
1 glass (50ml) sweet sherry	68
1 glass (50ml) dry sherry	58
1 vodka and diet mixer (25ml vodka)	56

Choose dry versions of all alcoholic drinks – for example dry cider or dry white wine – as these are lower in calories than sweet versions.

How much alcohol should I drink?

In terms of overall health, women should have no more than 2 to 3 units of alcohol a day and men no more than 3 to 4 units a day. However, in the *Shape-Up Healthy eating plan*, to help you lose weight, we recommend that:

 **Women should have** no more than
1 unit of alcohol each day.

 Men should have no more than
2 units of alcohol each day.

1 unit of alcohol =

1 small glass wine (100ml) of 10% 'ABV' or alcohol by volume (*NB Most wines are stronger than this.*)

½ pint (284ml) of ordinary strength beer, lager or cider

¼ pint of strong lager, beer or cider

1 single measure of spirits (25ml)

1 single measure of vermouth or sherry (50ml)

General guidelines for pregnant women or women trying to get pregnant advise avoiding alcohol completely, or drinking a maximum of 1 or 2 units of alcohol, once or twice a week.

Non-alcoholic and low-alcohol drinks

Choose non-alcoholic drinks carefully. Alcohol-free doesn't mean calorie-free. Choose tap water with ice and a slice of lemon, mineral water (sparkling or still), sugar-free squashes, or water flavoured with a hint of fruit. (This contains a small amount of sugar.)

Beware of low-alcohol or 'lite' beers or lager. These often contain more calories than the normal beers or lagers.

Want to cut down on your alcohol?

• Have at least one or two alcohol-free days a week.

• Choose smaller drinks – for example a half pint instead of a pint.

• Alternate alcoholic drinks with non-alcoholic drinks.

• Eat fewer savoury snacks when drinking. The salt in these makes you thirstier.

• Make alcoholic drinks last longer by extending them with mineral water or low calorie mixers. For example – have a white wine spritzer instead of white wine on its own.

- Be careful of strong beers and lagers which contain more alcohol than regular strength ones.

GOAL

Look back at your *Shape-Up Diaries* for the past few weeks. Using the information on pages 25-31, start to set yourself some healthy eating goals for changing the **balance** of foods you eat, so that your diet gets closer to the *Balance of Good Health* recommendations shown on page 40. Choose two or three goals to start with and make sure you achieve these before moving on. Here are some examples of SMART goals:

- ✔ 'I will eat chips on only one day of the week for the next two weeks. On other days I'll have lower fat alternatives such as pasta or rice.'
- ✔ 'I will use semi-skimmed or skimmed milk on cereals and in hot drinks for the next month.'
- ✔ 'I will have low-fat spread on toast and in sandwiches over the next week.'
- ✔ 'I will have a piece of fruit for my snack on at least five days over the next week.'
- ✔ 'I will make one main meal without meat, on at least one day of the week over the next four weeks.'

Fill in a *Shape-Up Goalsheet* on page 152, and then write your goals in the *Shape-Up Log* on page 154.

SHAPE-UP **STEP 3**
CUT DOWN THE QUANTITY

What happens in Step 3?

In Step 3 you will find out how to measure the quantity you are eating by counting the number of servings you have from each of the five food groups shown on page 40.

What are you aiming for?

In Step 2 you changed the balance of what you eat, and found out about how to make healthier choices. This will benefit your health and reduce your overall calorie intake. So you should at least stop putting any more weight on, and possibly lose some weight as well. If you have worked on Step 2 for about six weeks and you need to lose more weight, you will also have to pay attention to the amount of food you eat. It is not just the quality – the quantity matters too.

In order to lose weight, you will need to think about cutting down the quantity of food that you eat.

Food intake ⬆ + Physical activity ⬇ = Gain weight

Food intake ⬇ + Physical activity ⬆ = Lose weight

 Most women will lose weight if they eat or drink fewer than
1,500 calories
a day.

 Most men will lose weight if they eat or drink fewer than
1,800 calories
a day.

With *Shape-Up* you don't have to count calories. Instead we suggest that you count the number of *servings* you eat from each food group. By including a good mixture of foods, in the quantities we suggest on pages 62-66, you should be consuming 1,200-1,500 calories a day if you are a woman, and 1,500-1,800 calories a day if you are a man.

First you need to work out how many servings you're eating now. Using the information on the next pages, fill in a *Shape-Up 'How much am I eating? diary* like the one on page 68, keeping a record of the number of servings from each food group that you eat each day. Once you have done this, you will be able to set yourself a realistic goal for reducing the number of servings you eat.

How many servings should I aim for?

Below we show the recommended number of servings per day you should aim for, for each of the food groups.

	Women	Men
Bread, cereals and potatoes	7	8
Fruit and vegetables	*At least 5*	*At least 5*
Meat, fish and alternatives	2	2
Milk and dairy foods	3	3
Fatty and sugary foods		
– Fats	*No more than 2*	*No more than 2*
– Other fatty and sugary foods	*No more than 1*	*No more than 1*

How much is a serving?

On pages 62-66 we give information about how much food in each food group makes up a serving. Don't worry about exact amounts when referring to the servings.

Remember that a normal helping of food, which you may have in a meal, might contain more than 1 of our servings. For example, a sandwich made up of two slices of bread would be 2 servings from the 'bread, other cereals and potatoes' food group. We will explain this in more detail later in this section. See also the *Shape-Up Serving size guide* on page 148 in section 6.

We recommend that you eat a good **range** of foods. And with some food groups such as fruit and vegetables we actually recommend you eat more, as they are low in fat and calories and have many health benefits.

BREAD, OTHER CEREALS AND POTATOES

Women should aim to eat
7 servings
from this group each day.

Men should aim to eat
8 servings
from this group each day.

1 serving = for example:
- ✓ 3 tablespoonfuls of breakfast cereal
- ✓ 1 shredded wheat or weetabix
- ✓ 1 slice of bread or toast
- ✓ half a bread bun or roll
- ✓ 1 small pitta bread or chapatti
- ✓ 3 crackers
- ✓ 4 crispbreads
- ✓ 2 egg-sized potatoes or sweet potato
- ✓ 2 heaped tablespoonfuls of cooked rice
- ✓ 3 heaped tablespoonfuls of cooked pasta or noodles
- ✓ 1 medium-sized plantain or green banana
- ✓ 1 heaped tablespoon of pounded yam, fufu or gari
- ✓ 1 crumpet or English muffin
- ✓ 1 small slice of malt loaf

At first sight, 7 or 8 servings may seem like a lot to eat, especially if you have in the past tried restricting your carbohydrate intake to lose weight. In fact, it is important that you have enough of this food group. Go back to page 42 to remind yourself why.

Remember that the carbohydrate part of a meal may contain more than 1 serving. For example, two slices of bread or toast counts as 2 servings, one jacket potato counts as 2 servings, and a rice or pasta dish may be 2 or 3 servings each.

FRUIT AND VEGETABLES

Aim to eat
at least
5 servings
of fruit and vegetables each day.

Fruit
1 serving = for example:
- ☑ 1 large slice of melon or pineapple
- ☑ half a grapefruit
- ☑ 1 whole apple, banana or orange
- ☑ 2 whole plums or kiwis
- ☑ 1 cupful of raspberries or grapes
- ☑ 3 tablespoonfuls of stewed apple or canned peaches in juice
- ☑ 1 tablespoonful of sultanas or raisins, or 3 dried apricots
- ☑ a glass (150ml) of 100% juice (fruit or vegetable juice or smoothie), (maximum 1 per day)

Vegetables
1 serving = for example:
- ☑ 3 tablespoonfuls of broccoli or spinach
- ☑ 3 tablespoonfuls of carrots, swede or parsnips
- ☑ 3 tablespoonfuls of peas or sweetcorn
- ☑ 1 corn on the cob

Salad
1 serving =
- ☑ a bowlful of lettuce or tomato salad

It may not be as difficult as you think to reach the recommended amount!

Try to have fruit and vegetables across the day by including them in main meals, puddings and snacks. Look back at page 45 for ideas.

MEAT, FISH AND ALTERNATIVES

Aim to eat

2 servings
from this group each day.

1 serving = for example:

- ☑ 3 slices – or an amount similar in size to a pack of playing cards – of: lean beef, lean pork, lean ham, lean lamb, liver, kidney, chicken without skin, fish or oily fish
- ☑ 3 fish fingers
- ☑ 2 eggs
- ☑ 5 tablespoonfuls of tinned baked beans
- ☑ 5 tablespoonfuls of a dish based on lentils or beans or peas
- ☑ 2 tablespoonfuls of nuts or nut products (such as peanut butter) or seeds
- ☑ 100g (4oz) soya, tofu or quorn

MILK AND DAIRY FOODS

Aim to eat

3 servings
from this group each day.

1 serving = for example:

- ☑ 200ml (⅓ pint or a medium glass) of semi-skimmed or skimmed milk
- ☑ 1 small pot of low fat, plain or 'diet' yogurt
- ☑ 1 small tub of cottage cheese
- ☑ 1 small pot of fromage frais
- ☑ 40g (1½ ounces) of cheese (small matchbox-size), preferably reduced fat

FATTY AND SUGARY FOODS: FATS

Aim to eat
no more than
2 servings
of fats each day.

1 serving = for example:
- ☑ 1 teaspoonful of butter or margarine or spread
- ☑ 2 teaspoonfuls of low fat spread
- ☑ 1 teaspoonful of cooking oil, lard, dripping or ghee

Dressings and sauces
1 serving = for example:
- ☑ 1 teaspoonful of mayonnaise, salad cream or oily salad dressing
- ☑ 2 teaspoonfuls of low calorie mayonnaise or dressing
- ☑ 1 tablespoonful of gravy or white sauce

OTHER FATTY AND SUGARY FOODS

Aim to eat
no more than
1 serving
from this group each day.

1 serving = for example:
- ☑ 1 small pork pie or sausage roll
- ☑ 1 small bag of crisps
- ☑ 2 teaspoonfuls of cream
- ☑ 1 scoop of ice cream
- ☑ 1 small bar of chocolate
- ☑ 3 teaspoonfuls of sugar (for example in drinks)
- ☑ 1 heaped teaspoonful of jam or honey
- ☑ 1 chocolate biscuit or cream-filled biscuit
- ☑ 1 small doughnut, Danish pastry, pie or slice of cake
- ☑ 2 plain biscuits (for example, rich tea, ginger nuts, digestives or garibaldi)
- ☑ 1 small tube of sweets

DRINKS

Limit the amount of sugary drinks you have, and choose sugar-free soft drinks or mixers where possible. If you have one, count it as one serving of 'Other fatty and sugary foods'.

Alcoholic drinks

In terms of overall health, women can have up to 2 units of alcohol a day and men can have up to 3 units a day, but in the *Shape-Up Healthy eating plan* we recommend having less in order to control your overall calorie intake. So:

Women should have
no more than
1 unit
of alcohol each day.

Men should have
no more than
2 units
of alcohol each day.

1 unit of alcohol = for example:

1 small glass wine (100ml) of 10% 'ABV' or alcohol by volume. (*NB Most wines are stronger than this.*)

½ pint (284ml) of ordinary strength beer, lager or cider

¼ pint of strong lager, beer or cider

1 single measure of spirits (25ml)

1 single measure of vermouth or sherry (50ml)

Drink within the sensible limits. Spread your allowance through the week and have some drink-free days. For more information about alcohol see page 56

SHAPE-UP 'HOW MUCH AM I EATING?' DIARY

To get an idea of the quantity you are eating at the moment, fill in a *Shape-Up 'How much am I eating?' diary*. See the example on the next page. There is a blank diary on page 146.

This diary is different from the *Shape-Up Diary* on page 23 because it asks you to record the number of servings you have from each food group. See pages 61-66, and the *Serving size guide* on page 148, for how to measure servings.

We recommend that you complete this diary for seven consecutive days. Remember – it's important to chart weekdays and the weekend days.

At the end of each day, add up how many servings you have had from each food group. You can then compare them with the recommended number of servings shown at the bottom of the diary (or see page 61 for more details).

Please remember to keep this diary as you'll need to refer to it later.

EXAMPLE

When you write a food in the **Food/Drink** column, decide which food group it belongs to. Then, work out how many servings you have eaten from this group and write this number in the appropriate **Food groups** column. Use the **Serving size guide** on page 148 and look back to pages 61-66 to help you do this.

SHAPE-UP 'HOW MUCH AM I EATING? DIARY

Date 15 November

Day Thursday

FOOD GROUPS

Time	Food/Drink	Bread / Cereals / Potatoes	Fruit & Vegtables	Meat, Fish & alternatives	Milk & Dairy	Fatty & Sugary	
						Fats	Other fatty & sugary
7.45	BREAKFAST		1				
	small fruit juice	2			1		
	2 shredded wheat						
	200ml semi-skimmed milk						
10.45	MID-MORNING		1				
	Coffee with milk						
	Banana						
12.30	LUNCH						1
	Egg salad sandwich	2					
	2 slices of bread			1			
	2 teaspoons low fat spread						
	2 boiled eggs		1				
	lettuce, cucumber, tomato						
3.15	MID-AFTERNOON	1					
	Tea with milk						
	Slice of malt loaf				1		
7.15	DINNER						
	Chicken portion (no skin)	2					
	4 small boiled potatoes			1			
	Green beans			1			
	Courgettes			1			1
	Fresh fruit salad					1	
	2 teaspoons cream						
	Whole day: 1/3 pint semi-skimmed milk in tea and coffee						
TOTAL number of servings		7	6	2	2	1	1
RECOMMENDED number of servings		7 (women) 8 (men)	At least 5	2	3	2 max	1 max

GOAL

In Step 3 of the *Shape-Up Healthy eating plan* we have talked about cutting down the **quantity** of food you are eating. Use the information on pages 61-66 to think about where you can make changes in your diet to reduce the amount you are eating.

As before, set yourself two or three goals to start with. Make sure that your goals are SMART – **S**pecific, **M**easurable, **A**chievable, **R**elevant and **T**ime-Specific. For example, if you look back at your *Shape-Up 'How much am I eating?' diary* and find that you are eating 3 or 4 servings of fatty or sugary foods a day, your next goal might be 'to have no more than 1 serving of fatty or sugary foods on at least three days of the week, for the next two weeks'. Here are some other examples of SMART goals:

- ✓ 'I will eat no more than 7 servings from the bread, cereals and potatoes group, on at least four days next week.'
- ✓ 'I will eat less cheese. Over the next week on at least five days I'll have no more than 1 serving a day.'

Fill in a *Shape-Up Goalsheet* (see page 152) and then write your goals in the *Shape-Up Log* on page 154.

When you have achieved your goals and are happy that you are maintaining them, think about setting some more. This should enable you to gradually change your eating habits and keep up the changes that you have made.

Remember to keep a regular record of your weight, using the *Shape-Up Weight change record* on page 150.

Keeping going

It will take time for the changes you are making to become part of your lifestyle. To help you maintain new changes, or when things get difficult, see the information and advice in section 5.

GETTING MORE ACTIVE

3

GETTING MORE
ACTIVE

THIS SECTION AIMS TO:

increase your knowledge about
physical activity and how it relates to
your weight and your overall health,
and help you to make changes so that
you become more physically active.

3

It will help you to:

☑ decide what kind of activity is the most appropriate
for you, and

☑ get started on becoming more active, and keep going.

PREPARING YOURSELF FOR GETTING MORE ACTIVE

Why should you get more active?

The benefits of physical activity

Research has consistently shown that physical activity benefits people in lots of ways. It has been shown to:

- ☑ reduce the risk of heart disease
- ☑ reduce the risk of diabetes
- ☑ reduce the risk of some cancers
- ☑ reduce the risk of developing high blood pressure
- ☑ lower blood pressure in people who already have high blood pressure
- ☑ improve blood cholesterol levels
- ☑ help people maintain healthier joints and bones
- ☑ improve mood, and
- ☑ help people maintain a lower weight.

What's the connection between weight control and physical activity?

Overweight occurs when the amount of energy (calories) you take in from food is regularly greater than the amount of energy you use up in daily life. To lose weight you need to:

- ☑ take in less energy (ie. change your eating habits), and
- ☑ use up more energy (ie. increase your levels of physical activity).

Doing more physical activity will increase your chance of losing weight.

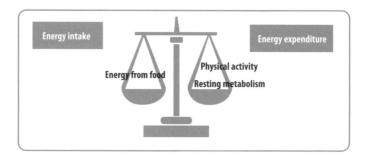

Different kinds of physical activity expend different amounts of energy, but any physical activity will expend some.

How tough does it have to be? Not necessarily very tough. To give you an idea, just walking one extra mile a day for a year could lead to a weight loss of about 8 pounds (3.8kg) – as long as you didn't increase the amount of food you ate.

Physical activity and weight control: what the research shows
- ☑ Activity doesn't have to be strenuous to benefit your weight.
- ☑ People who stick to a moderately active lifestyle achieve better weight control in the long term compared with people who aren't moderately active.

GETTING STARTED

People vary greatly in the extent to which they want or need to be more active as part of their weight control attempts. In order to see where physical activity fits in with your weight control plan, you need to answer the following questions:

- ☐ Do I need to do more physical activity?
- ☐ How much activity do I need to do?
- ☐ What sort of physical activity is best for me?
- ☐ Is it safe to exercise?

Do I need to do more physical activity?
This can be a difficult question to answer. The *Physical activity checklist* on the next page should help you identify whether you need to do more than you are currently doing. Complete the checklist and use the results and the information on pages 75-83 to identify specific targets for building more activity into your week.

Physical activity checklist

Use this checklist to find out if you are doing enough activity to encourage weight loss and maintain any weight loss. You can also use it at the end of every week to check your progress. Tick your answer to each question.

1 How often over the past week did you do a total of 30 minutes of physical activity that made you feel warm and breathe more heavily?

A ☐ 5 times in the week, or more
B ☐ 3-4 times in the week
C ☐ Twice
D ☐ Once
E ☐ Never

2 How often over the past week did you spend more than an hour at a time sitting down?

A ☐ Less than twice in the week
B ☐ 2-3 times
C ☐ 4-5 times
D ☐ 6-7 times
E ☐ More than 7 times (ie. more than once a day)

3 How often over the past week did you use the stairs instead of lifts?

A ☐ All the time/at every opportunity
B ☐ Most of the time
C ☐ Some of the time
D ☐ Rarely
E ☐ Never

4 How often over the past week did you walk or cycle instead of taking the bus or car for journeys under a mile?

A ☐ All of the time
B ☐ Most of the time
C ☐ Some of the time
D ☐ Rarely
E ☐ Never

Add up your score.
A = 4 points   B = 3 points   C = 2 points   D = 1 point   E = 0 points

16 points Excellent. You are certainly doing a substantial amount of activity already. Now you need to keep it up. If you are aiming to lose weight and maintain any weight loss, you should gradually increase to 60-90 minutes' activity a day. Look at steps 2 and 3 of the *Shape-Up Activity plan* on pages 78 and 79 for ideas.

13-15 points Well done. You are scoring highly on at least one of the questions. Are there any small changes you can make this week to increase your physical activity levels, to help you with your weight control plan?

9-12 points Why not pick out one of the questions on page 74 to work on? Be careful not to be too ambitious with your goals. Make only one or two small changes at a time.

0-8 points You are not yet doing enough physical activity to help with your weight control. Try to make one or two small changes next week. Remember not to be too ambitious with your goals. See step 1 of the *Shape-Up Activity plan* on page 77 to help you get started.

How much activity do I need to do?
Remember that, if you're not used to doing physical activity, you need to build up gradually. Use the *Shape-Up 3-step Activity plan* on page 77 as a guide for slowly increasing your activity level.

- **Adults should do at least 30 minutes' moderate intensity activity a day.** This will expend roughly 150 calories. For people leading sedentary lifestyles, 30 minutes is an excellent **initial** goal to work towards.
- However, **in order to maintain weight loss, you need to do 60 to 90 minutes' moderate intensity activity a day.** This should be the long-term goal for you to gradually work towards.
- The daily activity can be broken into bite-sized chunks. For example, three 10-minute walks will burn as many calories as one 30-minute walk.

You can choose from a whole range of different activities over the course of the day. Some examples are given below. As you can see, the more intense the activity, the less time you need to spend doing it in order to expend 150 calories.

Activity	Approximate time taken to expend 150 calories
Ironing	1 hour
Hoovering	50 minutes
Walking at a steady average pace	37 minutes
Food shopping pushing a trolley	37 minutes
Planting seeds and shrubs	32 minutes
Washing the car	28 minutes
Walking at a brisk pace	28 minutes
Mowing the lawn with a hand mower	28 minutes
Dancing	28 minutes
Cycling for pleasure or to and from work	25 minutes
Playing tennis	21 minutes
Swimming (leisurely)	21 minutes

Watching TV for an hour uses up about 100 calories. So, if you replace just one hour of TV-watching with a one-hour brisk walk each day, you would expend an extra 200 calories a day, which could result in about 2 pounds (1kg) weight loss in a month.

THE SHAPE-UP
ACTIVITY PLAN

The *Shape-Up 3-step Activity plan* will guide you in building up to a more active lifestyle. Read about the three steps and the different sorts of activity and then turn to page 81 and complete the exercise *Deciding which activities to do*.

The Shape-Up 3-step Activity plan

Step 1 Reduce the amount of time you spend sitting down.

Step 2 Increase lifestyle activity.

Step 3 Do more organised activity and sports.

SHAPE-UP STEP 1
Reduce the amount of time you spend sitting down.

In our modern society lots of things are automated and physical exertion is minimised. You need to seize any opportunity to reduce long periods of inactivity. Spending long periods of time sitting down – for example, sitting in front of the television for several hours – can contribute to weight gain.

If you lead a very inactive lifestyle, your first goal should be to reduce the amount of time you spend sitting down. Here are some small changes you can make to start off with:

- ☑ Stop using remote controls. Get up and operate your TV or video or CD player manually.
- ☑ Stand up during TV advert breaks, and walk around a little.
- ☑ Instead of asking others to fetch things for you, go and get them yourself.
- ☑ If you work in an office, get up from your chair and take regular breaks from your desk.

SHAPE-UP **STEP** 2
Increase lifestyle activity

Examples
- ☑ Walking
- ☑ Leisurely cycling
- ☑ Climbing stairs
- ☑ Housework
- ☑ Gardening

Physical activity doesn't necessarily mean working out in a gym or playing organised sport. In fact, walking has often been described as the perfect form of exercise.

Lifestyle activities are activities that we do in our everyday lives, like walking, climbing stairs or housework. We can all do lifestyle activities each day, and if we do them at **moderate intensity** these activities probably make the biggest overall contribution to energy expenditure.

To check if you are exercising at moderate intensity, you can use the 'talk test'. While you are exercising you should be breathing harder than usual and feel warmer, but you should still be able to hold a conversation. If you are so out of breath that you can't hold a conversation, slow down until you can.

Think about ways in which you can become more active in your daily life. Are there any journeys that you currently make by car or bus that you could do on foot or by bicycle? Activities such as gardening expend roughly the same amount of energy as a brisk walk and leisurely cycling. Stop using lifts and escalators – use the stairs instead. Get off the bus two stops earlier than usual and walk. Or take a walk at lunchtime when the weather is good.

Using a pedometer
Walking is probably the easiest way in which you can build moderate intensity activity into your lifestyle. Some exercise specialists have measured activity in terms of the number of steps we take each day. 10,000 steps a day is the recommendation for adults who want to stay in good health. This is roughly equivalent to 60 to 90 minutes' brisk walking. Doing 10,000 steps a day probably won't dramatically affect your weight loss, but it will certainly help

your fitness. For people who spend a lot of time sitting down, a good initial goal is to increase your daily step-count by 3,000.

A pedometer is a small, simple device that counts the number of steps you take. You attach the pedometer to your waistband or belt buckle. A pedometer is fairly unobtrusive, and is a great way to monitor your lifestyle activity level. Once you've measured the number of steps you take a day, check the box below to see how active you are.

Number of steps a day	Activity level
Under 5,000	Sedentary
5,000 – 7,499	Low active
7,500 – 9,999	Quite active
10,000 – 12,499	Active
12,500 or more	Highly active

Some pedometers can also measure the distance you have walked, and some even provide an estimate of how many calories you've used. Pedometers are relatively cheap and are available from most sports shops and department stores. For more information and advice on buying a pedometer visit our website www.weightconcern.org.uk

SHAPE-UP **STEP 3**
Do more organised activity and sport

The term 'organised activity' relates to specific activities which you need to schedule into your day. When you are feeling confident in your abilities and have increased your lifestyle activity as described in Step 2, you may want to try to add some more structured activity into your life.

There is a wide range of activities you can do to expend energy. **The most important thing is to find activities that are convenient and enjoyable for you, so that you're more likely to keep them up**. We've divided the exercises into two types: 'aerobic activity' and 'muscle fitness exercise'.

To lose weight, you need to take in less energy than you use. This needs to happen more or less every day. So you need to find ways to increase the amount of physical activity you do every day. Most people find that the easiest way to do this is to look for ways to increase the amount of lifestyle activities that they do.

Aerobic activity

Examples

- ☑ Jogging
- ☑ Swimming
- ☑ Aerobic classes
- ☑ Dancing
- ☑ Badminton
- ☑ Tennis
- ☑ Football

Aerobic exercise is the best type of activity for weight loss. The term 'aerobic' refers to activities that raise your heart rate, make you breathe harder and sweat a little. This type of exercise tends to use the larger muscles such as the legs and arms.

Aerobic activities use up more energy (calories) than lifestyle activities do, so this makes them good for weight control. However, you need to be reasonably fit to do many of them, so they are something to work towards. You shouldn't start doing **vigorous intensity** physical activity (any activity that makes you out of breath and sweaty) until you are much fitter. If you have high blood pressure or coronary heart disease (if you get angina, or if you have had a heart attack), you should get advice from your doctor before you start exercising.

If you are very overweight, some of these activities can be uncomfortable, so choose activities where your weight is supported – such as swimming or cycling.

Muscle fitness exercises

Examples

- ☑ *Resistance training:* weights, circuit training, toning classes (for example, body pump)
- ☑ *Stretching exercises:* stretching classes, yoga, pilates

If you have time, it is also a good idea to add some muscle fitness exercises into your schedule. There are two forms of muscle fitness exercise – resistance exercise and stretching exercises.

Resistance exercise will help keep your muscles strong, which can also help with weight control. As we age and become less active, our muscle tissue decreases. Muscles burn up energy so, if we have less muscle on our body, it means that we burn less energy.

Stretching exercises help to keep your joints flexible, which is important as we get older. Many people find stretching exercises relaxing and a useful way to wind down at the end of the day. Yoga classes include a lot of stretching exercises which can also be done at home.

Tai Chi is an excellent all-round form of exercise that is beneficial for all people but especially for older adults. It combines balance, stretching and resistance exercises.

✎_Deciding which activities to do

Which activities could I do?
Write down here some activities that you think you could realistically do.

_____

_____

_____

_____

_____

How would I do them?
Consider each of these activities in turn and think about how you would actually do them. For example:

Where will you do the activity?
For example: At home/At the leisure centre/Travelling to work/In the park

_____

_____

_____

_____

_____

When will you do it?
Which days of the week? At what time?

_____

_____

_____

_____

_____

Do you need to involve others?

Do you need someone to go with? Do you need other people to help with some of your other usual tasks? Do you need someone to look after children?

_____

_____

_____

_____

Do you need to travel to the activity?

How will you get there? What buses could you take? Do you need any special equipment? For example: Swimwear.

_____

_____

_____

_____

_____

Will I keep it up?

Thinking through the practical issues above will probably narrow down your list to two or three activities. Once you've done that, the final two most important questions for you when deciding on what activities to try are: 'Will I enjoy it?' and 'Can I do it regularly for most of my life?'

_____

_____

_____

_____

WHAT MIGHT GET IN YOUR WAY?

You'll need to think about any potential obstacles that might hinder your plans to become more active. Although this might seem like a negative thing to do at this time, it will be well worth it in the long run. Being prepared for challenges will help to ensure your success in the future.

Think about the various obstacles that you are faced with at home or at work that might get in the way of your plan to become more physically active. For more on this, see *Overcoming obstacles to following your healthy lifestyle plan* on page 118 in section 5.

FINDING OUT WHAT'S AVAILABLE

If you want to start taking exercise, it helps to have good knowledge about what options for physical activity are available to you. This will help you find something that you want to try or have enjoyed doing before. Below are some ideas for finding out what physical activity options there are.

Your local leisure and community service or local library

Contact the leisure and community service of your local authority. They can tell you about what is on offer, from organised walks to church hall aerobics. They will also be able to tell you about classes and programmes available for particular groups such as over-50s, women only, or people who have a heart condition. You should also be able to get information about leisure-pass schemes and discounts. Your local library can give you information about local activities too.

Your GP

Many GPs are now involved in 'exercise referral schemes'. This means that the GP can refer you to an organised programme of walking or other activities with specially trained staff to look after your needs. Ask if your GP takes part in any such schemes.

The internet

Several organisations have websites with information about opportunities for exercise. Here are some internet addresses to get you started:

- British Heart Foundation: www.bhf.org.uk
- Cyclists Touring Club: www.ctc.org.uk
- Sustrans (for cycling and walking networks): www.sustrans.org.uk
- Walking the Way to Health: www.whi.org.uk

IS IT SAFE FOR ME TO EXERCISE?

Overall, regular physical activity is a very safe thing to do. However, a small number of people need medical guidance before undertaking any physical activity. Fill in the *Pre-activity questionnaire* below and follow the advice given at the end.

Pre-activity questionnaire
Please tick all the relevant boxes.

		Yes	No
1	Has your doctor ever said that you have a heart condition and that you should only do physical activity recommended by a doctor?	☐	☐
2	Do you feel pain in your chest when you do physical activity?	☐	☐
3	In the past month, have you had chest pain when you were NOT doing physical activity?	☐	☐
4	Do you lose your balance because of dizziness, or do you ever lose consciousness?	☐	☐
5	Do you have a bone or joint problem that could be made worse by a change in your physical activity?	☐	☐
6	Is your doctor currently prescribing drugs for your blood pressure or for a heart condition?	☐	☐
7	Do you know of any other reason why you should not do physical activity?	☐	☐

If you answered 'Yes' to any of the questions above, you should get advice from your doctor before starting to do more physical activity.

You should also ask your doctor for advice:
- if you are over the age of 69 and are unused to regular physical activity, or
- if you are or think you might be pregnant.

Safety tips

Warming up and cooling down

Before starting any structured exercise it is important to warm up properly. This simply means exercising at a lower intensity of exercise than you intend exercising at for the main part of it. For example, for brisk walking, start off walking slowly and gradually increase your pace over 2-3 minutes.

Cooling down is the opposite of warming up, and is just as important. Spend 2-3 minutes cooling down by gradually slowing down after finishing the main exercise.

STOP exercising if you experience any of the following:

- ☐ an uncomfortable feeling or pain in the chest (which may spread to the arms, neck, jaw, back or stomach)
- ☐ nausea
- ☐ fatigue
- ☐ light-headedness
- ☐ cold sweat
- ☐ fainting.

Tips for exercising in hot and cold temperatures

Exercising when it's hot
- ☑ Make sure you are well hydrated before you do any exercise (240-300ml of water or just under half a pint) and drink water regularly during the exercise.
- ☑ Reduce the intensity of exercise.
- ☑ Wear lightweight, cotton, light-coloured clothing and try to keep as much of the surface of your skin exposed as possible. (Remember your sun block!)
- ☑ If you start to feel nauseous, dizzy or unusually fatigued, then stop.

Exercising when it's cold
- ☑ In the extreme cold it's generally best to find indoor alternatives.
- ☑ Wear lots of layers and remove them as necessary to avoid sweating.
- ☑ Try to stay dry.

"Every time I see a new video by somebody famous, I'm tempted to get it. But history tells me that I need to get out of the house to exercise. There are too many things waiting to be done when I'm in the house – which means too many excuses." *Judith*

> "I'm through with ambitious plans. I stick to my long walk in the weekend and allow myself more time to pick up the children from school so I don't have to drive." *Susan*

☑ Warm up properly and keep on the move. Avoid periods of no activity.
☑ Keep your head and hands covered. You lose a lot of heat through your head.

GOAL-SETTING AND SELF-MONITORING

Now that you have decided how to increase your activity level, it's time to set yourself some SMART goals to help you achieve your targets.

People are often over-ambitious with new activity goals. The following tips might help you to create more achievable ones.

It can be helpful to have both short and long-term SMART physical activity goals. For example:

☑ What will I have achieved by the end of today?
☑ What will I have achieved by the end of the week?
☑ What do I want to achieve in a month or six months' time?

Remember, it is important to start off slowly and progress gradually. In the first few weeks, focus on reducing the amount of time you spend sitting down and on trying to increase lifestyle activities such as walking.

Think long-term. Don't plan your physical activity just for the next few weeks. Think long-term and plan it for good.

GOAL

Once you have decided on some activities you will be able to manage, set yourself some SMART goals (**S**pecific, **M**easurable, **A**chievable, **R**elevant and **T**ime-Specific). Here are some examples of SMART goals:

- ✔ 'I will get off the bus a stop earlier all this week.'
- ✔ 'I will spend an hour less sitting watching TV in the evening, on at least three days this week.'
- ✔ 'I will walk to the train station rather than getting the bus on at least three days over the next week.'
- ✔ 'I will record my number of steps over the next week and aim to do 7,000 steps a day on at least five days.'
- ✔ 'I will go swimming once a week, for the next month.'

(For more information about SMART goals, see page 26.)

Complete a *Shape-Up Goalsheet* (see page 152) and then write your goal in the *Shape-Up Log* on page 154.

Keep a check on how much physical activity you are doing by recording it in your current *Shape-Up Diary*. Remember that continuing to self-monitor is an important part of behaviour change.

Remember that you are starting out on a journey towards lifelong physical activity. **It's better to achieve smaller changes in the short term that you can build on in the longer term, than to achieve big changes in the short term that you can't maintain in the longer term.**

KEEPING GOING

This can be the most difficult part of your plan. People who start to introduce more physical activity into their lifestyles often find it difficult to keep going at the new level. When life demands more of you, physical activity is often the first thing to go. It can be helpful to check from time to time whether your activity levels are high enough for your weight control targets. Use the *Physical activity checklist* on page 74 every now and then to review your progress.

How do I deal with a lapse?

Lapses are an inevitable part of any routine. Many different things can cause a lapse in your physical activity plan – such as illness, excess workload, holidays and business trips. If you have skipped any planned activity, see section 5 for information on how to deal with lapses.

SHOPPING, COOKING AND EATING OUT

4

SHOPPING, COOKING AND EATING OUT

4

THIS SECTION AIMS TO:

help you put into practice your knowledge of eating well and following a healthy, balanced diet.

It will help you to:

☑ look at your shopping pattern and give you tips for when you go shopping

☑ read food labels more critically

☑ choose healthier snacks

☑ make healthier meals and packed lunches, and

☑ make the most of eating out and social occasions.

SHOPPING

Your shopping pattern

What if you don't do the shopping?

If you are not the shopper of the household, it will still be useful for you to read this section. You may then want to talk about it with whoever does do the shopping. Remember that the foods available to you will affect what you can eat, regardless of who buys them.

Eating healthy foods will also be of benefit to the whole family, so you don't need to eat differently from everybody else.*

My shopping pattern

Which of the following apply to you?

- ☐ I end up buying unhealthy foods just because they're on special offer.
- ☐ I do my food shopping on an empty stomach or when I'm hungry.
- ☐ I go into a shop without a list and buy things that I fancy.
- ☐ I hardly ever write a shopping list.
- ☐ I shop whenever I think of it.
- ☐ I buy quite a lot of prepared foods.
- ☐ I write a shopping list and keep to it.
- ☐ I write a shopping list, but often don't stick to it.

You can only eat what's available to you at a particular time. Many people are determined to change their eating habits, but they will find this difficult if their shopping habits remain exactly the same. Try the *Shopping tips* below.

Shopping tips

- Plan what you (and the others in your household) are going to eat for the next few days or week and write a shopping list.
- Take a pen and tick off the items on the list as you go, so that you buy everything you need and don't stray from the list.

---

* Children need adequate energy and nutrients to grow properly. Low fat and high fibre foods are not recommended for children under 5 years. Your health visitor can give you more advice on this.

- Don't be swayed by special offers on unhealthy foods.
- Don't buy foods that you know you will not be able to resist – such as biscuits and chocolate.
- Don't go shopping when you're hungry.

Which snacks to choose?

A useful way to compare different snacks is to look at the label and check how many grams of fat a portion of the snack contains. **Aim for snacks with less than 3g of fat and less than 8g of sugar per portion.**

Another way of comparing snacks is to work out the percentage of calories which come from fat. Below we show the fat and calorie content of a range of popular sweet and savoury snack foods compared with a range of *healthier* sweet and savoury snack foods. Aim for snacks with less than 30% of their calories from fat. (To find out how to work out the figures for other snacks you eat, see page 98.)

SWEET SNACKS

High fat/high calorie sweet snacks

	Portion size	Kcal	Fat (g)	% calories from fat
Mars bar	1 bar (65g)	287kcal	12g	53%
Bounty	1 bar (60g)	284kcal	16g	51%
Plain digestives	2 (30g)	141kcal	6g	38%

Low fat/low calorie sweet snacks

	Portion size	Kcal	Fat (g)	% calories from fat
1 medium orange	245g	64kcal	0g	0%
1 medium apple	120g	42kcal	0g	0%
1 medium banana	135g	63kcal	0.3g	4%
10 dried apricots	80g	126kcal	0.5g	4%
Raisins	1 tbsp	82kcal	0.1g	1%
Sultanas	1 tbsp	83kcal	0.1g	1%
Grapes	100g	60kcal	0.1g	1%
Low fat fruit yogurt	150g pot	143kcal	1.5g	9%
Low fat hot chocolate drink (made with water)				
	1 sachet	40kcal	1.2g	27%

	Portion size	Kcal	Fat (g)	% calories from fat
Bran flakes (served with 125ml of semi-skimmed milk)				
	30g	160kcal	2.5g	14%
Malt loaf	2 slices	161kcal	1.4g	8%
Jaffa cake	2	73kcal	2g	25%
Ginger nut biscuit	2	91kcal	3g	30%
Garibaldi biscuit	2	72kcal	2g	25%
Fruit scone	1	158kcal	5g	28%
Sorbet	1 scoop	77kcal	0g	0%
Crumpet, with low sugar jam but no butter				
	2	156kcal	0.6g	3%

SAVOURY SNACKS

High fat/high calorie savoury snacks

	Portion size	Kcal	Fat (g)	% calories from fat
Croissant	1 (50g)	180	10	50%
Small sausage roll	1 (65g)	311	24	40%
Low fat salted crisps	30g	145	6	40%
Dry-roasted peanuts	25g bag	143	12	76%
Japanese rice crackers	80g box	458	28	55%
Prawn crackers	50g pack	282	18	59%
Vegetable samosa	1 (55g)	259	23	80%

Low fat/low calorie savoury snacks

	Portion size	Kcal	Fat (g)	% calories from fat
Plain breadsticks	Per stick	21	0.3	13%
Pretzels	100g	285	3.3	10%
Mini pitta bread	35g	93	0.4	4%
Bagel with marmite	84g	236	2.8	11%
Crispbread and low fat cottage cheese				
	3 + 45g	111	1	8%
Crunchy raw vegetables (eg. celery)				
	40g	3	0	0%
Brown roll with lean ham, tomato and scraping of low fat spread				
	152g	193	4.9	23%
Wholewheat crackers	3 (21g)	87	2.4	25%
Oatcakes	2 (26g)	115	2.6	20%
Matzo	1 (30g)	115	0.6	5%

You'll see that some foods that are low-fat can be high in calories, and vice versa. It takes time but it is worth working out in advance which snacks you want to have available and which you generally want to avoid. The section on *Labels* on page 95 will help you with this.

✎ Building up a store cupboard of foods

Here is a list of foods to keep in your store cupboard so that you have healthy foods available. Add your own favourites.

Food for the cupboard

- ☐ Breakfast cereals (All Bran, sultana bran, muesli, oats for porridge)
- ☐ Dried pasta
- ☐ Rice
- ☐ Barley
- ☐ Pizza bases

- ☐ Canned vegetables (corn, asparagus, tomatoes, peas etc.)
- ☐ Canned fruit in fruit juice
- ☐ Baked beans
- ☐ Kidney beans
- ☐ Lentils (canned or dried)
- ☐ Chick peas
- ☐ Cannellini beans

- ☐ Cans of tuna in water or brine, or other fish canned without oil

- ☐ Fruit loaf
- ☐ Crispbreads
- ☐ Pure fruit spread
- ☐ Marmite

- ☐ Long-life juices

- ☐ Dried fruit

"I think ahead about what I eat, rather than end up picking. And when I go shopping, I think about what I'm buying."

Add your own favourites.

_____

_____

_____

_____

Foods for the fridge or freezer

- ☐ Skimmed or semi-skimmed milk
- ☐ Low fat natural or fruit yogurt
- ☐ Eggs
- ☐ Cheese: low fat or reduced fat cheese, cottage cheese or mozzarella
- ☐ Bread
- ☐ Lean meat
- ☐ Tofu
- ☐ Quorn
- ☐ Frozen vegetables
- ☐ Frozen fruit

Add your own favourites.

_____

_____

_____

_____

LABELS

Understanding food labels

There is a lot of debate around food labelling at the moment, with campaigners demanding clearer nutritional information. Labels can be confusing, but the information they provide is essential if you want to make healthy choices. For most people this means learning how to read labels. Here we try to help you through the maze.

Food labels generally provide you with two sets of information: a list of the **ingredients** and the **nutrition information** about the product.

INGREDIENTS LIST

The ingredients are listed in descending order of weight. This means that the ingredient that weighs the most is listed first, and the one that weighs least is the last. The higher up the list you find fat or sugar, the more that product contains.

Some foods contain a number of different types of sugar or different types of fat. This makes it difficult to identify if the food actually contains large quantities of sugar or fat.

The following are all types of **sugars**:
- fructose
- maltose
- sucrose
- glucose
- dextrose
- syrup
- honey
- raw sugar
- cane sugar.

The following are all types of **fat**:
- animal fat (bacon, beef, chicken, ham, lamb, pork, or turkey)
- butter
- cocoa butter

- coconut
- coconut oil
- coconut cream
- egg and egg yolk solids
- hydrogenated vegetable oil or fat
- lard
- palm kernel oil
- palm oil
- vegetable oil
- shortening – vegetable or animal
- whole milk solids
- non-milk fat

NUTRITION INFORMATION

The *Nutrition information* label shows you how many calories, and how much protein, fat, carbohydrate and fibre there is in a food. Sometimes the vitamins and minerals in the food, such as calcium or iron, are listed too.

Nutritional labelling is voluntary (unless a nutritional claim is made, such as 'low-fat'), but all supermarkets now put labels on their packets. Labels usually come in one of two formats, such as the two sample labels shown below and on the next page.

On these two sample labels, we have highlighted the information you should check and compare when deciding which product to use.

Ginger Thin biscuits

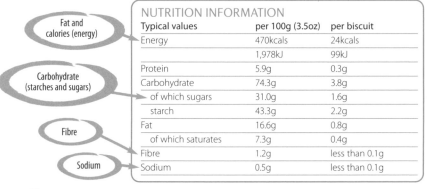

NUTRITION INFORMATION

Typical values	per 100g (3.5oz)	per biscuit
Energy	470kcals	24kcals
	1,978kJ	99kJ
Protein	5.9g	0.3g
Carbohydrate	74.3g	3.8g
of which sugars	31.0g	1.6g
starch	43.3g	2.2g
Fat	16.6g	0.8g
of which saturates	7.3g	0.4g
Fibre	1.2g	less than 0.1g
Sodium	0.5g	less than 0.1g

Fat and calories (energy)

Carbohydrate (starches and sugars)

Fibre

Sodium

Low fat yogurt

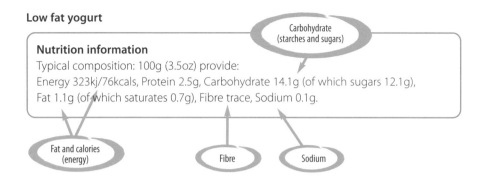

Nutrition information
Typical composition: 100g (3.5oz) provide:
Energy 323kj/76kcals, Protein 2.5g, Carbohydrate 14.1g (of which sugars 12.1g),
Fat 1.1g (of which saturates 0.7g), Fibre trace, Sodium 0.1g.

Carbohydrate (starches and sugars)

Fat and calories (energy)

Fibre

Sodium

HOW TO USE NUTRITION INFORMATION LABELS

Nutrition information labels are useful if you're comparing products
to find out which is a more suitable food choice. Most labels give
two sets of figures – one showing how much of the nutrients there
is in a food per 100g, and one set showing how much there is in a
typical serving.

As far as weight management is concerned, the three most
important things to look for on the label are total **fat**, **sugar** and
calories.

Making sense of food labels
The Food Standards Agency has produced this set of guidelines
to help you to make sense of food labels:

Per 100g	A lot	A little
Sugars	15g	5g
Fat	20g	3g
Saturated fat	5g	1.5g
Fibre	3g	0.5g
Salt	1.5g	0.3g
Sodium	0.6g	0.1g

Reproduced with permission from the Food Standards Agency

Fat and calories

Calories are a measure of how much energy (calories) a food will provide you with. On food labels, calories are usually given as kcals (see the examples on pages 96 and 97). Carbohydrate, fat and protein are all sources of energy. Your body needs a certain number of calories to work properly, just as a car relies on petrol to run. Fat contains the most calories, so this is the nutrient that we look at most on food labels.

Below we show you how to calculate the percentage of calories that comes from fat in a food. Remember that you should be aiming for no more than 30% of your calories to come from fat (see page 91). You may want to try calculating the percentage of calories from fat in some of the foods that you eat regularly. This will give you an idea of how healthy they are.

Some labels also indicate how much saturated fat is in the product. This is the type of fat that should be limited the most.

How to work out the percentage of calories from fat in a food

$$\frac{\textit{Number of grams of fat (in 100g of the food) x 9 x 100}}{\textit{Number of calories (in 100g of the food)}}$$

Look at the nutritional information label to find out the number of grams of fat in 100g of the food. Multiply this number by 9 (the number of calories in 1g of fat). Divide the result by the total number of calories contained in 100g of the food and multiply by 100. This gives you the percentage of calories from fat.

Example
To calculate the percentage of calories from fat in the ginger thin biscuits (see label on page 96):

$$\frac{\textit{16.6 (the number of grams of fat per 100g of biscuits) x 9 x 100}}{\textit{470 (the number of calories (kcal) in 100g of biscuits)}} = 32\%$$

Fat can be called lots of different things on a food label. For a list of the common sources of fat to look out for, see page 95.

Carbohydrate (starches and sugars)

There are two types of carbohydrate – starches and sugars. Starches are an essential part of the diet, but it is best to limit your intake of sugars.

Some labels include the information 'Of which sugars …' This will tell you how much of the carbohydrate in that food is made up of sugar.

Check the ingredients list to make sure that sugar is not among the first in the list. The nearer the top of the list sugar is, the more sugar the food contains.

Sugar can be called lots of different things on a food label. For a list of names of common types of sugar, see page 95.

Fibre

Fibre is essential in the diet for healthy bowels, and some types of fibre can actually help lower cholesterol – for example, the fibre in beans, pulses, oats, fruit and vegetables.

Choose high fibre foods where possible. These are ones which contain more than 6g of fibre per 100g.

Sodium

Sodium is a mineral and is mainly found in salt (as sodium chloride). Salt is in most foods, but the amount is very variable. Too much salt in the diet contributes to high blood pressure, which can increase the risks of several medical problems, including heart disease and strokes.

Most of us eat too much salt and much of this is hidden in processed foods (for example, tinned foods and ready-prepared meals). It is difficult to know how much salt is in a food just by looking at it, so food labels can be useful.

People in the UK eat an average of 9g of salt per day, but we should be aiming for no more than 6g per day – which is about 2g of sodium per day for women and 2.5g of sodium for men.

Many food labels only give you the figures for sodium. As a guide, 0.6g of sodium in a serving of food is a lot and 0.1g is a little.

Guide to shopping

Look for the following information on food labels to make healthy choices:

Snacks
Less than 3g fat
and less than 8g sugar per serving

Breakfast cereals
Less than 5g fat
and less than 10g sugar per 100g

Ready meals
Less than 10g fat
and less than 350kcal per portion

Pre-packed sandwiches
Less than 6g fat
and less than 280kcal per sandwich pack

TIPS FOR SMART SHOPPING

Below are four simple tips to help you to make healthier food choices.

1   **Look at the fat, sugar and calorie content per 100g.**
    How does this compare with similar products? Choose the product with the lower values per 100g. (However, not all foods give the 'per 100g' figures on the label, so you won't always be able to do this.)

2   **Do the fat, sugar, sodium and fibre content of the product match up to the guidelines in *Making sense of food labels* on page 97?**

3   **Check the ingredients list.** The ingredients in a product are listed in order of weight. The first ingredient on the list is present in the greatest amount, and the last ingredient present in the smallest amount. If fat or sugar is fourth in the list or lower, the product is likely to be a low fat/low sugar option. But remember that fat and sugar can come under many different names on a food label. See the lists of common sources of fat and sugars on page 95.

4   Take care with any nutritional claims such as 'reduced fat' or
     'low fat'. These foods may contain less fat, but may contain
     more sugar and a similar amount of calories per 100g as the
     standard product. Compare the labels of the 'reduced fat' or
     'low fat' product with the standard product, looking at the fat,
     sugar and calories per 100g. See the example below.

'REDUCED FAT' DIGESTIVE BISCUIT

Typical composition	Per biscuit (15.5g)	Per 100g
Energy	305kj	1972kj
	73kcal	469kcal
Protein	1.0g	6.5g
Carbohydrate	11.3g	73.4g
Of which sugars	3.5g	22.8g
Fat	2.6g	16.6g
Of which saturates	1.1g	7.2g
Fibre	0.4g	2.8g
Sodium	0.1g	0.6g

STANDARD DIGESTIVE BISCUIT

Typical composition	Per biscuit (15g)	Per 100g
Energy	297kj	1983kj
	71kcal	473kcal
Protein	1.1g	7.2g
Carbohydrate	9.4g	62.6g
Of which sugars	2.5g	16.6g
Fat	3.2g	21.5g
Of which saturates	1.5g	10.1g
Fibre	0.5g	3.6g
Sodium	0.1g	0.6g

Beware of nutritional claims

Nutritional claims can be misleading as they are often ambiguous. Below are some things to remember when you're reading the claims.

CLAIM	MEANING	
'No cholesterol'	The product contains no dietary cholesterol. This means that there is no cholesterol in the product. But it does not mean that it is low in fat or calories.	*The cholesterol that's in the food you eat has a relatively small effect on your blood cholesterol level. It's the saturated fat in food that raises the blood cholesterol level.*
'Low in cholesterol'	The product contains no more than 0.005% cholesterol. However, it may still be high in fat or calories.	
'Made with 100% vegetable oil'	This may still mean that the product contains palm, coconut or hydrogenated oil which are all saturated fat and therefore to be avoided.	
'Low fat' or *'Very low fat'*	A low fat claim on a high fat food such as sausages would mean that they have a lower fat content than other sausages. It doesn't mean that these sausages are lower in fat than other foods. Although low fat spreads have about half the fat content of butter or margarine (and very low fat spreads have about a quarter of the fat content), they are still high fat foods. A low fat spread still contains 40% fat which is high fat even though it has less fat than a so-called ordinary spread. A low fat yogurt contains less than 1% fat and contains less fat than an ordinary yogurt.	
'83% fat-free'	Don't be misled. This usually refers to the product's fat percentage by weight not calories, so the water in the product is included. For example, cuts of meat that are '83% fat free' by weight still provide 70% of their calories from fat, because of the water content.	
'High in polyunsaturates, low in saturates'	Many spreads claim to be 'high in polyunsaturates, low in saturates'. It is the amount of saturates in your diet that has most effect on your blood cholesterol, so this claim is good news but it doesn't mean low calorie.	

'Low calorie'	Can only be used at present if there are no more than 40kcal in both a serving and in 100g or 100ml of the product.
'Reduced calorie'	Can be used if the product has less than three-quarters of the calories of comparable products.
'Light' or 'Lite'	Can mean anything. For example, 'Light' spreads can contain anything from 38% fat to 60% fat. 'Light' or 'Lite' can refer to calories, colour, taste or alcoholic strength. You have to read the small print.
'Diet'	Don't assume anything. Read the label and compare it with similar products.
'No added sugar'	Usually means no added sucrose, which is one type of sugar. However, other sugars in fruit juice, and also honey and malt extract, are no lower in calories and can be just as bad for the teeth. Words indicating sugar include: sucrose, glucose, dextrose, fructose, maltose, honey, syrup, raw sugar and cane sugar.
'Reduced sugar'	Must contain at least 25% less sugar than an ordinary product.
'Low sugar'	Must contain no more than 5g of sugar per 100g, or no more than 5g per serving if a serving is greater than 100g.
'High in fibre'	Requires a fibre content greater than 6g fibre per 100g.

MAKING HEALTHIER MEALS AND PACKED LUNCHES

Healthier cooking tips

On pages 43-55 in section 2 you will find lots of tips on healthier cooking.

Lunch ideas

Taking a packed lunch to work is often a healthier option than eating food from the staff canteen or buying food from a shop or café. Making your own lunch means that you have complete control over what foods are in the lunch and you can make sure that the ingredients are low fat – for example, the spread or the sandwich filling. In many cases you'll save money too.

You will need to make time to prepare the packed lunch. Some people find it easier to make their lunch the night before and store it in the fridge.

Below are some lunch ideas:

Sandwiches

- ☑ Use different types of breads to add variety, such as wholemeal bread, a bagel, a roll, pitta bread or a tortilla wrap.
- ☑ Add some salad to the sandwich.
- ☑ Only use a thin scraping of low fat spread. With some fillings you won't need to add any spread at all.
- ☑ Choose lean meat or reduced fat cheese.
- ☑ If the filling is dry, use a small amount of low fat mayonnaise.
- ☑ Avoid the prepared tubs of sandwich spreads that are high in fat.

Low fat sandwich fillings

- ☑ Lean meat or poultry (such as chicken or ham) with salad
- ☑ Tuna and sweetcorn
- ☑ Lean ham and mustard
- ☑ Boiled egg and salad
- ☑ Lean ham and tomato
- ☑ Tuna and cucumber

- ☑ Low fat cream cheese with salad
- ☑ Cottage cheese with pineapple or chopped pepper
- ☑ Grated low fat cheese with celery and tomato
- ☑ Low fat hummous with grated carrot

Other lunch ideas
- ☑ Pasta salad. Use cooked pasta and add vegetables such as tomato, sweetcorn or celery, plus lean ham, chopped chicken, tuna or salmon.
- ☑ Rice salad. You could add some chopped apple or raisins to add variety.
- ☑ Couscous salad. Flavour it with herbs and add chopped vegetables.

Easy extras
A sandwich or salad may not be enough for your lunch. Below are some suggestions for extras to take with you to work.
- ☑ A piece of fresh fruit, such as an apple, banana, strawberries or plums
- ☑ Dried fruit, such as a mini-box of raisins or a few dried apricots
- ☑ Carrot, celery or cucumber sticks
- ☑ Cherry tomatoes
- ☑ A flask of vegetable soup
- ☑ Chicken drumstick (without the skin)
- ☑ Low fat yogurt

Ready meals
Many of us lead hectic lives and rely on a ready meal for those evenings when we don't feel like cooking. These can be a convenient way of eating a healthy, balanced meal, but make sure you choose the supermarket's healthy eating range of ready meals. And remember to check the food labels, as the meals in the healthy eating range may still be high in fat and calories.

- ☑ When buying a ready meal, look for less than 10g fat per portion **and** less than 350 calories (kcals) per portion. Many ready meal ranges produced by supermarkets aim at these levels, so you will find that you have a wide variety to choose from.

☑ Serve extra vegetables or a side salad with the ready meal to make it more filling.

☑ Try to avoid ready meals with cheesy or creamy sauces.

GOAL

If you want to set yourself a goal now, fill in a *Shape-Up Goalsheet* (see page 152) and then write your goal in the *Shape-Up Log* on page 154. Here are some examples of SMART goals:

☑ 'I will read the food labels on all the snacks I buy over the next week, and I'll only have snacks that have less than 3g of fat and less than 8g of sugar, on at least 5 days of the week.'

☑ 'I will fry food no more than once a week over the next month.'

☑ 'I will write a shopping list once a week, and take it with me when I do the weekly food shopping over the next month.'

EATING OUT AND TAKEAWAYS

Eating out is an enjoyable part of life. People in the UK on average eat out between two and three times a week. You may not think of yourself as someone who eats out a lot, but many of us get sandwiches for lunch even if we don't go to restaurants. Eating out is no longer something which is only for special occasions.

If you are eating out once a month or less frequently, you don't need to worry too much about what you eat at these times. However, if you're eating out more often than that, you need to be careful to find the right foods and places to eat in, in order to maintain your healthy eating plan. Eating out frequently can make it more difficult to eat healthily.

When choosing several courses for a meal, try to balance out higher with lower fat choices so that, even if a single dish does not match the *Balance of Good Health* (on page 40), the overall meal is closer. For example, if you're choosing fried fish for a main course, choose a lower fat starter such as melon, grapefruit or clear soup, or a low fat dessert such as fruit salad or sorbet.

The secret to success in following a healthy eating plan is making sure that you give yourself the maximum chance of choosing suitable foods. One way of doing this is by giving some thought to what you eat when you're out.

Eating out

Eating out is an enjoyable social activity. Just because you are now eating healthily doesn't mean that you have to stop eating out. But you will need to think carefully about the food choices that you are making.

- ☑ Choose foods which have been grilled, char-grilled, poached, stir-fried, steamed, or baked rather than fried. You can ask if the food can be cooked in a different way to how it appears on the menu.
- ☑ All the following words are likely to mean that extra fat has been added, so try to avoid these dishes: à la crème, alfredo,

au gratin, batter-dipped, battered, béarnaise, béchamel, beurre blanc, breaded, buttered, buttery, crispy, cheese sauce, cordon bleu, creamed, cream sauce, en croûte, escalloped, flaky, florentine, fried, hollandaise, meunière, milanese, pan-fried, parmigiana, puffed, rich, sauté, tempura.

- ☑ Watch out for foods with a rich or creamy sauce.
- ☑ Go for a lean meat or fish option.
- ☑ Try to have some vegetables or salad.
- ☑ Fill up on starchy foods (potatoes, rice or plain pasta).
- ☑ Ask for potatoes rather than chips.
- ☑ Ask for dressings and sauces to be served on the side, so you can choose how much to use.
- ☑ Choose fruit, fruit salad or a sorbet as a dessert.
- ☑ Go for either a starter or a dessert, but not both. Or share with someone else.
- ☑ Avoid being over-hungry by the time you get to the restaurant. This may cause you to overeat.
- ☑ Remember that you don't have to clear your plate.
- ☑ Eat slowly and enjoy your food.
- ☑ Alternate any alcoholic drinks with water, as your self-restraint may drop after a few drinks.

On the next few pages are some tips on foods to avoid at restaurants, and some tips for better choices.

BAKED POTATO BARS

Things to avoid

- Butter or margarine.
- Coleslaw, or food coated in mayonnaise, such as egg mayonnaise, tuna mayonnaise, or chicken mayonnaise.
- Cheddar cheese.

Tips for better choices

- Choose low fat fillings such as baked beans, cottage cheese, tuna, chicken or vegetables.
- Ask for a potato without butter or margarine.

PUB AND BAR MEALS, STEAKHOUSES, CARVERIES AND HOTELS

Things to avoid

- For a starter, avoid pâté, deep-fried mushrooms, deep-fried whitebait, egg mayonnaise, creamy soups or dips.

- For the main course avoid fried foods, pastry items, creamy or high fat dressings and sauces.

- Pastries, tarts, chocolate gateaux and cheesecakes are all high in fat and sugar, so only indulge on very special occasions.

- Coffee with cream.

Tips for better choices

- Choose à la carte and avoid buffets.

- For a starter, choose from: melon filled with fruit, fruit cocktail, fruit juice, consommé or vegetable soup, shellfish (with no dressing), grilled fish, or smoked salmon.

- For the main course, choose from: steamed, baked, poached or char-grilled fish, gammon with pineapple, roast chicken or turkey without skin or bread sauce, or a plain or vegetable omelette. If you're choosing steak, have a small one.

- Choose jacket, boiled or new potatoes, not chips.

- If you're having pasta, choose a tomato-based sauce.

- Include plenty of vegetables without a coating of butter or a rich creamy sauce. Or choose a side salad (without the dressing), and a roll.

- For dessert, choose sorbet, fruit salad, fresh fruit or jelly.

- If you're having milk in coffee, ask for semi-skimmed milk.

FAST FOOD OUTLETS

Things to avoid

- Burgers with added cheese or mayonnaise. These can have up to 30g of fat compared with an average of 10g of fat in a pure beefburger. Avoid having cheese or mayonnaise with chicken, fish and bean burgers too.

- Thick milkshakes. These contain about 9 teaspoonfuls of sugar and 6g of fat.

- Chicken nuggets, chicken in batter and fish burgers, as these are deep-fried. Nine nuggets could contain 25g of fat.

- Coleslaw as a salad as it's always smothered in mayonnaise.

Tips for better choices

- Burgers are a very high fat choice. Leaner burgers are now becoming available.

- A plain burger in a bun with salad but no dressing is your best choice in this sort of outlet.

- A plain grilled chicken breast or steak (not coated in batter or breadcrumbs).

- Salads (but be aware of high fat dressings).

- Choose 'diet' versions of fizzy drinks. Or even better, choose water, juice or semi-skimmed or skimmed milk.

SANDWICH BARS

Things to avoid

- Mayonnaise as a dressing or as an extra topping.

- Salad cream, unless they have low calorie salad cream.

- Sausage or bacon in sandwiches as they have probably been fried.

- Full fat cheese, especially if mixed with mayonnaise.

Tips for better choices

- Ask for granary or wholemeal bread.

- Ask for low fat spread instead of butter, or go without spread.

- Choose lean fillings such as ham, chicken, egg, tuna or cottage cheese, and include salad, tomato or grated vegetables.

- Ask for a low fat natural yogurt option instead of other dressings.

PASTA AND PIZZA RESTAURANTS

Things to avoid

- Garlic bread, especially if it has melted cheese on top.

- Cream or cheese sauces, for example in lasagne, cannelloni or carbonara dishes.

- Watch out for extra cheese on top of pizza or pasta dishes.

- Sausage, pepperoni and other fatty meats on pizza.

Tips for better choices

- Vegetable soup (such as minestrone) served with bread or grissini is a good starter.

- Choose any type of pasta served with tomato or vegetable sauces.

- If you're having pizza, go for a regular base or thick base rather than a thin base, as a regular or thick base pizza has a higher proportion of starchy carbohydrate base to topping.

- Ham, tuna and prawns are the lowest fat toppings.

- For extra toppings choose tomato, onion, green pepper, pineapple, sweetcorn, mushrooms or other vegetables, or chilli.

- Restaurants that serve stone-baked pizzas (rather than those cooked with added oil) are likely to be lower in fat.

INDIAN MEALS

Things to avoid

- Fried starters such as bhajees, pakoras and samosas.

- Naan bread and deep-fried poppadoms. (Avoid these to cut down on fat.)

- Ghee is used extensively in traditional Indian food. It is clarified butter and is high in saturated fat.

- Beware of meat curries swimming in fat.

- Rich shahi dishes such as pasandas, masalas and kormas which can be prepared with ghee, vegetable oil and a lot of added sugar.

Tips for better choices

- Tandoori dishes are usually a good choice, but check that they have not been cooked with fat.

- Dahl, a spicy lentil stew, is a good high fibre choice. Dhansaak is also made with lentils.

- In some restaurants, even the vegetable dishes can be high in fat. However, they are still lower in fat than meat dishes.

- Have a green undressed salad with your main course.

- Boiled rice usually accompanies the food.

- Choose low fat chapatti or tandoori roti.

- Madras or vindaloo curries may be better choices as some restaurants use vegetable oils in these dishes rather than the traditional ghee, which is made with butter. (From a weight point of view this won't make a difference, but you'll be eating less saturated fat.)

CHINESE MEALS

Things to avoid

- Fried starters such as prawn crackers, spring rolls, egg rolls and fried wantons.

- Spare ribs.

- Fried rice.

- Fried noodles.

- Meat or vegetables cooked in batter or deep-fried.

- Dim sum which have hot fat or lard poured over them or are deep-fried rather than steamed.

- Sweet and sour dishes or dishes with lemon sauce which often use battered and fried meat – which means extra fat.

- Fruit fritters.

Tips for better choices

- Try a broth-based Chinese soup such as hot and sour soup.

- Only choose dim sum which have been steamed.

- Stir-frying can be a healthy way to prepare foods. It's especially good for maintaining the flavour, as well as the vitamins, in fresh vegetables, especially when less fat is used. Include some vegetable stir-fry in your meal.

- Choose steamed or boiled rice or noodles.

- Try tofu dishes, provided the tofu has not been deep-fried first.

- Choose lychees for dessert.

CARIBBEAN MEALS

Things to avoid

- Fried snacks such as fritters and festival.

- High-energy milk drinks such as Nutriment and Supplegen.

- Home-made drinks such as Guinness punch or carrot juice, as these are usually made with sweetened condensed milk and/or high-energy milk drinks.

- Fatty meats such as belly pork, mutton and oxtail.

- Salads coated in mayonnaise, such as coleslaw or potato salad.

- High-sugar drinks including ginger beer, malt drinks and some 'juice drinks'.

Tips for better choices

- Steamed fish with tomatoes and onions or okra is low in fat, and steaming the vegetables holds in all the nutrients.

- Choose the soup of the day. A medium portion is normally enough for a main meal.

- Order a serving of callaloo or salad with your meal instead of sides like fried plantain or dumplings.

- Have jerk chicken with salad and either bread or plain rice.

- Before you order rice and peas, ask how it is cooked. If it's cooked with coconut milk/cream and butter, choose plain rice or boiled yam, or banana or plantain instead.

Lunch on the go

Do you ever buy your lunch from a supermarket or shop – for example, a ready-made sandwich or a salad bowl? There is a huge variety of sandwiches available, which can make it difficult to know what to buy. Below are some suggestions to help you choose healthier options.

- ☑ Choose sandwiches from the supermarket's or food manufacturer's healthy eating range.
- ☑ Avoid larger packs which offer three sandwich triangles rather than two.
- ☑ Look for less than 280kcal **and** less than 6g fat per sandwich pack.
- ☑ Avoid sandwiches with mayonnaise or salad dressings.
- ☑ Choose sandwiches which contain salad or vegetables – such as chicken salad sandwich or ham salad sandwich. This adds bulk to the sandwich and will fill you up.
- ☑ Watch out for salads and salad bowls. They may seem a healthier option but some contain very high amounts of fat. When choosing a salad bowl look for less than 280kcal per pack **and** less than 6g fat per pack.
- ☑ Avoid the temptation of picking up a packet of crisps or a chocolate bar as part of a meal deal. Many shops now include fresh fruit, fruit salads and dried fruit in meal deals, so choose these instead.

✎_How is eating out fitting into your new eating plan?

People who have followed the *Shape-Up* programme have told us that adopting a few strategies has helped them to enjoy eating out more. Some said that they had saved money by not paying for food that they did not feel good about eating.

Here are some sample strategies:

☐ If you eat out regularly with friends, ask them to try different restaurants or takeaways where you can make healthier choices.

☐ Ask for a broader selection of sandwiches to be delivered to a weekly work lunch meeting.

☐ Set an example to friends who eat at your home by serving the kind of foods that fit in with what you are trying to do for yourself.

Add your own ideas.

_____
_____
_____
_____
_____
_____
_____
_____
_____
_____
_____
_____

If you have the occasional lapse and find yourself eating foods that are high in fat and sugar, remember that it's only a lapse and not a catastrophe (see page 134 for more on dealing with lapses). Be sure to use the opportunities and ask yourself the two most important questions:

- **What led up to the lapse?**
- **What can I do to avoid it the next time I'm in a similar situation?**

KEEPING **GOING**

5

KEEPING **GOING**

THIS SECTION AIMS TO:

provide you with information
and advice to help you keep going
with the changes you have made to
your lifestyle.

5

It will help you to:

☑ understand and deal with the different sorts of 'triggers' for
unhealthy behaviour

☑ think your way out of difficult situations

☑ practise 'damage limitation' during the tempting times, and

☑ turn your lifestyle changes into long-term healthy habits.

OVERCOMING OBSTACLES TO FOLLOWING YOUR HEALTHY LIFESTYLE PLAN

Most people find it easy to make one or two changes when starting on a weight management plan. The difficult part is when you try to keep those changes going after the first rush of enthusiasm wears off. This section will teach you the techniques psychologists use to keep people motivated to achieve their goals.

Shape-Up works by helping people to focus on making changes to their behaviour that will lead to weight loss. But it goes one step further than just telling you what you can do to lose weight. It also teaches you how to work out what has happened when things go wrong, how to deal with it, and how you can make sure that you keep on track in the future.

This section looks first at the **things that can 'trigger' unhealthy behaviours of overeating or not being active enough**:

- Some triggers come from within the person. They can include the way you think and feel, as well as physical states such as hunger and thirst. We call these **internal triggers**.
- Other triggers to unhealthy behaviour come from outside the person. We call these **external triggers**. They can include things like the sight and smell of tempting, but unhealthy food.

This section also looks at **how to manage lapses** – those times when you stray away from your healthy eating plan or your activity plan.

Next, it looks at how **planning ahead** can help you maximise your chance of success.

And finally, we suggest ways of making sure you get **support from other people** – from friends and family, and perhaps from health professionals too.

All these techniques will help ensure that you keep going with your healthy eating and activity plans – and that you make those lifestyle changes permanent.

DEALING WITH EXTERNAL TRIGGERS

External triggers are things that trigger unhealthy behaviour and that come from 'outside' you. Some common external triggers to overeating are shown below. Which ones are most likely to throw you off your healthy eating plan?

✎ _Which are my most common external triggers?
These are external triggers that *Shape-Up* participants have identified. Rate to what extent they apply to you.

Seeing, hearing or smelling food
NOT AT ALL ├─────────────────────────────────┤ VERY MUCH SO

Seeing others eating
NOT AT ALL ├─────────────────────────────────┤ VERY MUCH SO

Seeing food adverts
NOT AT ALL ├─────────────────────────────────┤ VERY MUCH SO

Shopping
NOT AT ALL ├─────────────────────────────────┤ VERY MUCH SO

Preparing food
NOT AT ALL ├─────────────────────────────────┤ VERY MUCH SO

Not having healthy foods at home
NOT AT ALL ├─────────────────────────────────┤ VERY MUCH SO

Arguing
NOT AT ALL ├─────────────────────────────────┤ VERY MUCH SO

Being left alone
NOT AT ALL ├─────────────────────────────────┤ VERY MUCH SO

Having nothing to do
NOT AT ALL ├─────────────────────────────────┤ VERY MUCH SO

Other people (friends and family) offering me food
NOT AT ALL ├─────────────────────────────────┤ VERY MUCH SO

Other people (friends and family) tempting or teasing me to eat
NOT AT ALL ├─────────────────────────────────┤ VERY MUCH SO

Being in 'food' situations like a restaurant or party
NOT AT ALL ├─────────────────────────────────┤ VERY MUCH SO

Missing regular mealtimes and getting over-hungry
NOT AT ALL ├─────────────────────────────────┤ VERY MUCH SO

STRATEGIES TO HELP YOU WITH EXTERNAL TRIGGERS

Different people have different external triggers, and not everyone is aware of the things that trigger their behaviour. But once you know what your triggers are, you can use strategies to beat them. Here are three strategies to get you started.

1 Avoid the trigger. (Stimulus control)

One of the most effective ways to beat a trigger is to avoid it. Using stimulus control means trying to avoid the triggers that make you overeat or that make you inactive. For example:

- If looking at the ice cream tub in the freezer triggers the beginning of a binge, don't keep ice cream in the house for a while.
- If seeing yourself in a mirror in a clothes shop upsets you and triggers a binge, give up clothes shopping for a few weeks.

Some triggers can only be avoided for a while, and there are some that you can't avoid at all. But avoiding the trigger is just the first step. Later on you can use other strategies.

2 Do something else instead. (Response substitution)

Society and advertising encourage people to eat as a way of comforting or rewarding themselves. It can be difficult to avoid the situations which make you want comfort or distraction or a little treat. So one way around this is to find other types of comfort, distraction or reward. Try thinking about your own ideas for response substitution by doing the exercise below.

✎_My ideas for 'response substitution'

Apart from food, what else do I find comforting?

For example: A long soak in the tub while you do your phone calls, someone brushing your hair, lying on the couch listening to your favourite music, or writing a letter. What would work for you?

_____

_____

_____

_____

Apart from eating, what else helps me to take my mind off things?

For example: Dancing, doing a crossword, going for a walk, sewing, writing a letter or even a romantic novel, going to the cinema, watching a programme you've recorded, or reading travel brochures.

_____

_____

_____

_____

Apart from food, what else is a treat for me?

For example: Time off work, a new CD, a book, a magazine, looking at holiday photos, making a phone call, or applying a face pack.

_____

_____

_____

_____

Alternatives to eating

Some of the things *Shape-Up* participants have found to be good alternatives to eating are given below. Could you try any of these?

- ☑ Have a relaxing bath
- ☑ Walk in the park
- ☑ Read a novel
- ☑ Phone a friend
- ☑ Organise photographs into albums
- ☑ Do something very physically active
- ☑ Clean the car
- ☑ Organise a weekend away
- ☑ Go for a swim
- ☑ Have sex
- ☑ Do something around the house, like clearing out a cupboard, throwing things away, or reorganising a music collection.

Most people find it helpful to have a mix of 'organising-type' activities such as clearing out old clothes or sorting out your desk, and leisure activities such as watching a film, or reading the papers.

3 Learn to resist. (Resistance training)

It's not possible to avoid all the triggers which lead you to overeat, so it may be helpful to teach yourself how to resist in the presence of temptation.

Most urges to eat are 'learned'. For example, the more often you have a sweet snack while watching TV or walking home, the more you will want it in a similar situation. Research shows that, if you get animals used to eating whenever they get a puff of a certain scent, after a while they will start eating whenever they get the scent, even if they have just had a full meal. The scent 'switches on' the hormones that stimulate their appetite. It's called conditioning and was first described by Pavlov, a Nobel Prize physiologist in Russia.

The good thing about these conditioned (or learned) responses is that they can also be 'unlearned'. One method involves people exposing themselves to mild versions of the trigger that makes them want to eat, and then gradually working up to the most difficult situations. Let's say that the sight of a packet of 'Cheddars' in the sitting room is bound to set you off eating. You could start your resistance training with something easier – say a piece of Ryvita wrapped in cling film. Put it in full view and try to keep it there for a couple of days. If that works, move up to something harder – perhaps a cream cracker. Gradually give yourself harder tasks until finally you have a packet of Cheddars sitting, open but uneaten, for seven days.

You can apply the same approach to all sorts of things. Work out the steps, write them down, and gradually work through them. If you fail, go back a step or think up an intermediate step.

SUMMARY

How to deal with external triggers

1 Identify those things that reliably lead to deviation from your plan.
2 Make a plan about how you might overcome this trigger:
   • Stimulus control plan
   • Response substitution plan
   • Resistance training.
3 Make a SMART goal to help you deal with the external triggers, and set a reward for achieving this.

DEALING WITH INTERNAL TRIGGERS

Some triggers to overeating are not so obvious because they are 'inside' the person. They may include the way you feel about things or the way you think about things, but they can also include physical states of your body such as hunger or thirst.

Shape-Up suggests that there are four different sorts of internal triggers that make it difficult for people to stick to their lifestyle plans. These are:

- hunger
- cravings
- unhelpful thoughts, and
- emotions.

DEALING WITH HUNGER AND CRAVINGS

A regular eating pattern is the best way to keep overeating because of hunger at bay. This is covered in detail on page 35.

However, many people experience a strong desire to eat even when they can't possibly be hungry. For example, they might have a strong desire for a pudding at the end of a very filling meal. These intense desires – usually for a specific type of food – are known as cravings.

It can be difficult to distinguish between hunger and craving, and many people don't know the difference between the two. Because of this, they often eat when they don't need to and the excess calories can scupper the rest of the day's hard work. Do the quiz on the next page to learn how to tell hunger from a craving.

_Craving or hunger?

Which of the following eating temptations are cravings, and which are hunger?

Answers below.

		Craving	Hunger
1	You have eaten a large meal, but still want pudding.	☐	☐
2	Someone mentions iced buns, and you feel like eating.	☐	☐
3	You are always starving at certain times of the day.	☐	☐
4	You feel lightheaded after not eating all day.	☐	☐
5	You drive by a chip shop and the smell makes you want to eat.	☐	☐
6	Your stomach is rumbling.	☐	☐
7	You are watching a cookery programme and feel like eating something.	☐	☐
8	Your friend offers you half of her sandwich. You suddenly want to eat more.	☐	☐
9	You haven't thought about eating and you are getting the shakes.	☐	☐

Stop and think. Are you really hungry or is this just an urge or craving? Are you thirsty rather than hungry?

Knowing that you are having a craving doesn't always help you to resist the food you so desperately desire. However, there are some basic facts about cravings that should help you to resist temptation.

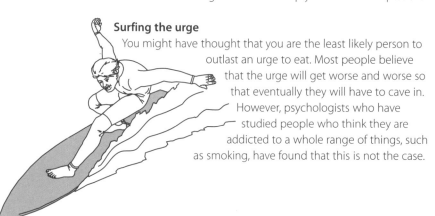

Surfing the urge

You might have thought that you are the least likely person to outlast an urge to eat. Most people believe that the urge will get worse and worse so that eventually they will have to cave in. However, psychologists who have studied people who think they are addicted to a whole range of things, such as smoking, have found that this is not the case.

Answers: 1, 2, 5 and 7 are usually cravings. 4, 6 and 9 signal hunger. 3 and 8 could be either.

Urges and cravings can be seen as a wave that comes upon you. The wave builds up more and more as if it can engulf you. You feel overwhelmed, and relieve these feelings by eating. However, like the wave, your craving can't stay high forever – it has to subside. Sometimes it helps to think of just such an image, perhaps of yourself as a surfer riding up and then down the wave. As you do that, remind yourself that these strong feelings will always subside within 15-30 minutes, even with no intervention. But there are things you can do to counter the feelings:

- ☑ Wait 20 minutes first.
- ☑ Distract yourself by doing something else that gives you pleasure. (Look back at *My ideas for 'response substitution'* on page 120.)

DEALING WITH UNHELPFUL THOUGHTS

The way in which you think about things often determines how you feel about a situation and the things that you do. Many people who have been trying unsuccessfully to manage their weight will have some unhelpful thoughts about a whole range of issues that affect eating and activity. See if you recognise in yourself any of the unhelpful thoughts below.

What unhelpful thoughts do I have?

Below are some of the most common unhelpful thoughts that can get in the way of successful weight management. Unhelpful thoughts are thoughts that tell you it is OK to behave in a way that you know will get in the way of your healthy eating plan or your activity plan. Think back to the last couple of times that you didn't stick to your plan. Put a tick by any of the following unhelpful thoughts that got in your way:

☐ Putting things off and starting again tomorrow – and then the next day and then the day after that …
"I've blown it now. I'll start again tomorrow."

☐ Thinking that food will help you cope with emotions or situations that you find difficult.
"I've had such a rubbish day. I'm going to treat myself to an evening off the diet!"

☐ Thinking that what you are trying to achieve is not important, or that it's not worth the effort of finding a different way to cope with a difficult situation.
"I'm tired of being made to feel guilty about my weight. A few extra pounds here and there isn't going to make that much difference."

☐ Thinking about what you need right now (for example, a chocolate biscuit) and ignoring what you need to do for the future (for example your increased risk of diabetes if you continue to put on weight).
"So what if I end up getting diabetes? I'll cope – I always do."

☐ Thinking that you have no control or choice about how to cope with situations in which you could choose a healthy or unhealthy way of behaving.
"There's nothing I can do about this party. I may as well enjoy the food rather than making myself miserable about it."

☐ Wishing that things were different and hoping that something will just happen without you having to try.
"It's not fair that I have to watch myself in this way. Other people don't have to keep a diary, so I don't see why I should."

☐ Thinking that there's no point in trying because the task is too great.
"I've got to keep this up for so long. I don't think I have the strength to keep it up."

We don't believe that particular thoughts are either good or bad, but you do need to evaluate your thoughts on the basis of whether they help you achieve what you set out to do. On the next few pages, *Shape-Up* will help you to identify and overcome unhelpful thoughts that make it difficult for you to stick to your healthy lifestyle plan. It will also help you to learn how to think in ways that make it easier for you to stick to your plans.

It may surprise you to know that it is possible to learn how to think differently about food, your weight and physical activity. The key to learning how to think differently is – as with many other things – practice.

Below we list all the 'unhelpful thoughts' that were on pages 125-126, and for each unhelpful thought we show an alternative, more helpful way of thinking.

Unhelpful thought	More helpful way of thinking
"I've blown it now. I'll start again tomorrow."	*"Yes, I've made a mistake but if I carry on I will have to work a lot harder for a lot longer than if I stop right now."*
"I've had such a rubbish day. I'm going to treat myself to an evening off the diet!"	*"To be honest unhealthy food won't really take away how rubbish my day was any more than a tasty healthy option. I'll look in my cookbooks for something that will cheer me up but won't break the calorie bank."*
"I'm tired of being made to feel guilty about my weight. A few extra pounds here and there isn't going to make that much difference."	*"I know that a few extra pounds does make a difference and I'm tired of not being able to get into any of my nice clothes."*
"So what if I end up getting diabetes? I'll cope – I always do."	*"I know I'd be able to cope if I get diabetes, but is that chocolate biscuit really worth all the extra effort I'll have to put in?"*
"There's nothing I can do about this party. I may as well enjoy the food here rather than making myself miserable about it."	*"I've always got a choice, even if it makes life a bit more difficult at times. These parties are part of my life. The only way I'm going to learn to control how much I eat at parties is by practising."*
"It's not fair that I have to watch myself in this way. Other people don't have to keep a food diary, so I don't see why I should."	*"It's neither fair nor unfair that I have to watch myself. It's just how things are. I know that keeping a diary helps, so I'm just going to keep doing it."*
"I've got to keep this up for so long. I don't think I have the strength to keep it up."	*"Anyone would give up if they thought about being on a diet forever. I'm just going to focus on what I can do right now and put the long term out of my mind."*

_Finding more helpful ways of thinking

Below we list some of the 'unhelpful thoughts' that *Shape-Up* participants have identified as being particularly problematic for them. See if you can turn the unhelpful thoughts into more helpful ways of looking at things. For each unhelpful thought we give some extra ideas to help you find a more helpful way of thinking. As with other behaviours, if you regularly 'practise' helpful thoughts, they will eventually become habitual ways of thinking.

ABOUT HEALTHY EATING

Unhelpful thought	More helpful way of thinking
"It takes too long to prepare healthy food."	_____ _____ _____ _____
	Ideas: ✓ You can eat healthily without cooking at all. ✓ Healthy foods can be very simple to buy and prepare. See section 4 *Shopping, cooking and eating out* for ideas. ✓ You can share the preparation with family or friends.
"Healthier eating is less filling."	_____ _____ _____
	Idea: ✓ Eating healthily means eating more starchy foods as these fill you up but still have a lot fewer calories and less fat. This means there are fewer calories per bite of food.
"I'll have to cook two different dinners a day for the family."	_____ _____ _____
	Idea: ✓ Start changing meals slowly at first. Make other changes as the family gets used to the healthier meals.

*"I can't be
bothered to eat
more healthily."*

Ideas:
- ☑ It might not take as much effort as you think, so why not give it a try? Weigh up the possible benefits against the effort you may need to make.
- ☑ Although it may seem an effort at the beginning, it can soon become a habit.
- ☑ Also, nowadays there is quite a wide range of healthy convenience foods available. See section 4 *Shopping, cooking and eating out*.

*"Healthy foods
don't taste
good."*

Ideas:
- ☑ Try changing small things one at a time.
- ☑ Experiment. Some foods you may like; others you may not.
- ☑ Traditionally, people have thought of diet foods as just being salad and cottage cheese, but in fact healthy foods include a much wider range of foods than you might imagine.

*"I can't afford to
eat more
healthily."*

Ideas:
- ☑ Eating less meat and more starchy foods can actually save you money.
- ☑ Canned or frozen fruits and vegetables are often cheaper and as nutritious as fresh.
- ☑ High fat takeaways often cost more than a home-prepared healthy meal.
- ☑ Buying fatty and sugary snacks means paying for empty calories which add to your weight.
- ☑ Shop in markets for low-cost fruit and vegetables.

*"My life is too
stressful to eat
more healthily."*

Ideas:

☑ Eating healthily and regularly can help you to feel more
energetic and better able to cope – and therefore more able to
combat stress. But if it's not the right time for you to make
major changes to your diet, you can always come back to it later.

*"My friends and
family won't
support me to
eat more
healthily. Or
they'll
undermine my
efforts at eating
more healthily."*

Idea:

☑ Learn to be more assertive about your needs. Explain to your
family and friends that following a healthy eating plan is very
important to you and you would really appreciate their help
and support.

*"I get home too
late."*

Ideas:

☑ You can make up quick meals, plan in advance, or freeze meals.
☑ If you need to use convenience foods, you can use low-calorie
ranges.

*"I'll have to give
up all my
favourite
foods."*

☑ You won't have to give them up, but if they're high in fat and
sugar, you will need to eat less of them.
☑ You can learn to prepare your favourite foods using less fat and
sugar.
☑ Explore new foods and find new favourites.

ABOUT BECOMING MORE ACTIVE

Unhelpful thought	More helpful way of thinking

"I don't have time for doing any activity."

_____
_____
_____
_____

Ideas:
- ✓ Get off the bus a stop or two early and walk the rest of the way.
- ✓ Try to take a 15-minute walk at lunchtime.
- ✓ Get your family to help share your household jobs.
- ✓ Encourage everyone to watch less TV.
- ✓ When the weather is good, try getting up 15 minutes early and taking a brisk walk before breakfast.
- ✓ Prioritise. You might get more done with the extra energy you can get from exercise. But remember that all exercise requires time which you would have spent doing something else. So think carefully about what you could do less of, or stop doing, in order to fit exercise in.

"Who'll look after the children?"

_____
_____
_____
_____

Ideas:
- ✓ Teach your children about the importance of exercise by taking part in a family activity like cricket, tennis or football.
- ✓ Make it fun for all of you.
- ✓ Walk to school with your children. Or walk just part of the way.
- ✓ Choose at-home activities such as gardening or using home exercise equipment or exercise videos.
- ✓ Negotiate for help with baby-sitting.

"I'm too tired to do any exercise."
_____
_____
_____

Ideas:
- ☑ Try exercising at the time of day when you're most alert – for example early in the day.
- ☑ Choose lifestyle activities like brisk walking that don't require a high degree of effort but leave you feeling less lethargic.
- ☑ Exercise with a partner or friend so that you can encourage each other.
- ☑ Challenge yourself to doing five minutes of physical activity before deciding whether or not you are too tired.

✎_Overcoming unhelpful thoughts

Now identify your own typical unhelpful thoughts and jot down some ideas on how to overcome them.

What unhelpful thoughts might be getting in the way of your attempts to change what you eat and how active you are? What could you think, or do, to help you to overcome those obstacles?

Unhelpful thought	What I could think, or do, to have more helpful thoughts

EMOTIONS

Many people say that they eat unhealthy foods because they are in a bad mood or feel stressed and need cheering up. Sometimes good moods can trigger unhealthy behaviour because you feel like celebrating. Food can therefore be used to help get rid of negative moods or enhance positive ones. This can be a problem for people who are trying to manage their weight.

If this happens to you, try to distract yourself from the mood. Discover and learn other ways to comfort, distract or reward yourself rather than using food. Make a plan about how you will teach yourself these. Ask yourself if you are having any unhelpful thoughts and deal with those. (See page 125.)

Strategies for dealing with internal triggers

Here's a summary of the strategies for dealing with the internal triggers to eating that we have talked about on pages 123-133.

Type of trigger and why it may lead to overweight	Strategies for dealing with the trigger
Hunger. If you don't have a regular eating pattern, you may get hungry more often and eat more than you need to.	• Get into a regular eating pattern. (See page 35.)
Cravings. Indulging your craving in a big way may make you eat more than you need to. It may lead you to give up on your healthy eating plan for that day.	• Distract yourself until the craving goes away.
Unhelpful thoughts. You have unhelpful thoughts that suggest that eating is the solution to a particular problem, or that minimise the importance of what you are trying to achieve.	• Ask yourself if the unhelpful thought is perhaps helping you to solve one problem, but creating others. • Challenge your thinking. Find more helpful ways of thinking. • Think about the last time you over-ate or didn't do any activity. How did you feel afterwards? Was it worth it? • Stop and remind yourself of what you are trying to achieve and why.
Emotions. You need to be comforted, distracted or rewarded, and eating seems like a good way to do this.	• Distract yourself from the mood. • Discover and learn other ways to comfort, distract or reward yourself. (See page 120.) Make a plan about how you will teach yourself these. • Ask yourself if you are having any unhelpful thoughts and deal with those. (See page 125.) • Ask yourself whether eating will change the problem you are currently facing.

SUMMARY

How to deal with internal triggers

1 Identify what your particular triggers are.
2 Brainstorm which strategies you could use for dealing with those triggers.
3 Make a plan to deal with one particularly important trigger and put it into action. Perhaps you could set yourself a SMART goal for dealing with it.

LAPSES AND RELAPSES

Single episodes of deviating from your healthy lifestyle plan are known as 'lapses'. They are a normal and expected part of the process of change and provide you with an opportunity to learn about the things that trigger unhealthy behaviour. In the words of other *Shape-Up* participants:

"I try to remember that one lapse doesn't mean that all is lost."

"When I had a lapse in eating, I used to skip the next meal so as not to feel so guilty. That just made me eat more later. Then I'd feel a loss of control and end up eating more. So the spiral continued. Now I try to go back to my plan as soon as possible after a lapse."

"Through thinking more about my lapses it made me think that they are to do with feelings – bad feelings, like guilt towards my children, or having to say no to someone. I would also eat in defiance, like when I'm angry with my partner for commenting about my eating. I do it to show who's boss!"

"One lapse led to another. I ate too much at lunch so I ditched gym after work. That made me feel bad so I over-ate again when I got home."

So, lapses are not a problem in themselves. They only become a problem because they tend to lead to other lapses. A series of lapses is called a 'relapse'. In other words: one lapse equals one individual failure; a relapse happens when you go back to old ways altogether. When psychologists help people to recover from lapses, they use the idea of 're-tracing your footsteps'. The diagram on the next page shows how this works for someone trying to manage their weight.

EXAMPLE
Re-tracing footsteps

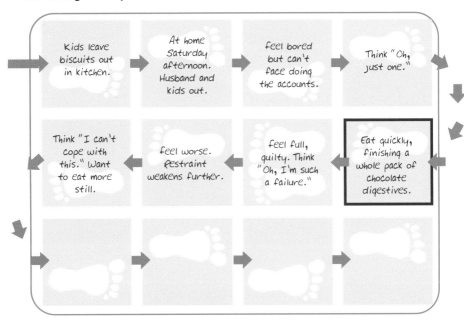

This is a common description of someone lapsing from an eating plan. But psychologists believe that lapses don't 'just happen'. Something will have led up to it. One way of understanding a problem really well is by concentrating on a single episode rather than the whole problem area. Thinking back in detail about a particular episode is like re-tracing your footsteps. First you need to be clear about what happened during the episode. Then you have to think about what happened before and after, including what thoughts and feelings you had before and after the event.

Stopping a lapse turning into a relapse

Unhelpful thoughts (as described on page 125) are often an important factor in whether a lapse becomes a relapse. Below we give some examples of both helpful and unhelpful ways of thinking about a lapse from a healthy eating plan. Tick the thoughts that you think will help a person get back on track with their plan.

☐ 'Oh well, that's it, I may as well give up for today.'

☐ 'I wish I hadn't had that – I didn't even want it. I'll make sure that I swim a couple of extra lengths tonight at the pool.'

☐ 'I'm good at organising the household, and holding down my job. I know I can follow my plan, so banish the negative thinking NOW.'

☐ 'My partner's right, I'm not good at anything. Me eating sensibly? Who am I trying to kid?'

☐ 'So what if I've blown it? I deserve a treat. Anyway, why not make it a treat day and finish the rest of the biscuits.'

☐ 'Everyone else is really good at sticking to their plans. That just proves I'm useless. Why don't I just forget all about it?'

☐ 'Apart from that, I've achieved quite a bit so far this week. If I carry on doing as well, I'll treat myself to that new novel at the weekend.'

☐ 'Everybody is different and we all work at our own rates. I won't get anywhere unless I keep trying.'

☐ 'OK, today's not been brilliant but, looking at the past week, there has been a definite improvement in what I've set out to try to do.'

Perhaps the most important thing you can do if you find yourself in the middle of a lapse is to stop what you are doing and give yourself time to think about what you want to do next. Try the following 'emergency plan' for getting yourself back on track.

What to do if you have a lapse
Memorise these steps:

- ☑ **STOP** doing what you are doing, and remove yourself from the situation.

- ☑ **RECOGNISE** that one lapse is not the end of the world and don't trap yourself with negative thinking.

- ☑ **LEARN** by thinking about what was happening around you, and inside you.

- ☑ **PLAN** what to do to stop your slip becoming a fall, and put your plan into action now.

- ☑ **BE POSITIVE** and carry on.

PLANNING

The secret to success in following a healthy lifestyle plan is being prepared so that you give yourself the maximum chance of having suitable foods available to you and opportunities to be more active. Many *Shape-Up* participants have told us that planning in advance was the key to helping them to maintain their lifestyle changes in eating and activity.

Here are some of their suggestions.

- ☑ Plan what you are going to eat for the next week and buy these foods in advance.
- ☑ Keep healthy snacks at home and at work, or in the car if you're going for a long journey, so that you are not tempted to buy a snack which is high in calories. (See page 91 for ideas for healthy snacks.)
- ☑ Take a healthy packed lunch to work (see page 104 for ideas), to avoid the temptation of buying a high calorie takeaway or sandwich for lunch.
- ☑ If you are going out for a meal and you know that you are going to eat late, have a small snack in the afternoon so that you don't overeat when you get to the restaurant.
- ☑ Think ahead about how you may feel when eating out:
  - At special occasions such as birthdays and Christmas, eating is often encouraged and there may also be some pressure to eat more than you had planned. It is enjoyable to let go when celebrating but often, if you are well prepared, you can avoid the anxiety that can come from trying to alter your diet and celebrate at the same time.
  - *Think about the event beforehand.* Think about your own desire to eat and the external pressures from others and how other people may act towards you. You could call ahead and ask what food will be served and then plan beforehand what you are going to eat.
  - *Rehearse in your mind how you would like to respond to difficult situations.* It's much better to be prepared than to find yourself having to react on the spot to situations and feelings. Without preparation you might find yourself responding in a way that you later regret.

☑ Take your trainers to work so that you can go for a walk at lunchtime or after work.

Add some of your own ideas for planning here.

_____

_____

_____

_____

GETTING SUPPORT FROM OTHERS

When you start to make changes in your lifestyle, you will notice the ways in which people and organisations affect your ability to change.

You may become aware of this when you first go shopping after planning to make healthier choices. You may find that some shops sell a wider range of healthy foods than others. Or you might notice it most in social settings. For example, it might be easier to order low fat options in certain types of restaurants. Or, if you have children and have decided to walk to school with them rather than drive there, you might have a full-scale rebellion on your hands.

"Now that I have to buy a lot more fruit and vegetables, I notice the limited choice and poor quality at my local greengrocers. I seem to be paying a lot for wrinkled apples."

"I have a lot of working lunches. With the best intention in the world, it is not always easy to choose low fat options. Should I go for the prawn mayonnaise, or the bacon and avocado sandwich?"

"I thought one way of increasing my activity is to walk instead of driving the children to school. When I mentioned the idea, guess what happened."

"My wife means well but her idea of encouragement amounts to cross-examination about my gym session and every time she sees me eat."

These are just a few of the many obstacles people come across when they try to make healthy eating and physical activity part of their lifestyle. So it makes sense to try and make the most of any support that you can get.

Would it help if you had support from other people?

This depends on what you are trying to do, your circumstances, and the sort of person you are. Some people say they work best on their own. Others do better if they have support. For example, one person may find it helpful to go for an early morning swim with a friend, while another might prefer to go alone.

Many people who have followed the *Shape-Up* programme said that getting more support helps them to make long-lasting changes to their lifestyle. But the type and level of support that people want vary from one person to another. The best support is the kind that you need, from the person most suited to provide it, at the time that you need it.

Getting help from family and friends

Friends and family can be a resource or a hindrance. For example, they might take an interest and offer constructive advice without being intrusive. Or they might criticise, tease, or belittle your attempts to change, or even try and talk you out of it.

There could be many reasons why family and friends are not as helpful as you would like them to be. Think about the last time people were unhelpful. Use the exercise on the next page to help you work out what you can do about it.

_How could people be more helpful?

The problem	What am I going to do to overcome this problem?

The problem

What am I going to do to overcome this problem?

Did they understand your reasons for wanting to make a change?
☐ Yes ☐ No

Did they fully appreciate how important it was to you?
☐ Yes ☐ No

Could they have been worried that you were not eating properly or that strenuous exercise would compromise your health?
☐ Yes ☐ No

Were they trying to protect you from disappointment?
☐ Yes ☐ No

Did they fear that your success would show them up?
☐ Yes ☐ No

Might they be afraid of having to change the way they relate to you once you have succeeded?
☐ Yes ☐ No

When trying to get more support from your family and friends, **communication** is key. Remember that they are not mind-readers, and they can only help you if you let them know what to do. So it is important to ask for their support and help, and tell them what works for you. And don't forget to thank people when they do something supportive. It will encourage them to do it again!

Can a health professional offer you support?

Shape-Up has been designed as a self-help programme that you can do on your own or as a member of a *Shape-Up Group*. You may already have a health professional offering you help – with your weight problem or with something else. It might be your doctor, a dietitian, an occupational nurse, a private therapist, or an exercise adviser. If so, why not ask them to help you work on a part of the *Shape-Up* programme? For example, they may be able to help you look at your *Shape-Up Diaries*, give you feedback or discuss your next goals with you.

For more information

See section 7 for further information, ideas for further reading, and websites and organisations which may be of help to you.

The *Shape-Up Change plan*

The *Shape-Up* programme has introduced several different skills that will help you to lose or maintain weight in a safe and controlled manner. You will have learned that not all of these will apply to you. You may also feel that you need to establish skills and confidence in one area before you feel ready to tackle another. Whatever your goal, it is vital to have a plan to help you achieve this.

After taking part in the *Shape-Up* programme, you may feel that you don't want to have a goal of weight loss, or that this is not the right time for you to make the changes required to achieve this goal. Many people feel that they would prefer to use their new skills and knowledge to prevent further weight gain. Others, after years of trying restrictive dieting, may feel that they can use the knowledge gained from the *Shape-Up* programme to develop a less tormented relationship with food and their weight.

Ultimately, the most appropriate goals to choose are those that fit with your priorities and beliefs about your weight.

Once you have worked on the *Shape-Up* programme for about 10-12 weeks (or for about 8 weeks if you're in a *Shape-Up Group*), you might want to review your overall goal and assess how well you have done at making some permanent lifestyle changes. Remember that people often fail at weight management because they try to do too many things at once. The *Shape-Up Change plan* on page 156 will help you to think systematically about what you have learned in *Shape-Up*, and will help you to plan the next steps to ensure your success.

EXTRAS

6

EXTRAS

THIS SECTION CONTAINS THE FOLLOWING ITEMS.
If you want to print out more copies of any
of them, visit www.weightconcern.org.uk.
Or you can photocopy them.

6

☑ **Shape-Up Diary** page 144
Use this to record exactly what you eat and how much activity
you do.

☑ **Shape-Up 'How much am I eating?' diary** page 146
Use this to record how many servings from each of the five food
groups you are eating.

☑ **Shape-Up Serving size guide** page 148
This will help you work out how many servings of each food
group you are eating. See page 61 for more information on this.

☑ **Shape-Up Weight change record** page 150
Each day or each week, record your weight.

☑ **Shape-Up Goalsheet** page 152
Each time you set yourself a goal, write it down on a *Shape-Up
Goalsheet*. This will help you make sure you have carefully
thought about and/or planned how you will reach your goal.

☑ **Shape-Up Log** page 154
Keep a record of all your goals in the *Shape-Up Log*.

☑ **Shape-Up Change plan** page 156
Once you have worked on the *Shape-Up* programme for about
10-12 weeks or for about 8 weeks if you're in a *Shape-Up Group*,
you can use this *Change plan* to review your overall goal and
assess how well you have done at making some permanent
lifestyle changes.

SHAPE-UP **DIARY**

Day   Date

FOOD AND DRINK

In this column, write down the actual time you eat or drink anything.

*In this column, write down **everything** you eat or drink. This includes any milk in your tea, spreads on bread, oil used for cooking, crisps with drinks, and even biscuit crumbs! Every morsel and sip contribute to your daily intake.*

Time   What did you eat or drink?

You can include any form of physical activity that makes you feel warm and breathe harder. This can include walking, cycling, moderate housework, gardening and DIY, as well as organised sport and exercise.

ACTIVITY

Did you do any physical activity of at least moderate intensity today that lasted at least 10 minutes? *'Moderate intensity' means activity that makes you feel warm and breathe harder than usual.* ☐ YES ☐ NO

If YES … What did you do?   How long did you do it for?

See page 78 for more about pedometers.

Pedometer count: [＿＿＿＿＿＿]   **WEIGHT** [＿＿＿＿＿＿＿＿＿]

SHAPE-UP **DIARY**

Day   Date

FOOD AND DRINK

Time   What did you eat or drink?

_____

_____

_____

_____

_____

_____

_____

_____

_____

_____

_____

_____

_____

_____

_____

_____

ACTIVITY

Did you do any physical activity of at least moderate intensity today that lasted at least 10 minutes? _'Moderate intensity' means activity that makes you feel warm and breathe harder than usual._ ☐ YES   ☐ NO

If YES … What did you do?   How long did you do it for?

Pedometer count: [   ]   **WEIGHT** [   ]

SHAPE-UP 'HOW MUCH AM I EATING?' DIARY

Day   Date

FOOD GROUPS

Time	Food/Drink	Bread / Cereals / Potatoes	Fruit & Vegtables	Meat, Fish & alternatives	Milk & Dairy	Fatty & Sugary	
						Fats	Other fatty & sugary
TOTAL number of servings							
RECOMMENDED number of servings		7 (women) 8 (men)	At least 5	2	3	2 max	1 max

SHAPE-UP 'HOW MUCH AM I EATING?' DIARY

Day   Date

FOOD GROUPS

Time	Food/Drink	Bread / Cereals / Potatoes	Fruit & Vegtables	Meat, Fish & alter- natives	Milk & Dairy	Fatty & Sugary	
						Fats	Other fatty & sugary
TOTAL number of servings							
RECOMMENDED number of servings		7 (women) 8 (men)	At least 5	2	3	2 max	1 max

SHAPE-UP **SERVING SIZE GUIDE**

How much is one serving?

FOOD GROUPS	FOOD	WHAT IS 1 SERVING?
Bread, other cereals and potatoes **Women** should aim to eat **7 servings** from this group each day. **Men** should aim to eat **8 servings** from this group each day.	Breakfast cereal	3 tablespoons
	Shredded wheat/weetabix	1 biscuit
	Bread/toast	1 slice
	Chapatti	1 small
	Crackers	3
	Crispbreads	4
	Pitta bread	1 small
	Roll	half
	Pasta/noodles	3 heaped tablespoons (cooked)
	Plantain/green banana	1
	Potatoes/sweet potatoes	2 egg-sized
	Rice	2 heaped tablespoons (cooked)
	Crumpet/English muffin	1
	Malt loaf	1 small slice
Fruit and vegetables Aim to eat at least **5 servings** of fruit and vegetables each day.	Apple/banana/orange	1
	Dried fruit (eg. raisins)	1 tablespoon
	Large fruit (eg. melon, grapefruit)	1 large slice/ $^1/_2$ grapefruit
	Plums/kiwis	2
	Small fruit (eg. grapes, raspberries)	1 cup
	Stewed or tinned fruit	2-3 tablespoons
	Fruit juice/vegetable juice/ 100% fruit smoothie	1 small glass (150ml)
	Green vegetables	3 tablespoons
	Root vegetables	3 tablespoons
	Small vegetables (eg. peas, sweetcorn)	3 tablespoons
	Salad	1 cereal bowl/1 tomato/7 cherry tomatoes
Meat, fish and alternatives Aim to eat **2 servings** from this group each day.	Lean meat (eg. beef, pork, ham, lamb, liver, kidney, chicken)	3 slices (total amount similar size of a pack of playing cards)
	Fish	size of a pack of playing cards

FOOD GROUPS	FOOD	WHAT IS 1 SERVING?
	Fish fingers	3
	Eggs	2
	Baked beans	5 tablespoons
	Nuts or nut products	2 tablespoons
	Pulses, beans, dahl	5 tablespoons
	Soya, tofu, quorn	100g or 4oz

Milk and dairy foods
Aim to eat **3 servings** from this group each day.

FOOD	WHAT IS 1 SERVING?
Milk	200ml or $^1/_3$ pint
Yogurt	1 small pot
Cottage cheese	1 small tub
Fromage frais	1 small pot
Cheese	40g or $1^1/_2$ oz (small matchbox size)

Fatty and sugary foods

Fats
Aim to eat no more than **2 servings** of fats each day.

FOOD	WHAT IS 1 SERVING?
Butter/margarine/spread	1 teaspoon
Low fat spread	2 teaspoons
Cooking oil/lard/dripping/ghee	1 teaspoon
Mayonnaise/salad cream	1 teaspoon
Oily salad dressing	1 teaspoon
Low calorie mayonnaise or dressing	2 teaspoons
Gravy/white sauce	1 teaspoon

Other fatty and sugary foods
Aim to eat no more than **1 serving** from this group each day.

FOOD	WHAT IS 1 SERVING?
Pork pie/sausage roll	1 small
Crisps	1 small bag
Cream	2 teaspoons
Sugar	3 teaspoons
Jam/honey	1 heaped teaspoon
Plain biscuits	2
Chocolate biscuit/cream-filled biscuit	1
Cake/pie	1 slice
Doughnut/Danish pastry	1 small
Ice cream	1 scoop
Chocolate	small bar
Sweets	small tube
Sugary drink	1

SHAPE-UP **WEIGHT CHANGE RECORD**

WEIGHT

WEEK	Mon	Tue	Wed	Thu	Fri	Sat	Sun	Weight change over the week _For example: Down by 1 pound_	Why has this happened? _What changes have I made to my lifestyle for this to happen?_

SHAPE-UP **WEIGHT CHANGE RECORD**

WEIGHT

WEEK	Mon	Tue	Wed	Thu	Fri	Sat	Sun	Weight change over the week For example: Down by 1 pound	Why has this happened? What changes have I made to my lifestyle for this to happen?

SHAPE-UP **GOALSHEET**

Remember to make your goals:
Specific **M**easurable **A**chievable **R**elevant **T**ime-Specific

MY GOAL IS:

_____

_____

_____

_____

_____

Today's date: _____ Review date: _____

Enter your goal and the date into your *Shape-Up Log* on page 154.

I will take the following steps:

1 _____

_____

2 _____

_____

3 _____

_____

4 _____

_____

I have thought about and/or planned for the following:

☐ Things that could get in my way and how I will overcome them
☐ People who might be able to help
☐ Time I'm going to give it
☐ How and when I'm going to review my goal
☐ How I will reward myself if I succeed.

Write about the outcome in your *Shape-Up Log* (see page 154).

SHAPE-UP **GOALSHEET**

Remember to make your goals:
Specific **M**easurable **A**chievable **R**elevant **T**ime-Specific

MY GOAL IS:

_____
_____
_____
_____
_____
_____

Today's date: **Review date:**

Enter your goal and the date into your _Shape-Up Log_ on page 154.

I will take the following steps:

1 _____
_____
_____

2 _____
_____
_____

3 _____
_____
_____

4 _____
_____
_____

I have thought about and/or planned for the following:

☐ Things that could get in my way and how I will overcome them
☐ People who might be able to help
☐ Time I'm going to give it
☐ How and when I'm going to review my goal
☐ How I will reward myself if I succeed.

Write about the outcome in your _Shape-Up Log_ (see page 154).

SHAPE-UP **LOG**

Please write in this *Shape-Up Log* each goal – large or small – that you set yourself throughout the *Shape-Up* programme.

Outcomes: ✔ = Achieved (Keep it up!)   ✳ = Keep trying.   ✗ = Not a goal for now

Goal	Date *I set the goal*	Review date	Outcome score	Review date	Outcome score	Review date	Outcome score

SHAPE-UP **LOG**

Please write in this *Shape-Up Log* each goal – large or small – that you set yourself throughout the *Shape-Up* programme.

Outcomes: ✔ = Achieved (Keep it up!)   ✳ = Keep trying.   ✗ = Not a goal for now

Goal	Date *I set the goal*	Review date	Outcome score	Review date	Outcome score	Review date	Outcome score

SHAPE-UP **CHANGE PLAN**

See page 142 for information on how to use this *Shape-Up Change plan*.

I want to achieve the following ...

_____

_____

I want to achieve this because ...

_____

_____

These are the steps I need to take to achieve this, and the order in which I need to tackle them ...

My goal: _____

Steps I need to take to achieve this goal (SMART goals)	Order in which I need to tackle these steps

I am prepared to tackle the following right now in order to achieve this ...

_____

_____

I need the following things to achieve this step (eg. help from other people, information, skills) and I am going to get them from the following places ...

What do I need?	Where/How am I going to get it?

I will know when I have achieved this step when ...

I will reward myself for achieving this step by ...

The following things might get in the way of me achieving this step ...

I am going to put the following things in place to try and overcome or limit
these barriers ...

I will set a date and time to review my progress ...

I will know it's time to move onto the next step when ...

FOR MORE
INFORMATION

7

FOR MORE INFORMATION

7

THIS SECTION:

gives you ideas for further reading, and a list of useful organisations and contacts.

FURTHER READING
COOKBOOKS

There are lots of low fat cookbooks. We suggest you go to your local bookshop or search on the internet and find which one suits you. This section includes details of some cookbooks which specialise in low fat recipes. More recent editions may be available.

Cooking for a Healthy Heart
By Jacqui Lynas. Published by Hamlyn, in association with Heart UK, 2004.
An easy-to-use guide with ideas for meals with low fat ingredients, fruit and vegetables, lean meats and low fat dairy products.

Fitness on a Plate: Anita Bean's Guide to Healthy Eating
By Anita Bean. Published by A & C Black, 2003.
An informative guide on nutrition and healthy eating for anyone who leads an active life – from an occasional gym-goer to a keen sportsperson. Clear nutrition advice on how to achieve a balanced diet with a number of healthy, low fat recipes.

Healthy Heart Cookbook

By Oded Schwartz. Published by Dorling Kindersley, in association with The Heart Hospital, USA, 2000.

Gives concise information about heart disease and nutrition as well as low fat cooking techniques and a variety of tasty recipes including vegetarian, Mediterranean and South East Asian dishes.

AFRICAN

Cooking the North African Way: Culturally Authentic Foods Including Low Fat and Vegetarian Recipes

By Mary Winget and Habib Chalbi. Published by Lerner Publishing Group, 2003.

CHINESE

The Chinese Way of Low-fat Cooking

By Yin-Fei Lo Eile. Published by John Wiley and Son, 1997.

Fresh Chinese: Over 80 Healthy Chinese Recipes

By Wynnie Chan. Published by Hamlyn, 2004.

Light and refreshing low fat dishes. Enjoy healthy, balanced Chinese food that includes easy-to-follow and quick-to-prepare recipes.

GREEK

Secrets of Fat-free Greek Cooking

By Elaine Gavalas. Published by Avery Publishing, 1999.

INDIAN

Fat Free Indian Cookery: The Revolutionary Way to Prepare Healthy and Delicious Indian Food

By Mridula Baljekar. Published by Metro Publishing Ltd, 2002.

The Low-Fat Indian Vegetarian Cookbook

By Mridula Baljekar. Published by Thorsons (imprint of Harper Collins Publishers), 2002.

This book has 250 low fat, healthy recipes. It also includes concise information about the different types of fats and their relation to heart health.

ITALIAN

Guilt-free Italian: Eat Well, Be Happy, and Stay Fit
Anne Sheasby. Published by Southwater, 2005.
This book includes over 160 traditional low fat, healthy recipes. The recipes are easy to follow and show the fat and calorie content.

99% Fat-free Italian Cooking: All Your Favourite Dishes with Less than 1 Gram of Fat
By Barry Bluestein and Kevin Morrissey. Published by Doubleday Books, 1999.

JEWISH

The Healthy Jewish Cookbook
By Michael Van Straten. Published by Kyle Cathie Ltd, 2005.

Healthy Jewish Cooking
By Steven Raichlen. Published by Viking Adult, 2000.
Traditional dishes adapted to lower-fat versions without losing the flavour.

KOSHER

Healthy Helpings: 800 Fast and Fabulous Recipes for the Kosher (or Not) Cook
By Norene Gilletz. Published by Woodland Publishing, 2004.
Low fat, high in flavour and nutritious recipes.

Secrets of Fat-Free Kosher Cooking
By D Bernstein. Published by Avery Publishing, 1998.

LATIN AND CARIBBEAN

Caribbean Light: All the Flavours of the Islands, Without the Fat
By Donna Shields. Published by Bantam Doubleday Dell Publishing, 1999.
Exotic, easy-to-cook low fat dishes with maximum flavour. Each recipe gives a nutritional breakdown of the amount of fat and calories per serving.

Healthy Latin Cooking: 200 Sizzling Recipes from Mexico, Cuba, the Caribbean, Brazil, and Beyond
By Steven Raichlen. Published by Rodale Press, 1998.
Some tasty, low fat, high flavour recipes. Each recipe includes the nutritional breakdown before and after making changes to the ingredients.

MEDITERRANEAN (General)
See also Greek, Italian and Turkish.

Low-fat No-fat Mediterranean
By Anne Sheasby. Published by Lorenz Books, 2005.
Over 200 low fat recipes from the Mediterranean region.

Mediterranean Light: Delicious Recipes from the World's Healthiest Cuisine
By Martha Rose Schulman. Published by Morrow Cookbooks, 2000.
A mix of healthy Mediterranean recipes from Greek, Italian and Turkish cuisine.

MIDDLE EASTERN
Persian Cooking: For a Healthy Kitchen
By Najmieh Batmanglij. Published by Mage Publishers, 2001.
95 low fat recipes with a particular focus on reducing the use of saturated fats.

The Secrets of Healthy Middle Eastern Cuisine
By Sanaa Abourezk. Published by Interlink Books, 2003.
A comprehensive guide to healthy middle eastern cooking, including a nutritional breakdown of dishes.

THAI
Green's Cuisine: Low Fat Food with a Taste of Thailand
By Daniel Green. Published by Book Promotion and Service Limited, 2003.

TURKISH
Cooking the Turkish Way: Culturally Authentic Foods Including Low-Fat and Vegetarian Recipes
By Kari Cornell. Published by Lerner Publications, 2004.

VEGETARIAN
Low-fat No-fat Vegetarian
By Anne Sheasby. Published by Lorenz Books, 2006.

1001 Low Fat Vegetarian Recipes
By Sue Spitler and Linda Yoakan. Published by Surrey Books, 2004.

FOOD AND NUTRITION

BBC Fat Nation: The Big Challenge
By Janette Marshall. Published by Dorling Kindersley, 2004.
Provides information on healthy eating for all ages.

Food and Nutrition (In the *Understanding* series)
By Dr Joan Webster-Gandy. Published by Family Doctor Publications, 2004.
Useful if you want further technical information about food and nutrition.

The New Glucose Revolution
By Jennie Brand-Miller, Thomas Wolever, Kaye Foster-Powell and Stephen Colagiuri. Published by Marlowe and Co, 2006.
An easy-to-read book for those who would like to learn more about the glycaemic index and how carbohydrates work in our body.

PHYSICAL ACTIVITY

BBC Fat Nation: The Big Challenge
By Janette Marshall. Published by Dorling Kindersley, 2004.
Provides information to help even the most reluctant exerciser to
improve their health.

Get Active
By the British Heart Foundation (BHF), 2005. Order via the BHF
website: www.bhf.org.uk/publications or phone 0870 600 6566.
A free booklet with information on the reasons why we should be
more active, and lots of ideas on how to fit more activity into your
everyday life. Includes examples of the different sorts of activity and
how to get started.

Great Shape: The First Exercise Guide for Large Women
By Pat Lyons and Debby Burgard. Published by Universe, 2000.
Shows how to be healthy at any size.

**Walking for Health and Happiness: The Complete Step-by-step
Guide to Looking Good and Feeling Your Best**
By William Bird and Veronica Reynolds. Published by Carroll and
Brown, 2002.
An essential guide for all those who are keen to become more
active, providing information on getting started and helping you to
get more out of any walk.

USEFUL CONTACTS

These contact details were up to date at the time of publishing this guide (January 2011).

Active Places
www.activeplaces.com
Active Places is a single database that holds information on sports facilities throughout England. It includes local authority leisure facilities as well as commercial and club sites. It will help you find out about the facilities, opening times and contact details in your local area.

British Association for Behavioural and Cognitive Psychotherapies
Imperial House
Hornby Street
Bury BL9 5BN
Phone: 0161 705 4304
www.babcp.org.uk
Can help you to find a cognitive behavioural therapist.

British Heart Foundation
Greater London House
180 Hampstead Road
London NW1 7AW
Phone (switchboard): 020 7554 0000
Heart Helpline: 0300 330 3311
Publications Orderline: 0870 600 6566
www.bhf.org.uk
The British Heart Foundation is a national charity fighting heart and circulatory disease. It funds research, education and life-saving equipment and helps heart patients return to a full and active way of life. It produces information on healthy eating and physical activity, and a series of booklets about heart conditions and treatment. It also runs a free, personalised service called *Heart Matters*, to help you live with a healthy heart.

The British Psychological Society

St Andrew's House
48 Princess Road East
Leicester LE1 7DR
Phone: 0116 254 9568
www.bps.org.uk
Can help you find a psychologist. Click on *E-services/Find a Psychologist*.

Cancer Research UK

Angel Building
407 St John Street
London EC1V 4AD
Phone: 020 7242 0200 (switchboard)
020 7121 6699 (supporter services)
www.cancerresearchuk.org
Dedicated to the prevention, treatment and cure of all forms of cancer. The website contains a wealth of information on healthy eating and activity.

Cyclists Touring Club

Parklands
Railton Road
Guildford
Surrey GU2 9JX
Phone: 01483 238337
www.ctc.org.uk
Campaigns for the rights of cyclists. Can provide information sheets on cycle routes in the UK.

Diabetes UK

Macleod House
10 Parkway
London NW1 7AA
Phone: 020 7424 1000
Diabetes Careline: 0845 120 2960
www.diabetes.org.uk
Offers information and advice for people with diabetes.

Eatwell
www.eatwell.gov.uk
The website provides useful information on healthy eating, food safety and understanding food labels.

The Fit Map.com
www.thefitmap.com
You can use this website to locate your nearest health club, gym or a personal trainer.

Fitness Industry Association
Castlewood House
77-91 New Oxford Street
London WC1A 1PX
Phone: 020 7420 8560
www.fia.org.uk
The trade organisation for the health and fitness sector. See their website for a list of health and fitness centres which are members of the Association.

Living Streets
4th floor
Universal House
88-94 Wentworth Street
London E1 7SA
Phone: 020 7377 4900
www.livingstreets.org.uk
Helps create streets and public spaces that people on foot can use and enjoy. Works at national and local level helping individuals and groups improve their local walking environment.

MIND (National Association for Mental Health)
Granta House
15-19 Broadway
London E15 4BQ
Phone: 020 8519 2122
www.mind.org.uk
A mental health charity working for a better life for everyone with experience of mental distress.

Sustrans

Phone: 0845 113 0065

www.sustrans.org.uk

For information on local walking paths and cycle ways.

Walking the Way to Health Initiative

Phone: 0300 060 2287

www.wfh.naturalengland.org.uk

An organisation and website for anyone with an interest in walking for health. It offers information, support and encouragement to walkers – both beginners and experienced.

Weight Concern

Phone: 020 7679 1853 (No helpline service available)

E-mail: enquiries@weightconcern.org.uk

www.weightconcern.org.uk

Weight Concern is a registered charity dedicated to fighting the UK's obesity epidemic. We provide independent, reliable information on obesity and weight management and campaign for better prevention and treatment. We also test new treatment programmes for adult and childhood obesity and provide training and education for health professionals.

Weight Wise

www.bdaweightwise.com

A website developed by the British Dietetic Association containing useful information on healthy eating, weight loss and physical activity.

APPENDIX

WHO CAN USE *SHAPE-UP*?

The *Shape-Up* programme was designed to help overweight adults manage their weight. The guidance on nutrition and physical activity was written with this population in mind.

Shape-Up is therefore not suitable for:
- people aged under 18 years
- women who are pregnant or breastfeeding, or
- people of a normal or low body weight.

People who are very overweight (with a BMI above 35), those with a current or past history of eating disorders, or those with psychological difficulties such as depression are likely to need additional support in managing their weight. While some of the ideas in *Shape-Up* might be useful to these groups of people, the programme may not be suitable on its own and additional support may be needed.

What next?
If you think that *Shape-Up* may be suitable for you, we recommend that you check with your doctor before beginning the programme. This is especially important if you have a health condition or are taking medication that may be affected by changes to your diet or level of activity. In most cases, the *Shape-Up* programme should still be suitable.

NUTRITION AND PHYSICAL ACTIVITY GUIDANCE

The nutritional guidance within *Shape-Up* follows current recommendations for a healthy, balanced diet. However, *Shape-Up* also recommends portion sizes equivalent to a total intake of 1,200-1,500 calories for women and 1,500-1,800 calories for men.

Physical activity guidance in the *Shape-Up* programme follows a three-step plan:
- reducing sedentary activities
- increasing lifestyle activity
- increasing organised activity and sports

This includes an initial recommendation of 30 minutes' moderate intensity activity a day, building up to 60 to 90 minutes a day for maintenance of weight loss.

Moderate intensity activity is defined as any form of exercise that makes you breathe harder than usual and feel warm, while still being able to hold a conversation.

The *Pre-activity questionnaire* on page 84 can help you decide whether it is safe to exercise.

SHAPE-UP
A SELF-HELP **GUIDE TO**
MANAGING YOUR WEIGHT

WEIGHTCONCERN
FIGHTING OBESITY WITH KNOWLEDGE

Acknowledgements

The *Shape-Up* programme has been developed by the charity Weight Concern, with support from Cancer Research UK.

The text of this self-help guide is based on *Shape-Up: A Lifestyle Programme to Manage Your Weight* by Jane Wardle, Lih-Mei Liao, Lorna Rapoport, Melvyn Hillsdon, Helen Croker and Carolyn Edwards.

Shape-Up would like to thank all the participants in the *Shape-Up* programmes who have inspired us to create this self-help programme.

Edited by Jane Wardle, Paul Chadwick, Alison Chipperfield, Helen Croker, Nichola Gokool and Lih-Mei Liao.

Produced by Wordworks, London W4 4DB.
Design by Heidi Baker.

Published by

WEIGHTCONCERN
FIGHTING OBESITY WITH KNOWLEDGE

Weight Concern
Website: www.weightconcern.org.uk
Phone: 020 7679 1853
E-mail: enquiries@weightconcern.org.uk

Registered Charity Number 1059686
Company number 3268842

© Weight Concern, 2006
Reprinted in 2011
ISBN 978-0-9540652-3-2

CONTENTS

INTRODUCTION

ABOUT THE SHAPE-UP PROGRAMME

Shape-Up is a programme which aims to improve your overall well-being and quality of life.

The aims of *Shape-Up* are for you to:
- ✓ limit further weight gain
- ✓ achieve modest weight loss
- ✓ become more physically active
- ✓ get into a regular eating pattern, which will make it easier to resist tempting, high calorie foods
- ✓ balance the different types of food that you eat, and
- ✓ reduce your tendency to overeat.

It also offers you information on how to manage difficult situations or 'lapses' and how to keep yourself motivated.

***Shape-Up* can be used by:**
- ✓ people who want to lose weight and keep it off in the long term, or
- ✓ people who want to avoid putting on any more weight.

What makes *Shape-Up* special?

Shape-Up is not 'just another diet'. And it's not just about losing weight. It uses psychological approaches to help you overcome the barriers that can get in your way when you're trying to change your eating habits and increase the amount of activity you do.

The idea for the *Shape-Up* programme came from a group of health professionals who had worked with overweight people. They found that overweight people had much more success in adopting a healthy lifestyle if they used advice from psychologists as well as from dietitians and specialists in activity and exercise. The *Shape-Up* programme combines expertise in psychology, nutrition, exercise and health promotion, to maximise your chance of success.

It's not a programme that you start and then finish a few weeks later. Instead it gives you the skills and knowledge that will help you to carry on with a healthy lifestyle for a lifetime.

How to use *Shape-Up*

We would advise you to see your doctor before beginning a weight management programme such as *Shape-Up*. This is especially important if you have any health conditions, or are taking any medicines that might be affected by changes to your lifestyle. This includes conditions such as diabetes, heart failure, high blood pressure or angina. In most cases the *Shape-Up* programme should still be suitable. For more information about the suitability of *Shape-Up*, see the *Appendix* on page 169 and the *Pre-activity questionnaire* on page 84.

There are five main sections in this *Shape-Up* guide:
1   Getting ready to shape up
2   The *Shape-Up Healthy eating plan*
3   Getting more active
4   Shopping, cooking and eating out
5   Keeping going.

It is recommended that everyone should work through sections 1, 2 and 3. It is best to start with section 1 as this will help you with all the other sections too.

It's up to you how long you spend on each section but we suggest that you aim to complete the sections in 15-20 weeks (or perhaps in less time if you're in a *Shape-Up* Group). This is the time you'll need to learn the new skills. After that it's a case of carrying on applying those skills.

Section 6 contains *Shape-Up Diaries*, *Goalsheets* and other materials that will help you to keep track of your progress, and section 7 contains sources of further information.